This book provides students with a fresh overview of the main theories of the state found in International Relations. Many IR scholars are proclaiming the state to be 'dead', while others lament the lack of an adequate theory of the state in IR. John Hobson seeks to resolve this confusion by introducing readers to state theory, arguing that existing schemas for interpreting theories of the state are limited, and proposes a new framework based around the 'agent–structure' debate. The book surveys realist, liberal, Marxist, constructivist, postmodernist, post-modernist feminist and neo-Weberian approaches to the state, and places each perspective's view of the state in relation to its theory of IR as a whole. It offers readers a unique introduction to state theory in IR, and will be of interest to students and scholars of sociology and politics, as well as IR.

JOHN M. HOBSON is Senior Lecturer in International Relations at the University of Sydney. He is the author of *The Wealth of States: A Comparative Sociology of International Economic and Political Change* (1997), and *States and Economic Development: A Comparative Historical Analysis* (with Linda Weiss, 1995).

GW00360514

THEMES IN INTERNATIONAL RELATIONS

This new series of textbooks aims to provide students with authoritative surveys of central topics in the study of International Relations. Intended for upper level undergraduates and graduates, the books will be concise, accessible and comprehensive. Each volume will examine the main theoretical and empirical aspects of the subject concerned, and its relation to wider debates in International Relations, and will also include chapter-by-chapter guides to further reading and discussion questions.

The State and
International Relations

John M. Hobson

CAMBRIDGE
UNIVERSITY PRESS

PUBLISHED BY THE PRESS SYNDICATE OF THE UNIVERSITY OF CAMBRIDGE
The Pitt Building, Trumpington Street, Cambridge, United Kingdom

CAMBRIDGE UNIVERSITY PRESS
The Edinburgh Building, Cambridge CB2 2RU, UK
40 West 20th Street, New York, NY 10011–4211, USA
477 Williamstown Road, Port Melbourne, VIC 3207, Australia
Ruiz de Alarcón 13, 28014 Madrid, Spain
Dock House, The Waterfront, Cape Town 8001, South Africa

http://www.cambridge.org

First published 2000
Reprinted 2002

Printed in the United Kingdom at the University Press, Cambridge

Typeset in Plantin 10/12pt [CE]

A catalogue record for this book is available from the British Library

Library of Congress Cataloguing in Publication data
Hobson, John M.
The state and international relations / John M. Hobson.
    p.   cm.
Includes bibliographical references and index.
ISBN 0 521 64354 6 (hb.) – 0 521 64391 0 (pb.)
1. International relations – Political aspects.
2. International relations – Sociological aspects.
3. State, The.   I. Title.
JZ1253.H63   2000
327.1′01   21–dc21   99–045364

ISBN 0 521 64354 6 hardback
ISBN 0 521 64391 0 paperback

Contents

Figures

Acknowledgements

I am grateful to many people who have, in their different ways, contributed to the making of this book. I thank Amitav Acharya, Brian Job, Chris Reus-Smit, Herman Schwartz, Colin Wight and three anonymous referees for their general advice and comments on the project. I would like to thank various people who read parts of the manuscript: Louise Chappell, Jane Ford, Martin Griffiths, Jeff Groom, David Mathieson, M. Ramesh, Len Seabrooke and especially Bob Howard and Steve Hobden, both of whom read the book in its virtual entirety. Warm thanks go to Michael Mann and Linda Weiss for all their support, help and encouragement. I particularly want to express my gratitude to Sushila Das and Louise Chappell, both of whom have taught me that there really is life after (and during) the next book, as indeed I thank Milly, Yves, Lisa and Steve. I especially thank John Haslam at Cambridge University Press for asking me to write this book, as well as for his patience and efficiency throughout. I am similarly most grateful to my copy-editor, Barbara Docherty. I also want to thank my colleagues and friends in the Department of Government for making Sydney University a pleasant and conducive place to work. Lastly, I thank the direct influence that my family has had on my life – Tim, Nora and Carole. I also wish to acknowledge the indirect influence of my great-grandfather, John Atkinson Hobson. To these four family members, I dedicate this book.

1 What's at stake in the 'second state debate'?: concepts and issues

Introduction: the two 'state debates' within the social sciences

If 'the state is dead', as so many International Relations (IR) scholars today contend, why do we need a book on 'the state and International Relations'? Indeed, it seems that the direction that the 'vanguard' of IR theory is currently taking is, if not in the opposite direction to the state, then at least 'away from the state'. Surely one of the common denominators that underpins the rapid rise of postmodernism, of critical theory and especially of constructivism along with feminism and Marxism, is an agenda that goes *beyond* the state: one that indeed seeks to displace state-centrism in general, and 'the state' as an object of enquiry, once and for all? At least, this appears to be the received wisdom within IR. But the argument of this book takes the form of a paradox: that it is neorealist state-centrism that denies the importance of the state in IR, while the various approaches listed above (along with liberalism), I argue, all take the state more seriously – a position which I readily concede contradicts my earlier statement (Hobson 1997: 1). This surprising conclusion emerges from introducing and applying a conceptual innovation that has largely been ignored by IR scholars – the 'international agential power' of the state – and reappraising each theory through this particular lens. This enables us to radically (re)view state theory in IR, such that in effect we end up by turning IR theory upside down.

Perhaps the key point to note here is simply that the conventional understanding of state theory in IR has been hampered by the interpretive tools of analysis that have been applied. As we shall see, when we consider the degree of international agential power (rather than domestic autonomy) that each theory accords the state, a new angle comes into view. This angle has in fact always been there, but has remained obscured as a result of the tools of analysis that have been applied – tools that are used within what I call the 'first state debate'. I reveal this alternative angle through the framework of what I call the 'second state debate'.

Across the spectrum of the social sciences a variety of theorists in different disciplines have situated theories of the state within two generic frameworks. The first comprises *normative* theories of the state, which consider what the most desirable or appropriate form of state and political community might be. The second comprises *explanatory* theories of the state, which consider who controls, or what forces shape, the state and its behaviour. Of course, in practice, the line that separates these two generic forms is fuzzy, given that normative concerns often creep into explanatory theory and, as one commentator put it, political philosophers often 'see what they think the state ought to be like in the state as it is' (Held 1984: 31). This volume is however, primarily interested in 'explanatory' state theory. The basic claim is that to the extent that it is possible to separate out the two forms of state theory, I suggest that we can discern two state debates within 'explanatory' state theory, both of which can be found across a variety of disciplines.

Within IR the first state debate emerged in its clearest form with the rise of interdependence theory in the 1970s – a debate that was a proxy for, or a means through which non-realists (especially radical pluralists) and realists fought each other for supremacy. The first state debate is concerned with the fundamental question as to whether 'states' predominate over 'social forces' and 'non-state actors'. Put differently, the debate revolves around the degree of autonomy that states have from non-state actors and social processes. Occupying one extreme are neorealists, who argue that the state, imbued with high autonomy, is the central actor in international politics. At the other extreme are liberals and radical pluralists, who insist that state autonomy is declining as states are being increasingly outflanked by economic processes (interdependence) and non-state actors (especially, though not exclusively, multinational corporations). Specifically they argue against the neorealist assumption that the state is a rational, coherent and autonomous actor that is primarily interested in the 'high politics' of security. By contrast, they claim that international interdependence is leading to the breakdown of states into incoherent entities, and that states are increasingly prioritising the 'low politics' of economics, distribution and welfare and ecological issues over military security (e.g. Burton 1972; Mansbach, Ferguson and Lampert 1976; Morse 1976; but see Keohane and Nye 1977, and especially Rosenau 1980 for a more complex approach). For these writers, neorealism's world of *states-as-billiard balls* is being transformed into a *global cobweb* of transactions that cuts across the increasingly porous boundaries of nation-states, rendering the sovereign state obsolete. This in turn led to the neorealist counter-attack, where theorists reasserted the continuing primacy and centrality of autonomous sovereign states. Thus the cobweb was blown away to reveal once more a harsh anarchic world comprising states-as-billiard balls (Gilpin 1975, 1981; Krasner 1976, 1978; Waltz 1979).

It is important to note that during the 1980s a parallel and comple-mentary 'state debate' was emerging within the disciplines of Sociology and Comparative Political Economy (CPE). With regard to the former, the work of Theda Skocpol was seminal, and her classic 1979 book, *States and Social Revolutions* was followed by the pioneering edited volume, *Bringing the State Back In* (Evans, Rueschemeyer and Skocpol 1985). This replicates the parallel state debate within IR. Here, neo-Weberians (rather than realists) were pitted against Marxists and liberals, with the former arguing that the state has high autonomy and primacy over society, while the latter reasserted the autonomy of social forces (e.g. Cammack 1989; Jessop 1990: 275–88). At the same time, a similar debate emerged in CPE and ran up to the early 1990s. Here 'statists' argued that the key to successful economic performance was based *not* on the ability of the state to conform to either 'market principles' (as in liberalism) or the needs of the dominant economic class (as in Marxism), but rested with strong or 'developmental' states imbued with high autonomy and bureaucratic 'proactivism'. This approach was most famously applied to explaining the meteoric rise of the East Asian Tigers (e.g. Johnson 1982; Wade 1990).

However, in recent years there has been a shift away from this 'state-centric versus society-centric' debate found in Sociology and CPE towards a 'second state debate'. A variety of sociological and compara-tive political economists are now arguing that there is an alternative theory of state 'autonomy': that state power derives from the extent to which states are embedded in society (Mann 1993; Evans 1995; Weiss and Hobson 1995; Hobson 1997; Weiss 1998). Now the debate has shifted away from 'state *versus* society' to one based on 'state autonomy *and* society', with the central question revolving around the issue: *to what extent do states structure society and to what extent do societies shape states?* Put differently, this second state debate in Sociology and Com-parative Politics/Comparative Political Economy examines the 'co-con-stitution' or 'mutual embeddedness' of states and societies. The obvious advantage of this approach (in contrast to the first state debate) is that it offers one possible resolution.

Returning to IR, the obvious questions are: (1) Has IR moved beyond the first state debate?, and (2) How useful is this debate? The first IR state debate did not end in the 1970s, but has continued on down to the present through a 'second phase', where Marxists, liberals and post-modernists assert the primacy of *globalisation* over the state (e.g. Camil-leri and Falk 1991; Brown 1995; Cox 1996: 296–313), while neorealists continue to reassert the primacy of the sovereign state (e.g. Krasner 1995). The first state debate, then, remains very much alive. But how useful is it? I suggest that it suffers from four fundamental limitations. First, it works within a binary, 'either–or' problematique based on 'state-centredness' *versus* 'international/global society-centredness'. Accordingly, this debate leads to stand-off between two intransigent and polarised camps. A second problem is that this stand-off is incapable of generating new research questions and agendas. Third, it tends to distort IR theory more generally, where all theories are simplified for the sake of 'winning the battle'. Accordingly 'straw-men' theories have been created, as both sides seek to simplify the 'other' in order to then knock them down. Fourth, it paradoxically suffers from 'state-blindness', in that both sides wittingly or unwittingly actually 'kick the state back out'. This is because both sides ultimately derive the state from international structures. Indeed, it could be argued that the first debate is not really about the state at all, given that both sides marginalise its importance; that perhaps the real contest is between *'international socio-economic structure-centredness'* versus *'international political structure-centredness'*. In this way, the first state debate paradoxically represents, to borrow Halliday's phrase, a 'non-encounter' on the state (Halliday 1994: 75–6).

Perhaps *the* most fundamental problem with the first state debate is that it fails to consider how the *state-as-an-agent* can determine or shape the international system. Thus while both sides of the first state debate tend to reify or exaggerate *international structure*, the second state debate is fundamentally organised around the 'agent–structure' dichotomy. I argue that all theories can be located within two continuums: the degree of agency that each theory accords the state-as-agent in the domestic and international arenas.

The 'second state debate': the two faces of state agential power

Perhaps not surprisingly, the sterility of the first state debate has given succour to the argument made by a host of writers across the social sciences that the state should be jettisoned as a theoretical object of inquiry (e.g. Easton 1981; Abrams 1988; Almond 1988; Ferguson and Mansbach 1988). I suggest, however, that we can retain the state as an analytical category by approaching it through the alternative lens of the second state debate. This new debate is *not* based around the question of 'state centrality' *versus* 'non-state actor centrality' (or state-centredness *versus* society-centredness), and does not *exclusively* focus on the question of state autonomy *versus* social autonomy. I focus on two categories here: the domestic, and international, agential powers of the state.

The 'domestic agential power' of the state

The first attribute of the state that this book examines is the domestic agential power of the state, which is equivalent to what theorists commonly think of as 'institutional state autonomy'. Thus domestic agential state power connotes the *ability of the state to make domestic or foreign policy as well as shape the domestic realm, free of domestic social-structural requirements or the interests of non-state actors*. This is broadly equivalent to the concept of state autonomy laid out by Skocpol and others (Skocpol 1979; Evans, Rueschemeyer and Skocpol 1985). This is charted along the x-axis of figure 1.1. Working with this definition, IR scholars generally conclude that neorealism (as well as Weberian historical sociology – WHS) attributes to the state the most autonomy or domestic agential power, while liberalism, Marxism, postmodernism and constructivism accord it the least. Put differently, 'autonomous' states loom large within neorealism and WHS, but appear to take a back seat in liberalism, Marxism, postmodernism and constructivism. At least, these are the familiar terms of the first state debate.

The issue of the degree of state autonomy or domestic agential power accorded within each theory constitutes the first aspect of the second state debate. Here we find that the received picture found in the first state debate is basically correct, though it glosses over the complexity of positions found not just between theories but, above all, within each paradigm. Realism, for example, produces three clear alternative positions, with Waltzian neorealism attributing very high or absolute domestic agential power to the state, while the modified neorealism of Gilpin and Krasner accords the state a varying or potential autonomy. In strong contrast, classical realism argues that pre-modern states have high domestic agency, while modern states have only low amounts. Marxists are divided between two positions; from the low domestic agential power found in classical Marxism to the 'relative' or 'moderate agential' power of the state approach found in orthodox neo-Marxism. Weberians are divided between the varying or potential domestic agential power found in the first wave, and the 'embedded autonomy' of the second wave. Some constructivists attribute low domestic agential power to the state (as in the international society-centric variant and

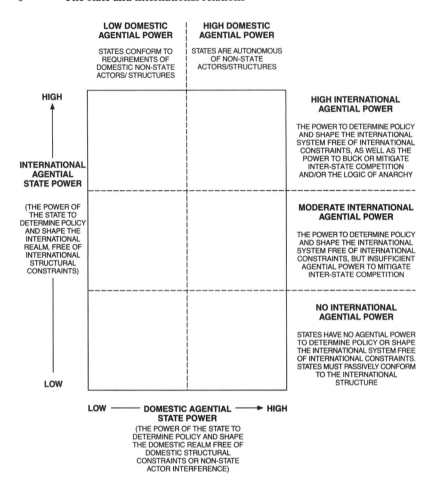

Figure 1.1 Configuring IR theory within the 'second state debate'

radical constructivism/postmodernism), while others accord it a moderate agential power (as in state-centric constructivism). And liberals range from granting the state very low domestic agential power (as in classical liberalism) through to moderate power (as in new liberalism and functionalism) and very high or absolute agential power (as in state-centric liberalism). Nevertheless, the distinct terrain that the second state debate maps out concerns the *international* agential power or capacity of the state.

The 'international' agential power of the state

If the domestic agential power of the state refers to the ability of the state to make domestic or foreign policy, and shape the domestic realm, free of domestic social-structural requirements or the interests of non-state actors, so the international agential power of the state refers to the *ability of the state to make foreign policy and shape the international realm free of international structural requirements or the interests of international non-state actors.* And at the extreme, high agential power refers to the *ability of the state to mitigate the logic of inter-state competition and thereby create a cooperative or peaceful world.* This 'international state power' must not be confused with the neorealist notion of 'state power' or 'state capability', which refers to the ability of states to effectively conform to international competition and the logic of what Waltz calls the 'international political structure'. In fact my definition of 'international agential state power' precisely inverts neorealism's notion of state capability.

With respect to international agential state power, all theories can be located along a continuum, ranging from low to moderate to high (as charted along the y-axis of figure 1.1). High international agential power refers to the ability of the state or state–society complex to buck the logic of inter-state competition and the constraining logic of international structure. All theories of IR recognise that inter-state competition exists and that the international political structure of anarchy also exists (where 'anarchy' refers to the fact that the international system is a multi-state system in which no higher authority or world state exists). This condition of potential or actual inter-state competition is sometimes referred to as the 'collective action problem', which assumes that cooperation between states is difficult or even impossible to achieve under international anarchy. High international agential state power enables the state to shape and reconstitute the international system as well as to solve the collective action problem and create a peaceful, cooperative world. Liberalism is the outstanding theory which accords such agential power to states. Classical liberalism stipulates that as states conform to individuals' social needs within domestic society, so they are able to create a peaceful world. State-centric liberalism (e.g. neoliberal institutionalism) stipulates that states have sufficiently high agency to reshape the international system and to solve the collective action problem. In establishing international institutions and regimes, states are able to reconfigure 'international anarchy' by enhancing the density of information, thereby creating a peaceful and cooperative world. High agential power is also accorded by some constructivists, classical realists and 'second-wave' Weberian historical sociologists (all of which are situated at the top of figure 1.1).

At the other extreme is international-systemic theory (neorealism, first-wave WHS and world systems theory – WST). Each theory fundamentally discounts the possibility that states have international agential power. For them, states have no choice but to conform to the international structure. Thus for neorealists and first-wave WHS, state conflict is an inevitable product of the international political structure, while for world systems theorists such conflict is an inevitable product of the capitalist world economy. In each case, states have no agential power to autonomously shape or modify the international structure. Accordingly these theories are situated at the bottom of figure 1.1.

In the middle are a range of theories. Marxism and postmodernism both assert that states can shape and determine the international system in accordance with national-level or domestic forces. Nevertheless, such theories stop short of granting the state high international agential power because, for them, states cannot overcome inter-state competition and solve the 'collective action problem'. For orthodox Marxists, in conforming to the needs of their domestic dominant economic classes, states come to create a highly conflictual international system. Nevertheless, it is simply not possible for states to create a peaceful world because for this to happen, states would have to be able to fundamentally reconcile the domestic class struggle – a logical impossibility for any Marxist. Likewise, postmodernists argue that states, through the process of engineering domestic legitimation (*normative statecraft*) create a conflictual world, in which the constructed appearance of 'threatening others' makes inter-state conflict not only inevitable, but the very condition of the continued reproduction of the state in the first place. These theories are situated in the middle layer of figure 1.1. (For a full summary of each theory's position, see figure 7.2.)

In sum therefore, we can define 'international agential state power' as the *ability of the state–society complex and the state as a unit-force 'entity' (whether it is imbued with high or low domestic agential power/autonomy, or is fragmented or centralised, or is 'imagined' or 'real') to determine or shape the international realm free of international structural constraints; and at the extreme, to buck or mitigate international structural constraints and the logic of international competition.*

Seen from this alternative angle, we necessarily reconfigure our understanding of how the different theories relate to each other over the question of the state. Now the fighters of the first state debate are juxtaposed into radically new positions. The debate is no longer between statism and realism 'as-for-the state' *versus* radical and pluralist theory 'as-against-the-state'. The counter-intuitive conclusion of this book is that the *non-systemic* approaches of liberalism, constructivism and postmodernism, classical Marxism and 'orthodox' neo-Marxism, second-wave WHS and classical realism succeed in attributing to the state far greater agency in the international realm than do the systemic approaches of neorealism, first-wave WHS and WST. If this conclusion appears surprising or counter-intuitive, it is only because IR theorists have either ignored the 'international' agential power of the state, or have simply confused it with institutional autonomy.

In this way, then, there is a great deal at stake in the second state debate – not just for understanding state theory, but for comprehending IR theory more generally. This of course begs the question as to why this approach has been previously ignored. The answer is that in the last twenty years, *international-systemic* theory has claimed dominance within IR theory. But the central limitation with systemic theory is that it denies the agency of the state; states are viewed as *Träger* – as passive receptors of an international structure – such that they have no choice but to adapt and conform to its constraining logic. It is precisely because the international structure constitutes the independent variable and the state the dependent variable that Waltz claimed that we do not need a theory of the state – by which he meant that we do not need to theorise the international agential power of the state. Moving away from systemic theory enables a consideration of how states and state–society complexes can autonomously shape the international system. It is this fundamental cleavage between systemic and non-systemic theory that constitutes the focus of the second state debate. In short, the second state debate redirects our attention away from pure international structural analysis and focuses on the degrees of agency that states and state–society complexes have to shape the international realm. In this way, then, when we view the ways in which IR theorises the state through the lens of the first state debate, the state all but disappears from view. But viewed through the more sensitive lens of the second state debate, we find that the state is very much brought back into focus.

A relationship between the two faces of agential power?

As noted, most IR scholars confuse the state's autonomy (domestic agential power) with its international agential power, and assume that they are one and the same thing. They are, however, distinct. Thus, for example, neorealism grants the state high domestic/no international agential power, while classical liberalism and international society-centric constructivism grant it low domestic/high international agential power. Does this suggest an inverse relationship between these two faces of power? No, because there are a whole range of theories which argue for high domestic and high international agential power (e.g. state-centric liberalism, classical realism), while others stipulate low domestic and moderate international agential power (classical Marxism and post-modernism), or moderate domestic and moderate international agential power ('orthodox' neo-Marxism), or moderate domestic and no international agential power (WST). In short, the fact that there is no intrinsic relationship between the two faces of agential state power suggests that these two 'attributes' are distinct.

Two further classificatory schema

Clearly, the second state debate is much more complex than the first state debate and raises a whole series of issues, which are discussed more fully in the second section of chapter 7 (pp. 223–35). While this basically concludes the discussion of the second state debate for the moment, nevertheless there is one further problem to confront. To be able to fully understand each theory, we need to apply two further classificatory schemas: the 'modes of causality problem' and the 'levels of analysis problem'. Categorising theory according to these two frameworks enables us to reveal a much more varied and nuanced set of approaches than is sometimes recognised by IR theorists.

The 'modes of causality problem'

This problem essentially refers to the *number of independent variables that a theory employs in order to explain outcomes*. All theories can be located within a trichotomy which ranges from 'parsimony' to 'modified parsimony' to 'complexity'. Parsimonious theory insists that outcomes (international relations and state behaviour) can be explained through *one exclusive* variable (e.g. Waltzian neorealism and classical liberalism). At the other extreme lies 'complexity', which explains outcomes through two or more independent variables (e.g. second-wave WHS). In between lies 'modified parsimony' (e.g. Gilpin's 'modified neorealism', J.A. Hobson's new liberalism, first-wave WHS or Coxian critical theory). Because so many scholars confuse modified parsimony with complexity, it is vital to clearly define this methodological approach.

Modified parsimony is a variation on parsimonious theorising in which one basic causal variable is primary but is supplemented by a set of *intervening* variables. These variables intervene between the basic causal variable and outcomes. What, then, is an 'intervening variable'?

As the term would imply, an intervening variable lies part-way between the basic independent causal variable (the *explanans*, or that which explains), and the dependent variable or outcomes (i.e. the *explanandum*, or that which is to be explained). It has much less causal power than an independent variable. An intervening variable is in effect a 'contingency', which is added on to the basic causal variable. Thus intervening or contingent variables have only a 'relative' rather than a full explanatory status or autonomy. Put in more 'colloquial speak', we could give the following example. If a woman walks along a beach, she will leave a set of footprints in the sand. The basic or independent causal variable is the movement of the leg, while the footprint is the outcome or the dependent variable. If the woman then puts on a pair of running shoes, the print left in the sand will of course be different to the original footprint. But the basic causal variable is still the independent movement of the leg. The shoe is an intervening variable: it modifies the final outcome, but does not constitute a basic causal variable because, without the movement of the leg, no print would be created. In sum, therefore, modified parsimony enables a richer and more empirically sensitive analysis to that provided by pure parsimony, but the addition of supplementary or intervening variables does not fundamentally *transform* the parsimonious approach into a complex one.

The 'modes of causality problem' has direct ramifications for the 'levels of analysis problem'. Indeed, the 'modes of causality problem' helps bring into focus various crucial aspects that have been hitherto ignored in the 'levels of analysis problem'.

The 'levels of analysis problem'
In his famous book, *Man, The State and War* (1959), Kenneth Waltz outlined a three-fold typology that could be used to categorise or pigeon-hole all theories of conflict and war. Originally formulated as a means of classifying theories of war, I use it here to categorise theories of IR more generally. First-image theory explains state behaviour and IR through the role of individuals; second-image theory argues that state behaviour and IR is determined by causal developments at the national state/societal level, while third-image theory argues that outcomes are determined by international structures.

However while this schema is a useful analytical first cut, it suffers from two central limitations. First, it is limited in that it cannot be used to consider those theories which seek to explain developments at the national rather than the international level. Peter Gourevitch's (1978) well used concept of 'second-image-reversed' theory begins to address this, but needs to be broadened. To overcome this I suggest that we add a 'fourth image', which captures those theories which argue that developments at the national or sub-national level shape international outcomes, while developments at the international/global level also shape the national realm (cf. Reus-Smit 1996: 187). Examples of this are found in second-wave WHS, Morgenthau's and Carr's classical realism and Ruggie's constructivism. Second, it is unable to consider theories which use more than one level to explain outcomes. Here I synthesise the 'modes of causality problem' with the 'levels of analysis problem', by suggesting that we need to differentiate *strong* and *weak* images. A 'strong'-image approach accords primacy to one exclusive level, and is utilised by 'parsimonious' theory (e.g. Waltzian neorealism). By contrast, a weak-image approach is utilised by 'modified parsimonious' theory, which accords causal primacy to one spatial level, but adds in the 'intervening' effects from one or various other levels (e.g. modified neorealism, as in Gilpin and Krasner). But note that the addition of intervening variables does not convert the theory into a fourth-image approach. This is because a fourth-image approach is congruent with 'complex theory' rather than 'modified parsimony'.

We have now laid out the framework of the second state debate. Equipped with these various concepts we can now turn to discussing each major theory with respect to its position within the debate.

Discussion questions

- Why in the last twenty years have mainstream IR theorists in general chosen *not* to 'problematise' the state? Or, why do some IR scholars reject the need for a theory of the state?

- What are the first and second 'state debates' as they have been conducted within IR, Sociology and Comparative Politics/Comparative Political Economy?

- How can it be claimed that IR's 'first state debate' has not really been about 'the state'?

- How and why has the first state debate distorted IR theory and IR theories of the state?

- What are the two faces of state agential power in the 'second state debate', and what is the difference between low, moderate and high international agential power?

- How does the introduction of the concept of 'international agential state power' lead beyond the first state debate?

- What is the 'modes of causality problem'?

- Why does 'modified parsimony' stop short of 'complexity'?

- What is the 'levels of analysis problem'? Why and in what ways, if at all, do we need to modify and extend the basic categories?

- Why is a 'strong'-image approach congruent with 'parsimonious' theory, and a 'weak'-image approach congruent with 'modified parsimony'?

Suggestions for further reading

While IR state theory can help improve the theories of the state developed in Sociology, Political Science, Comparative Politics/Comparative Political Economy and Political Geography, among others, nevertheless the reverse is also true: that IR needs to become more aware of theories of the state found outside of the discipline. Excellent introductory texts include those by Dunleavy and O'Leary (1987), Held (1987), Schwarzmantel (1994) and Pierson (1997).

For readings in the first state debate within Sociology, the classic statist text remains Evans, Rueschemeyer and Skocpol (1985), and especially Theda Skocpol's chapter 1. Two further key texts are those of Krasner (1978) and Skocpol (1979). Good examples of the Marxist response can be found in Cammack (1989) and Jessop (1990: 275–88). The standard statist position within CPE's first state debate can be found in Johnson (1982) and Wade (1990). The second state debate within Sociology and CPE has been advanced in the works of Mann (1993), Evans (1995), Weiss and Hobson (1995), Hobson (1997) and Weiss (1998). Chapter 3 of Mann (1993) is a good starting point for an introduction to the various theories of the state, especially within Sociology. This chapter also implicitly opens up the second state debate within Sociology and CPE. For the first state debate within IR, the standard 'first-phase' texts that insist that the state is being undermined by 'interdependence' are Burton (1972), Mansbach, Ferguson and Lampert (1976) and Morse (1976), while Camilleri and Falk (1991) is an excellent introduction to the second-phase approach, in which 'globalisation' is seen to be transcending the sovereign state. The key statist and neorealist 'defences' of the sovereign nation-state can be found in Gilpin (1975, 1981), Krasner (1976, 1995) and Waltz (1979: chapter 7).

It is vital to follow up the discussion of the 'agent–structure' debate. In Sociology, good introductions can be found in Layder (1994) and Thrift (1983). Two important positions are found in Giddens (1984) and Archer (1995). The 'structurationist' resolution to the agent–

structure problem has been adapted and imported into IR, initially by Wendt (1987), and see especially, the important debate conducted within the journal, *Review of International Studies* (Hollis and Smith 1991; Wendt 1991). For an important recent discussion, see Wight (1999). Finally, it is important to follow through on the 'levels of analysis problem'; Waltz (1959) is the standard starting point. Singer (1961) is also an important discussion which argues, in contrast to the position adopted in chapter 7 of the present volume, that it is *not* possible to produce a single model that combines two or more of the levels.

Part 1

Traditional theories of the state and
international relations

2   Realism

Introduction: the two realisms of international relations theory

Conventional wisdom conflates neorealism and classical realism (e.g. Gilpin 1986; Grieco 1993a: 135). But my interpretation suggests two clearly differentiated realisms and two distinct theories of the state, as revealed within the framework of the second state debate. These two positions are juxtaposed in figures 2.1 and 2.7 (p. 46). There is a relatively strong consensus among realists and non-realists as to what constitutes 'neorealism'. I summarise the approach through 'six principles', outlined on the left-hand side of figure 2.1. In essence, neorealism is highly parsimonious, such that although the state has high domestic agential power (or high institutional autonomy), nevertheless it has no international agential power to determine policy or shape the international system free of international structural constraints. For neorealism, states are in effect 'passive bearers' (*Träger*) of the international political structure. This contrasts with what I call 'the six principles' of classical realism which boil down to the essential claim that while states' domestic agential power varies through historical epochs, nevertheless all states have at all times (albeit to varying degrees) sufficient levels of international agential power to shape the inter-state system. Both Carr and Morgenthau emphasise that, under certain circumstances, states can create a peaceful world. Morgenthau (1948/1978: chapter 32) argues that the regaining of high domestic agential power can enable the state to create the necessary conditions for a peaceful world (i.e. enable the generation of high international agential state power). Carr (1945, 1951) argues that the eclipse of the sovereign state after 1945 through the corrosive effects of global moral norms, enables the development of a post-sovereign global community of free and equal individuals. This suggests in Ashley's (1981) terms, an 'emancipatory realism' which stands in radical contrast to 'technical neorealism', in which the state has no choice, or international agency, and must technically adapt to the

17

THE 'SIX PRINCIPLES' OF NEOREALISM (THE PASSIVE/ADAPTIVE STATE)	THE 'SIX PRINCIPLES' OF CLASSICAL REALISM (THE STATE-AS-AGENT)
(1) THE 'CONTINUITY 'ASSUMPTION BECAUSE THE ANARCHICAL STATES SYSTEM IS ONTOLOGICALLY SUPERIOR TO THE UNITS AND IS AN AUTONOMOUS AND SELF-CONSTITUTING REALM, INTERNATIONAL POLITICS (IP) NEVER CHANGES BUT HAS ALWAYS BEEN A REALM OF NECESSITY AND VIOLENCE. ACCORDINGLY, THE NEOREALIST METHOD SEEKS TO UNCOVER THE ESSENTIAL A-HISTORICAL LAWS OF MOTION OF IP	**(1) HISTORICAL VARIABILITY** THE ONTOLOGICAL SUPERIORITY OF THE STATE OVER THE SYSTEM MEANS THAT IT CONSTITUTES AN INDEPENDENT AGENTIAL VARIABLE IN IP. THUS AS STATES CHANGE, SO DOES THE INTERNATIONAL SYSTEM
(2) THE 'POSITIONAL' OR 'RELATIVE GAINS' ASSUMPTION ANARCHY AND POWER DIFFERENTIATION REQUIRES STATES TO PLACE A PREMIUM ON SHORT-TERM 'RELATIVE GAINS' OVER LONG-TERM 'ABSOLUTE COOPERATIVE GAINS'. THIS IS BECAUSE IF STATE *B* GAINS MORE FROM COOPERATION THAN STATE *A*, STATE *A* FEARS THAT STATE *B* MIGHT SUBSEQUENTLY USE THAT POWER AGAINST *A*. THEREFORE STATE *A* ESCHEWS COOPERATION, PREFERRING TO DEFECT AND GO IT ALONE	**(2) RELATIVE AND ABSOLUTE GAINS** STATES HAVE NOT ALWAYS PURSUED RELATIVE GAINS (E.G. SEVENTEENTH TO NINETEENTH CENTURIES). MOREOVER, STATES MIGHT COME TO COOPERATE IN THE FUTURE THROUGH SUPER-INTELLIGENT MORAL DIPLOMACY (MORGENTHAU), OR THEY MAY BE RE-SOCIALISED INTO HIGHER MORE COOPERATIVE POLITICAL FORMS (CARR)
(3) THE POLITICAL 'SOVEREIGNTY' ASSUMPTION AUTONOMOUS NATION-STATES ARE THE CENTRAL ACTORS IN IP. THE SOVEREIGN STATE IS THE HIGHEST FORM OF POLITICAL EXPRESSION AND WILL REMAIN SO DESPITE ECONOMIC INTERDEPENDENCE OR GLOBALISATION	**(3) 'SOCIAL' SOVEREIGNTY** STATE SOVEREIGNTY CHANGES THROUGH TIME VIA EXTENSION OF DOMESTIC CITIZENSHIP RIGHTS. FOR CARR THE STATE IN ITS 'SOCIALISED NATIONAL' FORM IS NOT THE HIGHEST FORM OF POLITICAL EXPRESSION BUT THE HIGHEST STAGE OF A MORALLY AND FUNCTIONALLY OBSOLETE POLTICAL COMMUNITY
(4) THE SURVIVAL 'RATIONALITY' ASSUMPTION THE SOVEREIGN STATE IS A UNITARY AND HERMETICALLY SEALED ACTOR THAT RATIONALLY PURSUES ITS NATIONAL INTEREST OF 'MILITARY SURVIVAL', WHICH IS UNCHANGING	**(4) VARIABLE 'SOCIAL' RATIONALITY** THE STATE IS NOT UNITARY, AND IS SHAPED BY STATE–SOCIETY RELATIONS AND INTERNATIONAL NORMS. AS THESE CHANGE, SO DOES STATE RATIONALITY
(5) THE HIGH DOMESTIC AGENTIAL STATE POWER ASSUMPTION (BILLIARD-BALL MODEL) STATES HAVE HIGH DOMESTIC AGENTIAL POWER. STATES ARE LIKENED TO 'BILLIARD BALLS' NOT SIMPLY BECAUSE THEY CONFLICT AND 'BOUNCE OFF EACH OTHER', BUT ABOVE ALL BECAUSE THEIR INTERNAL OR DOMESTIC PROPERTIES ARE IRRELEVANT TO STATE BEHAVIOUR AND INTERNATIONAL POLITICS. ALTHOUGH GILPIN AND KRASNER ALLOW FOR VARIATIONS IN DOMESTIC STATE AUTONOMY, THESE DO NOT OVER-RIDE THE DETERMINING NATURE OF ANARCHY	**(5) VARIABLE DOMESTIC AGENTIAL STATE POWER** NOT ONLY DOES A STATE'S DOMESTIC AGENTIAL POWER VARY THROUGH TIME, BUT IT SIGNIFICANTLY DETERMINES STATE BEHAVIOUR AND INTERNATIONAL POLITICS. HIGH DOMESTIC AGENTIALⱭPOWER ENABLES HIGH INTERNATIONAL AGENTIAL STATE POWER. LOW DOMESTIC AGENTIAL POWER LEADS TO MODERATE INTERNATIONAL AGENTIAL POWER
(6) NO INTERNATIONAL AGENTIAL STATE POWER AND THE 'A-MORAL' ASSUMPTION STATES HAVE NO AGENCY TO SHAPE IP NOR MITIGATE THE LOGIC OF ANARCHY, AND MUST IGNORE INTERNATIONAL MORALITY AS A BASIS FOR ACTION/POLICY. THEY MUST PURSUE THE TECHNICAL MEANS TO SURVIVE (I.E. ADAPTATION) IN A HOSTILE EXTERNAL WORLD OF COMPETING STATES. NORMS HAVE NO AUTONOMY TO PROMOTE INTERNATIONAL PEACE	**(6) VARIABLE INTERNATIONAL AGENTIAL STATE POWER AND MORALITY** IN THE SEVENTEENTH TO NINETEENTH CENTURIES, STATES HAD HIGH INTERNATIONAL AGENTIAL POWER AND CREATED A RELATIVELY PEACEFUL INTERNATIONAL REALM. BY CONTRAST, IN THE MODERN ERA, STATES HAVE ONLY MODERATE INTERNATIONAL AGENTIAL POWER (AND THEREFORE INTER-STATE CONFLICT IS NORMAL). EITHER WAY, THOUGH, STATES ARE GRANTED MUCH HIGHER LEVELS OF INTERNATIONAL AGENTIAL POWER THAN ASCRIBED IN NEOREALISM

Figure 2.1 Juxtaposing the two realist theories of the state and IR

system's requirements. Moreover, I argue that Carr's 'realism' has much in common with Critical theory, while both Carr and Morgenthau also draw on constructivist insight.

Neorealist parsimony: the passive-adaptive state under socialising anarchy

Waltz and the 'passive-adaptive' state

It is commonly thought that neorealism involves a fundamental paradox: it insists on the absolute centrality of the autonomous state in International Politics (IP), and yet it denies the possibility of a theory of the state. Actually, Waltz does have a theory of the state, though it is highly 'minimalistic': the state is exclusively derived from the systemic reproduction requirements of the anarchical state system. In exclusively focusing on international structure, the state is denied international agential power either to shape the international political structure or to buck its constraining logic. To understand this, though, we must first understand Waltz's overall theory of IP outlined in his *Theory of International Politics* (1979).

Waltz's theory begins with the 'continuity' problematic (principle (1), figure 2.1). What primarily struck Waltz was the high degree of continuity of outcomes that allegedly marked IP through the millennia. As he put it, '[t]he texture of IP remains highly constant, patterns recur and events repeat themselves endlessly. The relations that prevail internationally seldom shift rapidly in type or in quality. They are marked by a dismaying persistence' (Waltz 1979: 66, 1986: 329). This refers to Waltz's observation that international politics is, and always has been, a realm of conflict between states, whether these have been empires, city-states or nation-states. The key that unlocks Waltz's theory involves understanding the theoretical move that is required to meet and explain such 'continuity'. To explain continuity, Waltz is forced (or chooses) to construct a theory in which there are a minimum of explanatory variables, which themselves are subject to little change or transmutation. Thus 'parsimony' or 'elegance' is fundamental to Waltzian neorealism (Waltz 1979: chapter 1). To create such a parsimonious (narrow) theory, Waltz insists that empirical complexity (or reality) must be simplified and reduced down to one key factor. He singles out the international political structure as the sole determining variable of IP, in turn producing a positivistic theory which seeks to uncover the essential 'laws of motion' of international politics (Waltz 1979: chapters 3–4).

The fundamental problem with previous IP theory, Waltz argues, has

been its 'reductionist' methodology. His unconventional (if not con-
fusing) way of defining 'reductionism' refers to theory in which 'the
whole [the international system] is understood or explained by its parts
[i.e. the units]' (Waltz 1979: 18, 19). Reductionism (associated with a
'second-image' approach which focuses on national-level variables, as
well as first-image theory which focuses on the individual) is avoided
through a 'third-image' approach, which relies on the *international*
political structure as *the* independent variable (Waltz 1959). The vital
move is to define the international political structure itself in highly
parsimonious terms, which requires that 'unit-force' (domestic-force)
variables be omitted (Waltz 1979: chapter 5, especially 65). Why must
unit-level variables be omitted? Because, at the domestic level, there are
an indefinite number of variables – economic, social, technological,
ideological, political, etc. – *which are constantly changing*, and yet, for
Waltz, IR has not changed but has always remained the same. 'If
changes in international outcomes are linked directly to changes in
actors, how can one account for similarities of [international] outcomes
that persist or recur even as actors vary?' (Waltz 1979: 65, 1986: 329).
So to avoid 'reductionism' and preserve parsimony in order to explain
'continuity', it is crucial to ensure that the international political structure is defined only in *systemic* ways, with a rigid exclusion of non-
systemic, unit-force/national variables. How is this achieved?

Waltz's definition of international political structure

There are three basic features or tiers of domestic political structures,
though only two for the international political system:
(1) the *ordering principle*, or the 'deep structure' – a phrase coined by
    Ruggie (1986: 135)
(2) the *character* or *differentiation* of the units
(3) the *distribution of capabilities*, or the 'surface structure', as Ruggie
    termed it (1986: 136).
The deep structure provides the key.

(1) The ordering principle (deep structure)   There are two types of ordering principle: 'anarchy' and 'hierarchy'. Hierarchy characterises
domestic political structures, while anarchy characterises international
systems. Under (domestic) 'hierarchy', the units (i.e. individuals)
'specialise' in a *harmonious and interdependent* division of labour. Thus
some specialise in producing cars, others houses, others vegetables, etc.
Because they specialise, they come to rely on others for goods that they
need but do not themselves produce – hence entailing cooperation and

interdependence. Such harmony and interdependence is possible only because the problem of security has already been solved by the state. By contrast, in anarchic international systems, the units (i.e. states) must follow adaptive 'self-help', because there is no higher authority (world state) which can solve the security problem. They cannot specialise but *must compete and be independent*, since interdependence promotes vulnerability. Why does the absence of a world government lead to self-help and competition?

Waltz draws on the 'domestic analogy', which is based on the argument made by Thomas Hobbes in his classic book, *Leviathan* (1651). Hobbes argued that before the advent of the modern state – in what is known as the 'state of nature' – there was a 'war of all against all'. Thus men were free but highly insecure, since there was no higher authority which could have prevented them from preying on each other. Hobbes' solution was the construction of a state or higher coercive authority (termed the 'leviathan') through the 'social contract', whereby all individuals agreed to surrender their freedom to the state in order to gain security. Applying this framework to international relations (the 'domestic analogy'), Waltz assumes that states in the inter-state system are like Hobbes' individuals within the state of nature – even though ironically, Hobbes denied, or at least heavily qualified, such an assumption, by arguing that the international state of nature was in fact 'less intolerable to men than was the pure [domestic] state of nature' (Suganami 1986: 145; Walker 1987: 73). Just as individuals compete with each other in pursuit of their own interests in Hobbes' domestic state of nature so, for Waltz, individual states compete with each other in the anarchic realm of international politics: 'Among states, the state of nature is a state of war . . . Among men [in the state of nature] as among states, anarchy, or the absence of government, is associated with the occurrence of violence' (Waltz 1979: 102). And precisely because there is no world leviathan or world state, there is nothing to prevent inter-state conflict from recurring. In short, order is possible only if there exists a higher coercive authority. States are free to pursue their own national interest but are forever insecure, because war can break out at any time. Accordingly, if states are to survive, they must eschew cooperation in favour of 'self-help'. Cooperation is ultimately dangerous because, in lowering their guard, states become vulnerable to predators (here Waltz borrows Rousseau's story of the stag-hunt).

Because the ordering principle is so important but is invisible – or, as Waltz put it '[t]he problem is: How to conceive of an order without . . . [a visible] orderer' (Waltz 1979: 89) – he draws on microeconomic theory by way of analogy in order to understand the nature or power of anarchy. Drawing on Adam Smith's discussion of the market, Waltz claims that just as the market emerges as a result of the spontaneous actions of individuals and firms (who do not seek order but only self-interested personal gain), so the international political structure emerges out of the spontaneous actions of self-interested states pursuing their own selfish national interests. But, once formed, the international system constrains the actors (i.e. the states). For Smith, it was the structure of the market system that determined the self-help and adaptive behaviour of individuals (and firms), just as for Waltz the anarchic system determines the adaptive behaviour of states. Smith's famous claim was that through the competition of selfish individuals, an 'invisible hand' of market competition ensured the reproduction (and betterment) of society overall (Smith 1776/1937: 423). Similarly, for Waltz, through the competition of selfish states, the 'invisible hand of anarchy' ensures the reproduction of the anarchic state system. And just as for Smith the market selects appropriate behaviour for survival by rewarding those who conform to the logic of the market with high profits and those who do not with bankruptcy, so for Waltz the international political structure selects out states according to whether their behaviour conforms to anarchy (i.e. the requirement of military survival), rewarding those who conform with survival or even great power, and those who do not with decline, defeat or extinction (Waltz 1979: 89–93). The crux of the argument is captured in the discussion of the second tier, in which the state effectively drops out as a basic causal variable in IP.

(2) Character of the units In a hierarchy (i.e. in domestic structures) the units are *differentiated according to function*: all units are 'unlike' and specialise in *different* functions, and accordingly enter into an *interdependent* system of mutual cooperation (without which specialisation could not occur). But under international anarchy, states are 'like units' and are *minimally differentiated in terms of function* (i.e. they all perform the same function). Thus while they differ greatly in terms of capability, functionally they are all alike – that is, they are all sovereign, having a centralised political system with a legitimate monopoly of violence and rule-making, and are not subject to a higher political authority either domestically or internationally (Waltz 1979: 95). The reason why they are all the same derives from the 'socialising' logic of anarchy. Failure to emulate the successful practices of the leading states (i.e. to conform to the logic of anarchic competition) leads to the opening up of a 'relative power gap' and therefore, heightened vulnerability or even extinction. Survival dictates convergence or functional homogeneity. Waltz's funda-

mental argument is that the 'the second [tier] is not needed in defining international political structure, because so long as anarchy endures, states remain like units' (Waltz 1979: 93, 101). Why does the second tier drop out?

Waltz effectively 'black-boxes' the state – that is, unit-forces are held constant. It is this manoeuvre that informs the 'billiard-ball' metaphor. States are like billiard balls, not simply because they constantly clash, but because billiard balls are solid such that their internal properties do not vary, and above all, do not affect their external behaviour. Herein lies the crux of Waltz's understanding of the state: *that because states are 'like units' (due to the 'socialising' effects of anarchy), their particular attributes cannot enter into the definition of the international political structure as an independent (i.e. determining) variable, precisely because their internal attributes do not vary.* Of course, they differ greatly in terms of regime form, ideology, etc. but, as we have seen, these have purposefully been ignored. The fact that states (e.g. liberal/authoritarian, capitalist/socialist) have fought wars irrespective of their type or form, suggests that unit-forces are not relevant (Waltz 1979: 66). In short, Waltz accords the state no determining agential power or influence in IP. Accordingly, the state must be dropped as an independent causal variable in IP. It is for this reason that Waltz argues that we do not need a theory of the state.

It also aids understanding if we clarify what Waltz is *not* saying. He is *not* saying that domestic variables are irrelevant to international politics. As he argued in a lesser-known book, *Foreign Policy and Democratic Politics* (1967), domestic variables must be utilised if we are to explain the *foreign policies* of states. But a *structural* explanation does not try to explain the details of each country's foreign policies. It merely tries to tell us 'a small number of big and important things' about the general tendencies and characteristics of international politics (Waltz 1979: chapter 1: 71–2, 121–3, 1986: 329, 344, 345).

(3) Distribution of capabilities   While states are all functionally alike, nevertheless they are differentiated in terms of power capability (i.e. *power differentiation*). Here Waltz refers to 'strong' and 'weak' states. Strong states or great powers are in effect 'power-makers'; they can change the behaviour of other states, whereas weak states are in effect 'power-takers', having no choice but to follow the great powers. Under anarchy, power differentiation ensures that all states must follow self-help – or decline and perish. But does not the inclusion of capability allow unit-forces back into the definition, as is sometimes charged by his critics (e.g. Gabriel 1994: 85)? No, Waltz answers, because having

abstracted (i.e. ignored) every aspect of the state except power, 'what emerges is a positional picture, in which states are understood by their placement in the system as opposed to their individual attributes' (Waltz 1979: 99). Or again,

[a]nd yet one may wonder why only [state] *capability* is included in the third part of the definition, and not such characteristics as ideology, form of government, peacefulness, bellicosity, or whatever. The answer is this: Power is estimated by comparing the capabilities of a number of units. Although capabilities are attributes of units, the distribution of capabilities is not. The distribution of capabilities is not a unit attribute, but rather a system-wide concept. (Waltz 1979: 97–8)

Thus because it is the 'systemic' or 'positional' picture that matters, Waltz succeeds in once again keeping the state out of the definition of the IPS.

Waltz's 'minimalist' or 'functionalist' definition of the state – the passive 'military-adaptive state'

We have effectively arrived at Waltz's approach to the state by analysing his 'systemic' approach (summarised in figure 2.2). Because the state resides within an independent and self-determining anarchic international system, it can be granted no serious ontological (determining) status or international agential power. Although states are very much the key units of the system, they have no determining influence. Thus no formal theory of the state is required, much as microeconomics does not require a theory of the firm. Nevertheless, Waltz has a *minimalist* definition of the state: what we term the 'theory of the passive military-adaptive state'. Before defining this, let us examine its core aspects, which have an *institutional* foundation.

The institutional means of adaptation: high/absolute domestic agential state power   The most fundamental institutional means that underpins adaptive behaviour is the 'sovereignty' of the state, in which the state has high or absolute domestic agential power (or institutional autonomy from all non-state actors). This does not imply that the state can do simply as it pleases, but merely that 'the state is free of external or internal interference [by non-state actors] to decide for itself how it will cope with external challenges. States develop their own [adaptive] strategies . . . It is no more contradictory to say that sovereign states are always constrained [by the system] and often tightly so than it is to say that free individuals often make decisions under the heavy pressure of events' (Waltz 1979: 96). In short, the state is granted high (absolute) domestic agential power and can operate wholly independently of domestic (and

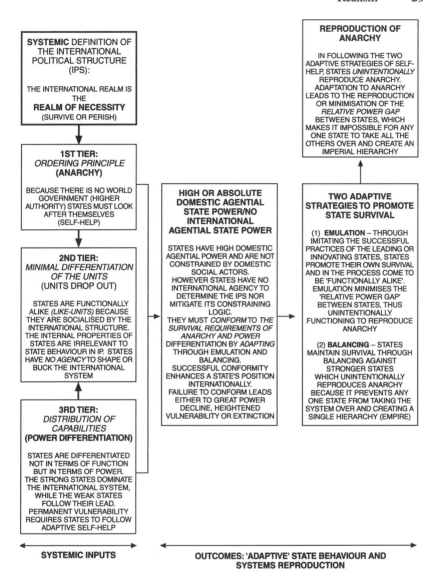

Figure 2.2 Waltz's systemic functionalist theory of the passive 'military-adaptive' state

international) social forces. In short, it can buck the logic of domestic non-state power forces. But the key point is that the state has no agential power either to shape the international realm/structure or to mitigate or buck its constraining logic. Instead, the state must conform to anarchy (i.e. its survival dictates). Thus despite having high domestic agential power, the state is effectively imprisoned within an 'iron cage of anarchy'. In turn, anarchy and power differentiation dictate two adaptive strategies that states must conform to if they are to survive.

No international agential state power to mitigate anarchy: two technical modes of adaptive state behaviour Recall that states are 'like units': '[c]ompetition produces a tendency toward the sameness of the competitors' (Waltz 1979: 127). Why? Because the logic of anarchy and power differentiation – i.e. where some states are more powerful than others and can thus threaten the survival of the weaker states – requires states to adapt and conform to the survival dictates of anarchy. How? States adapt by *'integrating' into the international system, which enables them to conform to the structure's dictates*. Integration implies two main adaptive strategies which states employ so as to survive:

(a) *Adaptation through emulation:* due to power differentiation under anarchy, states must imitate or emulate the successful practices of the leading state(s), since failure to do so leads to heightened vulnerability. Thus there is in play a 'demonstration effect' such that the successful practices of the leading state(s) pressurise the other states to emulate their practices – or perish. Thus, for example, when Prussia defeated Austria (1866) and France (1870) through its superior military staff system, other states imitated these practices very soon after, since failure to do so would have left them vulnerable. Even chiliastic (non-conformist or recalcitrant) states will become integrated into the system, and may even engage in great power politics (as the USSR did after 1917). 'The close juxtaposition of states promotes their sameness through the disadvantages that arise from a failure to conform to successful practices. It is through this "sameness", an effect of the system, that is so often attributed to the acceptance of so-called rules of state behavior. *Chiliastic [i.e. recalcitrant] rulers occasionally come to power* [who initially seek not to conform to the systems's requirements]. *In power most of them quickly change their ways* [for fear of defeat or extinction]' (Waltz 1979: 128, emphases mine). Note however, that Waltz does *not* say that all states necessarily will follow this policy – merely that if they don't they will perish or decline (Waltz 1979: 73–4). As Waltz put it, '[a] self-help system is one in which those who do not help themselves [i.e. adapt], or who do so less effectively than others will fail to prosper, will lay themselves open to dangers, will suffer' (Waltz 1979: 118).

Thus just as states or individuals cannot buck the market in microeconomic theory without suffering economic loss, so for Waltz states cannot buck the logic of anarchy (and hence socialisation) without suffering political loss (i.e. defeat in war or great power decline). Accordingly, all states that remain in the system will 'display characteristics common to competitors'. Moreover, '[a]s in economics, competitive systems are regulated by the 'rationality' of the more successful competitors . . . Either their competitors emulate them or they fall by the wayside' (Waltz 1979: 76–7). In this way states come to resemble each other. In the process, by conforming to the successful practices of the system's leaders in order to promote their survival, states unintentionally reproduce the anarchic state system. Emulation promotes 'systems maintenance' because it *reduces the relative power gap between states*, making it more difficult for a leading state to transform anarchy into hierarchy (i.e. empire).

(b) *Adaptation through balancing:* states adapt through socialisation by becoming involved in balancing. While states 'imitate' the great powers as a means of minimising the relative power gap, this does not fully eradicate fundamental differentials in power across the system. To ensure survival, therefore, states must also 'balance'. Thus weak states balance with other weak states against stronger ones. But, for Waltz, balancing does not entail genuine cooperation between states. He makes two arguments here. First, alliances are merely temporary and expedient. Thus while the United States was a military ally of the USSR during the Second World War, shortly afterwards they were on opposite sides in the 'Cold War'. Secondly, in contrast to Bull and Morgenthau, Waltz argues that the balance of power is not an institution that 'actors consensually [and collectively] agree upon' (1979: 121). They balance merely to maintain their own individual survival. While for Bull the system is *intentionally* maintained by states in part through the balance of power, for Waltz the system is *unwittingly* maintained as states balance, because its subversion into a hierarchy through the creation of a world empire is ultimately prevented. Although there has been a long line of would-be imperialists who have tried to subvert the anarchical structure of the system to create a hierarchical empire – e.g. Louis XIV, Napoleon Bonaparte, Adolf Hitler – none has succeeded because the others have defensively ganged up through balancing, thereby unintentionally maintaining a multi-state system.

In sum, while states have high domestic agential power (the ability to conduct policy free of domestic constraint), nevertheless, they have *no* international agential power to conduct policy free of international constraint nor the ability to buck the logic of anarchy. A key part of the argument is that these adaptive strategies *unintentionally* enable what might be termed 'states systems maintenance'. Thus the adaptive strategies of 'emulation' and 'balancing' promote systems maintenance because they *reduce the relative power gap between states*, making it impossible for a leading state to transform anarchy into hierarchy (i.e. empire). Thus, for Waltz, international structural change is not possible since anarchy will always remain. This is why Ruggie (1986) claims that Waltzian neorealism has only a 'reproductive' rather than a 'transformationist' logic. Thus Waltz manages to transplant what he describes as Adam Smith's 'brilliant insight' in microeconomic theory into the study of IP. Smith famously argued that as the units follow their own individual interests regardless of others, so the market system is successfully and unwittingly reproduced – i.e. without any of the actors actually intending such an outcome (see chapter 3, p. 66). Thus just as for Adam Smith, the 'invisible hand' of market competition results in order so, for Waltz, the 'invisible hand of anarchy' leads to anarchic multi-state systems maintenance. In this way, 'Order may prevail without an orderer; adjustments may be made without an adjuster; tasks may be allocated without an allocator' (Waltz 1979: 77).

This discussion can be reinforced by considering the two interpretations of Waltz that currently exist: what I call a minority 'statist' or 'agent-centric' reading (e.g. Ashley 1986: 271–3; Wendt 1987, 1991; Dessler 1989; Finnemore 1996: chapter 1; cf. Buzan, Jones and Little 1993: chapters 6–7), and a majority 'systemic' reading (e.g. Ruggie 1986: 134–5; Hollis and Smith 1991), which has been pursued in this chapter. Because the issue of state agency is so important to this volume, it is vital to resolve this particular debate. The minority statist view holds that Waltz invokes an individualist ontology which gives primacy to the actions and (international) agency of the state, such that the system is the product of prior state behaviour. Here the system is *epiphenomenal* to (i.e. completely determined by) state interests, a position which precisely inverts the 'systemic' interpretation developed in this chapter. Proponents of the agent-centric interpretation typically cite various arguments that Waltz has made, most notably:

(1) that structures 'do not determine behaviors and outcomes . . . [and] may be successfully resisted' (Waltz 1986: 343)

(2) that '[i]nternational-political systems, like economic markets, are individualist in origin, spontaneously generated, and unintended . . . [S]tructures are formed by the co-action of their units' (Waltz 1979: 91); that '[n]either structure nor units determine outcomes. Each affects the other' (Waltz 1986: 328, 338); that structure shapes and shoves rather than determines (Waltz 1986: 343); and finally, that the structure is 'not fully generative' (Waltz 1986: 328).

In favouring the systemic interpretation, I shall critically respond to each point in turn. First, while Waltz often tells us that structure is sometimes resisted, it is central to his theory that such 'chiliastic' recalcitrance can *never* be successful and will always be punished by the system (Waltz 1979: 128). Only if it can be demonstrated that recalcitrant behaviour can go unpunished by the system could the 'statist' interpretation be correct; a concession that would thoroughly undermine Waltz's whole theory. Regarding (2), while it is true that Waltz frequently claims that the units spontaneously give rise to the system, and that the units reproduce anarchy (implying the priority of the units over the system), nevertheless they do so precisely because they follow adaptive self-help policies that are *dictated by the survival imperatives of the system itself*. Indeed states *do* play a fundamental role in reproducing anarchy, but this is achieved only by their ability to conform to anarchy through the adaptive strategies of 'emulation and balancing'. Moreover, only if it could be demonstrated that states intentionally reproduce anarchy could the 'statist' interpretation be correct (as in state-centric liberalism). But Waltz never strays from his central claim that states reproduce anarchy through the *unintended consequences* of their adaptive/conformist behaviour. As Hollis and Smith (1991) point out, if the 'statist' interpretation was correct, then Waltz would have contradicted his whole theory because it would render it in Waltz's own terms 'reductionist' – the very 'other' that he has negatively defined himself against (see Waltz 1979: 18–102). With respect to Waltz's point that the system is not 'fully generative' while it is true that Waltz genuinely recognises that a great deal of social and political life is not generated by the structure, nevertheless the key point is that everything which is not generated by the system is for Waltz precisely irrelevant to international politics – denigrated as mere 'process'.

To conclude, the 'statist' or 'international agent-centric' interpretation is problematic because it ultimately rests on the assumption that states have autonomy from anarchy and the distribution of power – a logical impossibility for Waltz. In short, for Waltzian neorealism states have no international agential power and are unequivocally 'all product and . . . not at all productive' (Ruggie 1986: 151). *Contra* Wendt (1991: 388–9), this is a thoroughly *systemic* ontology. Thus Waltz's 'adaptive' theory of the state may be summarised as:

The sovereign 'positional' state, imbued with a high degree of domestic agential power follows its national interest or survival imperative, but has no international agential power and must adapt (i.e. conform) to the short-term anarchical requirements of the inter-state system (via emulation and balancing), which in turn unintentionally functions to reproduce the anarchical state system.

In short, *the state functions as a factor of anarchic systemic cohesion.*

It is wrong to assume that Waltz has no theory of the state, as others have noted (Buzan, Jones and Little 1993: 117–19; Hobden 1998: 66–9). It is merely a minimalist and functionalist one, in which the state is denied international agential power and is defined by the external functional requirements of the state system. It seems that what Waltz means when he says that we do not need a theory of the state is a different point: that we must not allow a neorealist theory of the state to grant the state international agential power. Thus, as neo-Weberians argue, the irony is that for all the talk of states, state power and state autonomy, the state is *under-theorised* and rendered all but irrelevant to the determination of IP – it is merely a 'passive victim of systemic anarchy' (Hobson 1997: chapters 1, 7).

The Waltzian 'two-step' variation: Gilpin and the 'process' of adaptive state change (modified neorealism)

Many argue that Waltz's theory is severely constrained by its static, a-historical, positivistic, deterministic and highly parsimonious framework (Ashley 1981, 1986; Cox 1986; Ruggie 1986; Walker 1987). Some IR scholars have suggested that such a critique would not apply to other neorealist works, most notably Robert Gilpin's *War and Change in World Politics* (1981), which allegedly views international *change* as a fundamental aspect of IR and brings not only social processes, but above all the state back in as unit-force variables (e.g. Gabriel 1994; Guzzini 1997; Schweller and Priess 1997). My interpretation suggests that Gilpin's work is a variation of Waltz's systemic approach (though Gilpin would not accept such a reading, see Gilpin 1986: 302–3), and that he succeeds only in producing a modified parsimonious or weak third-image approach. However, I argue that while both Waltz and Gilpin do indeed take different routes, they end up squarely within the same structuralist problematic and accordingly deny the state any inter-national agential power. How do the similarities arise?

First and foremost, both authors work essentially within a rigorous 'continuity' problematic (principle (1), figure 2.1). The primary purpose of *War and Change in World Politics* was to counteract the claim made by liberals and interdependence theorists in the 1970s that the world had fundamentally changed, and to reassert the centrality of international anarchy (the subject of the first state debate). In this book (and others – see p. 38), Gilpin sought to reinstate the *timeless* quality of IR, such that war and the rise and decline of the great powers is as fundamental to IR today as it was in the time when Thucydides was writing, in the fifth century BC. Even at the end of the twentieth century, Gilpin argues, states can still be understood as self-regarding entities within an anarchic international realm (Gilpin 1981: chapters 1, 6). Secondly, Gilpin's conception of change is precisely equivalent to Waltz's. For both theorists, change refers to surface changes *within* the system (i.e. changes in the distribution of power or changes of the units), as opposed to changes *of* the deep structure of the system (i.e. a transition from anarchy to hierarchy) (Gilpin 1981: chapter 1). More-over, both authors discount the possibility of a *fundamental* change in the system's *ordering principle*.

These first two points are derived from the third point of similarity between Waltz and Gilpin: that in Gilpin's model the logic of anarchy is the basic or primary causal variable and the state must passively adapt to the system's constraining logic (see figure 2.3). Gilpin precisely repli-cates Waltz's theory of the state, such that adaptive states – i.e. those that can emulate the successful practices of the leading states – will rise to the top of the international system, while maladaptive states sink to the bottom. However, Gilpin modifies Waltz's conceptual schema (what I call the 'Waltzian two-step'), by adding on two sets of contingent *intervening variables*: varying domestic agential state power and socio-economic fetters. These intervening variables enable Gilpin to supple-ment Waltz, only insofar as it enables him to specify *how* great powers rise and decline (a story that Waltz does not tell). Gilpin thus adds empirical sensitivity to Waltz's schema, but does not change the funda-mental approach.

The first intervening variable is that of the varying domestic agential power of the state. Gilpin relaxes Waltz's notion of *absolute* domestic agential state power or autonomy, by arguing that states can have varying degrees of domestic agency. He in effect argues that when domestic state agency is moderate or low, the state has difficulty in adapting and maintaining its power in the international system. Thus

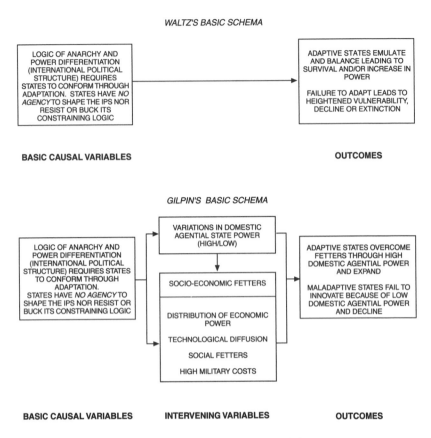

Figure 2.3 Gilpin's 'two-step' variation on Waltz

high domestic agency enables the state to better conform to inter-state competition under anarchy, and hence grow stronger; low domestic agency undermines the ability of the state to develop its power base, leading to great power decline (Gilpin 1981: 96–105). Gilpin's basic assumption is that the state will seek an expansionist foreign policy, and will continue to expand until countervailing forces – or what we might call 'fetters' – intervene. Most importantly, states come up against internal and external *fetters* which undermine either an expansionist foreign policy, or prevent a challenger from emerging only if the state has insufficient domestic agential power to overcome such obstacles. These fetters constitute the second set of intervening variables, which are economic, social and technological in nature. These entwine with the domestic agency of the state. Under conditions of low domestic agency, these non-political fetters undermine the state's position in the system; under conditions of high domestic agency such fetters can be overcome, enabling the state to expand its power base. These fetters comprise technological diffusion, internal social fetters and high international military costs:

(1) *Technological diffusion (changes in the distribution of economic power):* when a society harnesses a high rate of technological and productive innovation it expands. But, over time, the economy inevitably goes into decline, as the rate of technological innovation slows and the locus of innovation shifts to more adaptive rival states (Gilpin 1981: 160–2, 175–82). Hence the more adaptive states, endowed with relatively high levels of domestic agential power, are able to overcome fetters or obstacles and thereby successfully imitate and improve upon the leading technologies of the innovating states, enabling them to catch up and take the lead.

(2) *Internal social fetters as countervailing forces:* often domestic social arrangements prevent the absorption or introduction of new forms of technology, as noted above, or social forces push for higher taxation for public welfare consumption, the effect of which is to crowd out (i.e. reduce) investment, thereby undermining national economic growth (Gilpin 1981: 96–103, 163–5). Again it is the low domestic agential power of the state that prevents it from overcoming these obstacles to economic expansion.

(3) *High international military costs – foreign policy costs exceed domestic revenues:* this is associated specifically with great powers or 'hegemons'. High defence expenditures such as welfare spending, 'crowd out' investment, thereby leading to economic slowdown, in turn undermining the state's military base (Gilpin 1981: 163–5). A great power can maintain its power only by keeping its resources in balance with its military commitments. This is complemented by the international problem, consistent with neorealist hegemonic stability theory (see p. 41), whereby rival states 'free-ride' on the international public goods which the leading state exclusively provides, in turn promoting their growth at the hegemon's expense (Gilpin 1981: 168–74).

Gilpin (1975, 1981) applies this model in order to explain the decline of British hegemony after 1873 and US hegemony after 1973 (see the left-hand side of figure 2.4). Thus the decline in British economic growth after 1873 was determined first through a shift in the location of industrial innovation to the Continent. That is, continental states (especially Germany) enhanced their technological power through

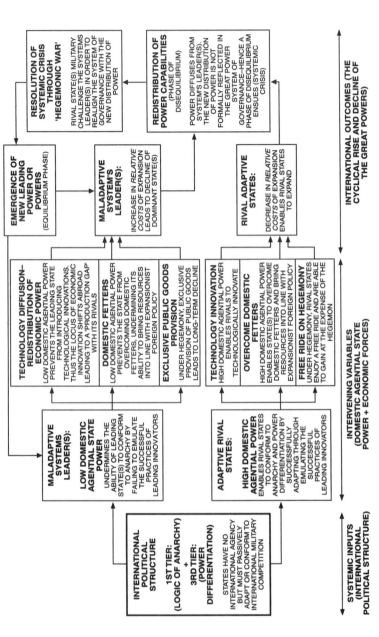

Figure 2.4 Gilpin's systemic 'cyclical' theory of the 'military-adaptive' state and the rise and decline of the great powers

superior state adaptation, while conversely the British state became increasingly *maladaptive*, failing to imitate the new successful practices of continental technological innovation. Secondly, British decline was premised upon the shift to a rentier economy through increased overseas investment and a service-based economy (deindustrialisation). Instead of *emulating* the successful new manufacturing developments achieved on the Continent, the British state demonstrated *maladaptability* – happy to complacently sit back and allow capital to leave the country at the expense of reinvigorating the domestic economy. This further promoted the shift in the distribution of economic power away from Britain. Thirdly, the *maladaptability* of the British state and its inability to overcome domestic fetters at a time when defence expenditures increased (i.e. increases in the relative costs of hegemony through rising private and public consumption), undermined its military power base. In short, in each case the low domestic agential power of the state led to maladaptability which, in failing to overcome countervailing fetters, undermined the state's military power as well as the economic base upon which its 'hegemonic' power rested (Gilpin 1975: 88–97). Thus after 1873 the distribution of power shifted away from unipolarity under British hegemony towards multipolarity (led by Germany), culminating in the latter challenging the former through 'hegemonic war' (1914–18). A similar set of factors undermined the US economy after 1970. And the American state also allowed – and indeed intentionally promoted – greater overseas foreign direct investment (FDI) through its multinational corporations (MNCs), at the direct cost of reinvigorating the domestic economy through a planned industrial policy programme (Gilpin 1975: chapter 7). Thus state maladaptability – or the inability of the state to adjust to inter-state competition imparted by low domestic agential power – resulted in US and British hegemonic decline in their respective periods. Put succinctly, 'the United States contracted a disease of the strong: refusal [or an inability] to adjust to change' (Keohane 1984: 179).

Changes in the distribution of power

Gilpin has thus traced the dynamics that lead to the rise and decline of great powers that was missing in Waltz, and simultaneously provides an account of changes in the distribution of capabilities (also missing in Waltz). While IP has remained the same since the time of Thucydides (the 'continuity' assumption), any given international order is in the process of constant change, as the distribution of power is constantly shifting. We can aid the discussion by drawing on Stephen Krasner's 'tectonic plate' metaphor (Krasner 1983b: 357–8). Beginning at the top of figure 2.4, a system begins with an equilibrium phase in which the dominant state(s) stands at the top and governs the system (i.e. the first plate). Progressing down figure 2.4, through time the distribution of power diffuses from the dominant maladaptive state(s) to more adaptive rival challengers (the second plate). In time, the system enters a phase of disequilibrium (the two plates shift out of phase). The subsequent resolution of this disequilibrium phase through 'hegemonic war' (i.e. a 'volcanic eruption)', leads to the establishment of a new international order which reflects the new distribution of power, thereby bringing the plates back into line (Gilpin 1981: 10–15, chapter 5). With a new state atop of the system, the cycle begins anew.

The critical variable is the ability of a state – through high domestic agential power – to harness through superior adaptation the economic, fiscal, social and military means which enable it to move towards the top, or keep it there. Thus it is the adaptiveness of rival states and maladaptability of the leading state(s) that accounts for international change – i.e. shifts in the international distribution of power.

The logic of anarchy and the adaptive state in 'systems change'
The common assumption that neorealism cannot explain systems change (e.g. Cox 1986; Ruggie 1986) is, I suggest, partially incorrect. Gilpin *is* able to explain the transition from feudal heteronomy to modern sovereignty by focusing exclusively on anarchy and the adaptive state (although he is *unable* to envisage change beyond the present system). The triumph of the nation-state over its feudal and imperial predecessors occurred because it was *better able to adapt* to the rise in military costs generated by the 'military revolution' (1550–1660) (Gilpin 1981: 116–27). Thus the cost of technological–military innovations – gunpowder, the gun and the professional army – increased exponentially through the military revolution, bringing about a fiscal crisis of feudalism. This crisis was founded upon the small and inefficient size and nature of the feudal unit, which was unable to generate sufficient revenues to meet these spiralling costs, and was therefore unable to meet the new conditions of warfare. The ensuing fiscal crisis could be resolved only by the emergence of a more adaptive form of state – namely, the more centralised 'nation-state' which, by harnessing capitalism, could enhance tax revenues. In short, anarchy dictated the emergence of a new and more adaptive state. *Contra* Ruggie, therefore, an exclusive focus on the logic of anarchy can explain 'historical systems change', an ironic conclusion given that Waltz himself missed this point in his reply to Ruggie's criticism (see Waltz 1986: 323–30).

Gilpin's systemic theory of the 'passive-adaptive state'

So we have seen that Gilpin clearly opens up the 'black-box' of state–society relations, as well as international economic relations, in order to explain adaptive and maladaptive state behaviour and changes in the distribution of power. To do this, he relaxes Waltz's assumption that the state has absolute autonomy from non-state processes. For Waltz, the second level drops out because of the centrality that he accords to the first and third tiers. Gilpin does the same. Non-systemic processes – domestic agential state power on the one hand, and economic, technological and social forces on the other – are salient only to the extent that they *enable a state to either conform, or fail to conform, to the primary logic of anarchy and power differentiation: they enable or constrain state behaviour, but do not define it – that is left to the system of anarchy.* What makes this structuralist is the point that while some states might choose not – or be unable - to adapt to anarchy, so they will be punished by the system. Hence the state is denied any international agential capacity, and has no choice but to rationally adapt to the external environment. The state, state–society relations and international economic relations are, therefore, reduced to the military dictates of anarchy. As Rob Walker so aptly puts it, despite the fact that Gilpin 'tempts' us with a sensitive and complex historicist approach, nevertheless the central conclusion of his work is that 'a Thucydides reborn would have little difficulty in explaining our contemporary agonies' (Walker 1987: 66).

In the end, Gilpin reproduces Waltz's systemic neorealist logic. As Waltz put it: 'Actors may [or may not] perceive the structure [of anarchy] that constrains them and understand how it serves to reward some kinds of behavior and to penalize others . . . those who conform to accepted and successful practices more often rise to the top and are likelier to stay there. The game one has to win is defined by the structure that determines the kind of player who is likely to prosper' (Waltz 1979: 92, 128). By adding in various 'contingent' or intervening variables, Gilpin is able to tell us *how* some states are able or unable to conform to anarchy. But the crucial point is that while states are accorded varying degrees of domestic agential power, they are, in classic Waltzian fashion, denied international agential power to determine the international structure, let alone mitigate or buck its constraining logic. They must conform to anarchy; if not, they decline. Thus, once again, international structure is reified and the international agential power of the state is denigrated. This systemic theory of the 'passive-adaptive' state, and of IP more generally, furnishes Gilpin's account of the rise and decline of hegemons and great powers. And it is upon this systemic theoretical base that hegemonic stability theory rests.

The neorealist theory of the passive-adaptive state and
hegemonic regimes (modified neorealism)

As noted in chapter 1, the first-state debate emerged in the 1970s, with
Marxists and pluralists arguing that MNCs, international regimes and
global interdependence were eroding the salience of the sovereign state,
and were effectively transcending anarchy and self-help as the organising
principles of world politics. The neorealist response was developed in
large part by Robert Gilpin and Stephen D. Krasner, who developed
what is known as 'hegemonic stability theory' (HST). Here Gilpin and
Krasner sought to reestablish the *timeless* importance of anarchy and the
distribution of power as *the* fundamental bases upon which interdependence, free trade, international regimes and the MNC are founded. In
short, HST sought to reverse the causal relationship between economics
and politics that liberalism and Marxism prescribe. Consequently, given
the continuing relevance of anarchy, it was axiomatic that the sovereign
state was still primary. Specifically Krasner (1976, 1995) argued that
contemporary interdependence and the importance of the free trade
regime could be explained by US hegemonic power under a unipolar
distribution of power. But the paradox was that in reasserting the
centrality of anarchy and the sovereign state, HST fundamentally
denied the state any international agential power.

The neorealist foundations of hegemonic stability theory
Neorealism argues that, under anarchy, cooperation is not possible,
given the survival imperative which dictates that states must prioritise
'relative gains' (self-help) over 'absolute (international cooperative)
gains'. Anarchy gives rise to the 'collective action problem', in that states
must eschew collaboration in order to survive. However, HST modifies
this formula arguing that cooperation *is* possible, but only under a
unique distribution of power – *hegemonic unipolarity* – and only for the
short term. In the long run, cooperation dissolves as hegemony declines
and the distribution of power inevitably shifts to multipolarity. As figure
2.5 shows, 'hegemony' is introduced as an intervening variable that can
transform states' short-term preferences into long-term 'cooperative
gains' preferences. Thus a hegemon can persuade 'others to follow a
given course of action which might not be in the follower's short run
interests if it were truly independent' (Kindleberger 1981: 243). Nevertheless, given the 'long-run tendency for hegemony to decline', it is
inevitable that states will eventually revert back to their traditional or
'natural' preference for pursuing short-term 'relative gains'. The key
difference between neorealism and neoliberal institutionalism is that, for

WALTZ'S BASIC SCHEMA

BASIC CAUSAL VARIABLES   OUTCOMES

HEGEMONIC STABILITY THEORY'S BASIC SCHEMA

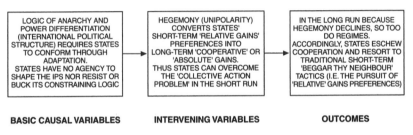

BASIC CAUSAL VARIABLES   INTERVENING VARIABLES   OUTCOMES

Figure 2.5 Hegemonic stability theory's variation on Waltz

the latter, states have high international agential capacity and voluntarily cooperate through international regimes while, for neorealists, cooperation can be enforced only by a coercive hegemon. For neorealists, hegemonic regimes are determined by a unique configuration of the distribution of power (i.e. unipolarity), while for neoliberals, regimes acquire a full autonomy from the distribution of power (see pp. 94–104).

A 'hegemon' fulfils five defining criteria:

(1) The leading state must have a preponderance of economic and military power (superior power base).

(2) A hegemon must be a *liberal* state, because only liberal states have the *will* to pursue hegemony: authoritarian states prefer imperialism; moreover, only liberal states are concerned to create an open and liberal world order.

(3) There must be a rudimentary consensus among the major states for hegemony (Gilpin 1987: 72–3).

To the usual three, two more can be added:

(4) That a hegemon has the necessary 'far-sightedness' to set up regimes which can enhance long-term global welfare.

(5) A hegemon must be willing to make short-term sacrifices in order to secure long-term collective/global benefit (cf. Keohane 1984: 146, 180–1). The basic function of hegemony is to overcome the 'collective action problem' by altruistically creating and maintaining liberal international trading and monetary regimes – especially fixed exchange rates and free trade – as well as acting as the global policeman. In the process, the hegemon converts the short-term 'relative gains' preferences of states (i.e. their 'natural' preferences) into 'long-term' cooperative gains preferences.

What, then, are these altruistic sacrifices that hegemons make? With respect to the United States, the benign hegemonic sacrifices were basically four-fold. First, the United States has performed the role of world policeman (globocop) and militarily shielded the Western Alliance. But in spending disproportionately more than its allies, the latter have been able to allocate more resources to promoting economic development (Gilpin 1987: 343–9). Secondly, the United States endured assymetrical gains from trade with its major trading partners until the late 1950s, allowing Europe and Japan to erect tariff barriers against US exports, while the United States allowed industrial imports in on a relatively free trade basis (thereby promoting global trade). Thirdly, the United States was responsible for setting up and maintaining liberal international economic regimes (especially free trade) and for providing the global currency. Finally the United States made sacrifices in investment and aid, passing on outright grants and loans to Europe, principally through Marshall Aid, and in general acted as 'lender of last resort' (Gilpin 1975: chapter 5, 1981: chapter 4, 1987: 72–80, 85–92, 123–42; Kindleberger 1973). The result was relative peace, interdependence and the rapid growth of the world economy. The theory argues that similar hegemonic sacrifices, with similar results, were achieved by Britain between c. 1820 and 1873.

The theory argues that there are two phases of hegemony: *benign* (i.e. altruistic) and *predatory* (i.e. selfish). The former results in the exclusive provision of public goods by the hegemon, which broadly characterises the initial phase of hegemony (i.e. 1945–73 for America and c. 1820–73 for Britain). This is followed by the predatory phase in which the declining hegemon eschews its policy of self-sacrifice and pursues its own selfish national interest (i.e. Britain after 1873 and the United States from 1973 to the present). Although the benign phase was not always *wholly* altruistic – the United States enjoyed certain private gains or privileges from hegemony such as 'imperial taxation' (Gilpin

1975: 153–6, 217–19) – these were, however, insufficient to outweigh the costs of leadership, making hegemonic decline inevitable.

Hegemonic decline, the shift from unipolarity to multipolarity and the passive-maladaptive state

The key point for neorealism is that hegemonic regimes are unstable and precarious because they can be successfully maintained only by a strong hegemon (figure 2.6). Thus HST argues that regimes are 'effective', but that they lack 'robustness' or 'resilience'; that they are effective only as long as hegemony lasts (Hasenclever, Mayer and Rittberger 1997: 86–7). Because of the 'long-run tendency for hegemony to decline' regimes are, therefore, only short-lived. Why, then, does hegemony (and, therefore, hegemonic regimes) decline?

The conventionally received view is that for neorealists, the exercise of hegemony is necessarily 'self-destructive' or 'self-liquidating' (Keohane 1989: 252). This is supposedly because of the 'free-rider' problem associated with the exclusive provision of public goods by the hegemon (Olson and Zeckhauser 1966; Kindleberger 1981). Hegemons provide *public goods* – goods which are consumed by all states such that their consumption by one state does not reduce the amount available for others. Conventional wisdom assumes that hegemonic decline derives from the fact that the hegemon provides public goods from which all other states benefit, but that its 'rivals' do not contribute to the payment or upkeep of these goods or 'regimes'. They therefore enjoy a 'free-ride' at the expense of the hegemon's altruistic behaviour, which leads to the hegemon's long-term relative decline and hence the decline of hegemonic regimes. While this 'international public goods provision' thesis of hegemonic decline is not an insignificant component of the theory, I nevertheless argue that hegemonic decline rests primarily upon the theory of the 'maladaptive' state. The conventional reading is problematic for two reasons. First, if the hegemon is as 'far-sighted' and benign, as HST assumes, why can it not predict its own future demise and therefore change its short-term behaviour to pre-empt or avoid any future decline? More damaging still, to hinge the whole theory on the argument that the leading state is self-sacrificial to the point that it actually undermines itself, is to contradict the fundamental neorealist assumption that states are 'positional' and are motivated by self-interest. Indeed, it would break the cardinal neorealist rule that weak states are unable to undermine the leading states in the international system. But neorealist integrity is retained (and saved) by its theory of the maladaptive state which, I argue, lies at base of the 'hegemonic decline' thesis.

As we saw on pp. 33–5, Gilpin (1975, 1981) argues that the decline in

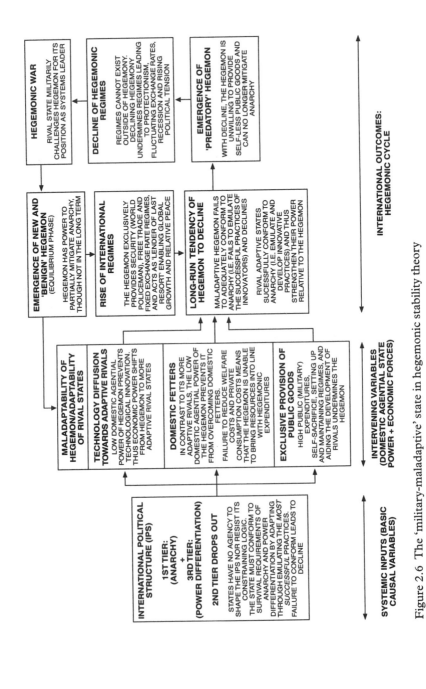

Figure 2.6 The 'military-maladaptive' state in hegemonic stability theory

HEGEMONIC WAR

RIVAL STATE MILITARILY CHALLENGES HEGEMON FOR ITS POSITION AS SYSTEMS LEADER

DECLINE OF HEGEMONIC REGIMES

REGIMES CANNOT EXIST OUTSIDE OF HEGEMONY. DECLINING HEGEMONY UNDERMINES REGIMES LEADING TO PROTECTIONISM, FLUCTUATING EXCHANGE RATES, RECESSION AND RISING POLITICAL TENSION

EMERGENCE OF 'PREDATORY' HEGEMON

WITH DECLINE, THE HEGEMON IS UNWILLING TO PROVIDE SELF-LESS PUBLIC GOODS AND CAN NO LONGER MITIGATE ANARCHY

EMERGENCE OF NEW AND 'BENIGN' HEGEMON

('EQUILIBRIUM PHASE')

HEGEMON HAS POWER TO PARTIALLY MITIGATE ANARCHY, THOUGH NOT IN THE LONG TERM

RISE OF INTERNATIONAL REGIMES

THE HEGEMON EXCLUSIVELY PROVIDES SECURITY (WORLD POLICEMAN), FREE TRADE AND FIXED EXCHANGE RATE REGIMES, AND ACTS AS 'LENDER OF LAST RESORT' ENABLING GLOBAL GROWTH AND RELATIVE PEACE

LONG-RUN TENDENCY OF HEGEMON TO DECLINE

MALADAPTIVE HEGEMON FAILS TO ADEQUATELY CONFORM TO ANARCHY (I.E. FAILS TO EMULATE THE SUCCESSFUL PRACTICES OF INNOVATORS) AND DECLINES

RIVAL ADAPTIVE STATES SUCCESSFULLY CONFORM TO ANARCHY (I.E. EMULATE AND DEVELOP INNOVATIVE PRACTICES) AND THUS STRENGTHEN THEIR POWER RELATIVE TO THE HEGEMON

MALADAPTABILITY OF HEGEMON/ADAPTABILITY OF RIVAL STATES

TECHNOLOGY DIFFUSION TOWARDS ADAPTIVE RIVALS

LOW DOMESTIC AGENTIAL POWER OF HEGEMON PREVENTS TECHNOLOGICAL INNOVATION. THUS ECONOMIC POWER SHIFTS FROM HEGEMON TO MORE ADAPTIVE RIVAL STATES

DOMESTIC FETTERS

IN CONTRAST TO ITS MORE ADAPTIVE RIVALS, THE LOW DOMESTIC AGENTIAL POWER OF THE HEGEMON PREVENTS IT FROM OVERCOMING DOMESTIC FETTERS.

FAILURE TO REDUCE WELFARE COSTS AND PRIVATE CONSUMPTION COSTS MEANS THAT THE HEGEMON IS UNABLE TO BRING RESOURCES INTO LINE WITH HEGEMONIC EXPENDITURES

EXCLUSIVE PROVISION OF PUBLIC GOODS

HIGH PUBLIC (MILITARY) EXPENDITURES, SELF-SACRIFICE, SETTING UP AND MAINTAINING REGIMES, AND AIDING THE DEVELOPMENT OF RIVALS UNDERMINES THE HEGEMON

INTERNATIONAL POLITICAL STRUCTURE (IPS)

1ST TIER: (ANARCHY)
+
3RD TIER: (POWER DIFFERENTIATION)

2ND TIER DROPS OUT

STATES HAVE NO AGENCY TO SHAPE THE IPS NOR RESIST ITS CONSTRAINING LOGIC. THE STATE MUST CONFORM TO SURVIVAL REQUIREMENTS OF ANARCHY AND POWER DIFFERENTIATION BY ADAPTING THROUGH EMULATING THE *MOST SUCCESSFUL* PRACTICES. FAILURE TO CONFORM LEADS TO DECLINE

INTERNATIONAL OUTCOMES: HEGEMONIC CYCLE

INTERVENING VARIABLES (DOMESTIC AGENTIAL STATE POWER + ECONOMIC FORCES)

SYSTEMIC INPUTS (BASIC CAUSAL VARIABLES)

British economic growth after 1873 was determined not by free-riders as such, but through the state's maladaptiveness or inability to adapt to the successful practices of the more adaptive 'rival' states. Thus continental states (especially Germany) enhanced their power through *superior state adaptation*, while conversely the British state became increasingly *maladaptive* (see pp. 33–5 for full details). And as noted above, precisely the same processes of maladaptive state behaviour applied to the United States after 1973. Thus in explaining hegemonic decline, the free-rider problem is substantially diminished, while the maladaptive behaviour of the hegemon is considerably upgraded. Stephen Krasner adopts a slightly different version of the maladaptive state in his *Defending the National Interest* (1978). He places special emphasis on the low domestic agential power (i.e. low institutional autonomy) of the US state (as of course does Gilpin). The domestic structure of the state was weak owing to its fragmented and dispersed nature, enabling private groups varying degrees of access to, and influence over, government policy. This was prevalent in trade policy where commercial private interests in Congress had considerable say because of the state's *lack of insulation*. Thus domestic protectionist interests initially hampered America's ability to shift to free trade. Conversely, after 1970, with the rise of foreign competition and imports, domestic groups turned back to protection, thus pushing the state to abandon its outright pursuit of external free trade. But the essential neorealist theory of the maladaptive state is fundamental to Krasner's account of US hegemonic decline, since he argues that the lack of insulation of the state from strong domestic pressure groups (i.e. low domestic agential state power) undermined the state's ability to adapt to systemic requirements.

The passive-adaptive state in hegemonic stability theory

My interpretation suggests that the 'theory of the adaptive/maladaptive state' lies at the base of hegemonic stability theory as well as neorealism more generally. That is, differentials in national state adaptability is the motor that informs changes in the distribution of power and hence the rise and decline of hegemons and hegemonic regimes (as depicted in figure 2.6). As we have seen, both Gilpin and especially Krasner relax Waltz's assumption of the absolute domestic agential power of the state, and allocate considerable analysis to state–society relations in their explanation of IR. This begs the all-important question: has HST/ modified neorealism succeeded in going beyond neorealist parsimony, and invoked 'second-level variables' to explain IP, thereby endowing the state with international agential power? I suggest that HST is a 'weak' third-image or 'modified parsimonious' theory, which conceives of state–society relations as only *intervening* variables. Thus while these intervening variables succeed in adding empirical sensitivity, the approach does not transcend Waltz's *systemic* schema. These intervening variables are ultimately reduced to the geopolitical dictates of anarchy. The crucial point is that *domestic interest groups and domestic state weakness can only constrain the ability of the state to conform to anarchy; they cannot fundamentally affect the structure of the international system and the logic of anarchy, nor change the rules of state behaviour under anarchy – namely following self-help policies of adaptation.* Thus low domestic agential state power prevents the state from conforming or adapting to anarchy, leading to punishment by systemic anarchy through hegemonic or great power decline, while high domestic agential power enables conformity and the rewards of great power or hegemonic expansion. Either way though, the state has no international agential power to shape the international political structure. Of course modified neorealists and what Rose (1998) calls *neoclassical realists* as well as 'structural realists' (Buzan, Jones and Little 1993) might object and point out that states can choose not to adapt or conform to anarchy, or, that the nature of state–society relations might prevent them from doing so. But such behaviour will simply be punished by the system and lead to state decline, as Waltz tells us (Waltz 1978: 118). In the end, states have no agency to shape the international system and have no choice but to passively adapt to the systemic requirements of anarchy (or suffer the consequences).

The key point here is that Gilpin and Krasner have pushed neorealism as far as it can go with respect to integrating unit-level forces. Nevertheless, given that unit-level forces are no more than intervening variables, anarchy remains primary. The same conclusion applies to 'neoclassical realism' which, as Rose (1998) concedes, also conceives of unit-level forces as intervening variables. In the last instance, *all* neorealist theories reify the international structure and deny the state any genuine agency to shape the international political structure. They succeed only in 'kicking the state back out' as an agent in IP. But this should not be entirely surprising, given that HST was developed precisely to demonstrate and explain that world politics has never changed because of the timeless effects of the logic of anarchy. By contrast, classical realists accorded considerable levels of international agential power to the state.

Classical realist complexity: the 'socialising state' with international agential power

As figure 2.7 shows, I suggest that classical realism to an extent problematises the state, endows it not only with *variable* degrees of domestic agential power, but above all insists that the international system is created by the international agential powers of the state at the unit level. In short, in radical contrast to neorealism, classical realism 'brings the state (the second tier) back in' as an independent agential variable in IP. The key differences are listed in figure 2.7.

Compared to neorealism, classical realism places the state more at the centre of analysis, such that IP is derived for the most part from changes in the state's domestic agential power – independent of anarchy or changes in the international distribution of power (see also figure 2.1, p. 18). In addition, both Carr and Morgenthau emphasise the importance of norms. Although to an extent both authors tie norms to the domestic agential power of the state, they also ascribe autonomy to norms, which promotes both a 'practical realism' as well as an 'emancipatory realism' (cf. Ashley 1981). To an important extent, therefore, classical realism has much more in common with constructivism and critical theory than is often recognised. But the most significant point is that, for classical realism, systemic parsimony is largely avoided.

From Waltzian adaptability to Morgenthau's intelligent state

Waltz (1979: chapter 3) famously argued that classical realism is non-systemic – or, in his terms, 'reductionist' – in that it explains the whole through its parts. Surprisingly this stands in contrast to the conventional understanding of Morgenthau, which conflates Morgenthau with neo-realism (e.g. Hoffmann 1981; Smith 1986). But this has been challenged by a minority of authors who differentiate classical realism from neo realism (Ashley 1981; Walker 1987; Griffiths 1992). I side with the minority interpretation, although I argue that Morgenthau, unlike Carr, does on occasion derive the state from the system. There are in fact two discernible strands in Morgenthau: in Rosecrance's (1981) terms, a 'static' or systemic approach (similar to the 'technical' approach of neorealism and represented in the top half of figure 2.8, p. 49), and a 'dynamic' or *non-systemic* approach that departs from neorealism (i.e. a 'practical' realism represented in the bottom half of figure 2.8, p. 49). But, *contra* Rosecrance, I argue that the dynamic rather than the static approach is the dominant aspect of Morgenthau's theory. The conflation of Morgenthau with neorealism is usually traced to his 'six principles of

Figure 2.7 The two realist approaches to the state

	NEOREALISM	CLASSICAL REALISM (MORGENTHAU'S NON-SYSTEMIC THEORY)	CLASSICAL REALISM (CARR)
DOMESTIC AGENTIAL STATE POWER (ABILITY OF STATE TO DETERMINE POLICY FREE OF DOMESTIC SOCIAL CONSTRAINT)	**HIGH:** STATES HAVE ABSOLUTE DOMESTIC AGENTIAL POWER. ALTHOUGH GILPIN AND KRASNER ALLOW FOR VARIATIONS IN DOMESTIC AGENTIAL STATE POWER, NEVERTHELESS STATES ARE DETERMINED BY ANARCHY	**VARIABLE:** PERIOD 1: 1648– NINETEENTH CENTURY HIGH: IN THE ARISTOCRATIC INTERNATIONAL STATE HAS HIGH INSULATION FROM THE MASSES PERIOD 2: TWENTIETH CENTURY LOW: UNDER NATIONALISTIC UNIVERSALISM STATE HAS LOW INSULATION FROM THE MASSES PERIOD 3: POST-TWENTIETH CENTURY POTENTIALLY HIGH: UNDER SUPER-INTELLIGENT DIPLOMACY THE STATE MAY REGAIN ITS INSULATION FROM THE MASSES	**VARIABLE:** PERIOD 1: 1648–1792/1815 HIGH: UNDER THE MONARCHICAL NATION THE STATE HAS HIGH INSULATION FROM THE MASSES PERIOD 2: 1792/1815–1870/1919 HIGH: UNDER THE BOURGEOIS NATION THE STATE HAS HIGH INSULATION FROM SOCIETY PERIOD 3: 1919–1945 LOW: UNDER THE SOCIALISED NATION THE STATE HAS LOW INSULATION FROM THE MASSES PERIOD 4: POST-1945 WITHERS AWAY: POTENTIAL TRANSCENDENCE OF THE SOVEREIGN STATE AFTER 1945
INTERNATIONAL AGENTIAL STATE POWER (ABILITY OF STATE TO DETERMINE POLICY AND SHAPE THE INTERNATIONAL SYSTEM FREE OF INTERNATIONAL CONSTRAINTS AND, AT THE EXTREME, TO BUCK THE LOGIC OF INTER-STATE COMPETITION)	**NONE:** SYSTEMIC ANARCHY WHOLLY DETERMINES STATE BEHAVIOUR AND IP STATES HAVE NO AGENTIAL POWER TO SHAPE THE INTERNATIONAL SYSTEM NOR BUCK THE LOGIC OF ANARCHY (HOWEVER HEGEMONS CAN MITIGATE ANARCHY, BUT ONLY IN THE SHORT RUN. MOREOVER, ALL OTHER NON-HEGEMONIC STATES HAVE NO AGENCY)	**VARIABLE: INTERNATIONAL AGENTIAL STATE POWER DETERMINES IP** PERIOD 1: 1648– NINETEENTH CENTURY HIGH: HIGH INTERNATIONAL AGENTIAL STATE POWER TO MITIGATE ANARCHY OUTCOME: RELATIVE PEACE IN IP PERIOD 2: TWENTIETH CENTURY MODERATE: MODERATE INTERNATIONAL AGENTIAL POWER LEADS TO A CONFLICTUAL INTER-STATE SYSTEM OUTCOME: 'WAR OF ALL AGAINST ALL' PERIOD 3: POST-TWENTIETH CENTURY POTENTIALLY HIGH: STATES MAY ACQUIRE HIGH DEGREES OF INTERNATIONAL AGENCY AND THEREBY PROMOTE A FUTURE PEACEFUL INTERNATIONAL ORDER OUTCOME: GLOBAL PEACE	**VARIABLE: INTERNATIONAL AGENTIAL STATE POWER DETERMINES IP** PERIOD 1: 1648–1792/1815 HIGH: UNDER THE MONARCHICAL NATION STATES HAVE HIGH DEGREES OF INTERNATIONAL AGENTIAL POWER OUTCOME: RELATIVE PEACE IN IP PERIOD 2: 1792/1815–1870/1919 HIGH: UNDER THE BOURGEOIS NATION STATES HAVE HIGH INTERNATIONAL AGENTIAL POWER OUTCOME: RELATIVE PEACE IN IP PERIOD 3: 1919–1945 MODERATE: UNDER THE SOCIALISED NATION STATES HAVE ONLY MODERATE INTERNATIONAL AGENTIAL POWER. ACCORDINGLY THE MORAL BOUNDARY SHRINKS FROM THE INTERNATIONAL BACK TO THE NATIONAL REALM OUTCOME: 'WAR OF ALL AGAINST ALL' PERIOD 4: POST-1945 WITHERS AWAY: AFTER 1945 THE SOCIALISED NATION IS TRANSCENDED BY AUTONOMOUS GLOBAL NORMS OUTCOME: GLOBAL PEACE

political realism', which are laid out in chapter 1 of his most famous text *Politics Among Nations* (1948/1978).

Here Morgenthau asserts that (1) 'politics is governed by objective laws rooted in human nature'; (2) the 'national interest' is defined as the maximisation of national power; ((4), (5) that foreign policy must be detached from morality; ((6), (2) that the sphere of politics must be separated out from all others, whether these are economic, legalistic, moralistic, etc. Typical summary statements of his approach usually cited are: 'the struggle for power [between states] is universal in time and space' (Morgenthau 1948/1978: 36); and '[a]ll history shows that nations active in international politics are continuously preparing for, actually involved in, or recovering from organised violence in the form of war' (Morgenthau 1948/1978: 42). These statements clearly suggest a systemic 'neorealist' approach.

But even in chapter 1, there is a hint of a radically different picture (i.e. his 'dynamic' non-systemic approach), articulated in his principle (3): that although interest is defined as power, such a concept 'is not fixed once and for all' (Morgenthau 1948/1978: 8). Echoing Carr, he states that,

> the contemporary connection between interest and the nation state is a product of history, and is therefore bound to disappear in the course of history. Nothing in the realist position militates against the assumption that the present division of the political world into nation states will be replaced by larger units of a quite different character, more in keeping with the technical potentialities and the moral requirements of the contemporary world. (Morgenthau 1978: 10)

This suggests a sensitivity to the issues of historical (systemic) change and morality, which sits uneasily or in contradiction with the universalist, systemic, static and 'rationalist' (i.e. materialist) criteria of the other five principles (see figure 2.1, p. 18). It also questions the neorealist notion that the modern nation-state is the highest form of political expression. Most significantly, I argue that this dynamic approach comprises the bulk of Morgenthau's following thirty-one chapters, although the static (systemic) approach is also on occasion evident. In contrast to conventional understanding, my subjective interpretation suggests that there are two theories of the state in Morgenthau: a minor systemic approach (as in Waltzian neorealism), where the state is denied any international agential capacity; and a major non-systemic approach, in which the state is granted considerable international agential power. This leads to an awkward and contradictory analysis given that it is not possible to reconcile the two approaches. We begin with Morgenthau's static 'adaptive theory of the state', before examining the major aspect of his approach found in his 'non-systemic' theory of the state and IP.

Morgenthau's minor (first) 'systemic theory' of the state: the 'passive-adaptive (intelligent) state'

Morgenthau's first theory of the state is systemic (or third-image) and is depicted in the top half of figure 2.8. This theory derives state behaviour from the system of anarchy to which the state must adapt in order to gain technical control in a hostile environment (as in Waltz). Here, the state has high domestic agential power (internal sovereignty), but no international agential power either to determine the international structure or to mitigate its constraining logic. As in Waltz, the state achieves this through various adaptive strategies. While Morgenthau focuses on 'emulation' and 'balancing' (the fundamental aspects of Waltz's adaptive strategies), he also adds 'intelligence' which comprises the *demystification* of rival states' foreign policies, the *bluffing* of opponents in terms of one's own foreign policy (FP) intentions and national strength, and the *evaluation* of rivals' power bases. First, it is vital that a state, when choosing its FP, is able to intelligently read or demystify the FPs of other states and distinguish between three types of FP: 'imperial', 'status quo' and 'prestige'. Imperialism is the most threatening. Note that this is not necessarily the same as a policy of empire; 'imperialism' refers to a policy which seeks to change the distribution of power within the states system to the advantage of a particular state. The policy of the 'status quo' refers to a FP in which a 'satisfied' state has no desire to change the distribution of power in its favour (usually the policy of a dominant power). The policy of 'prestige' is more modest than the first two, and is employed by all states to demonstrate their power to other nations through diplomatic ceremony (pomp and circumstance) and through the display of military force at home.

The first problem for the intelligent state is to decipher these different FPs. If statesmen choose the wrong counter-policy, disaster can ensue. Thus to counter an imperialist FP, a strategy of 'containment' is necessary. Appeasement is the wrong policy and courts disaster. Here Chamberlain's Munich settlement is singled out for special (if not vitriolic) criticism (Morgenthau 1948/1978: 6, 70). Appeasement is, however, the correct strategy to counter a status quo policy. Intelligence is required to *demystify* the ideological cloaks with which statesmen dress up their particular FPs (which is most acute under imperialism). Without this ability, statesmen will be hindered in applying the correct counter-policy, as Neville Chamberlain found out to the detriment of the world in 1939. Moreover, it is vital for all statesmen to be able to

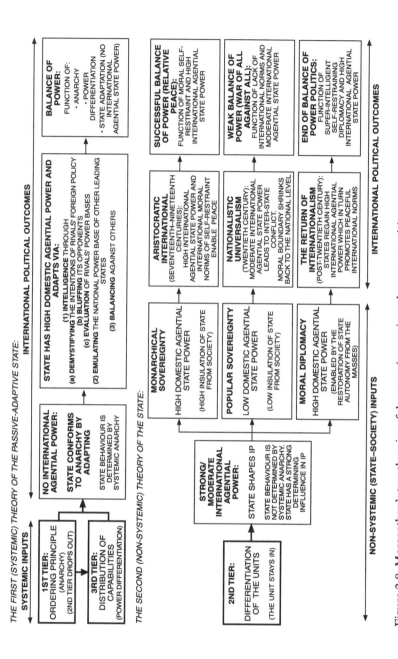

Figure 2.8 Morgenthau's two theories of the state (systemic and non-systemic)

dress up their FPs in an ideological cloak in order to 'bluff' the enemy. As in *Star Trek*, the element of surprise that was achieved by the Klingon battleship cruisers' cloaking device gave them considerable initial tactical advantage over the Federation star ships. In a crude sense, IP is almost akin to a type of poker game in which all the actors are seeking to bluff their opponents as well as to read through any bluffs made by their opponents. Moreover, statesmen are advised not to over-play their bluff since they could eventually be found out on the battle-field (Morgenthau 1948/1978: 68–103). Statesmen also on occasion need to be able to bluff their own domestic populations in order to gain popular support for a given FP.

The third aspect of intelligence is the need to *evaluate* the national power bases of their opponents, and to adapt the state's national strength to that of others through *emulation* (as in Waltz). There are eight factors of national strength that statesmen must consider – nine if we include 'geographical position' (1948/1978: 117–55). These com-prise: self-sufficiency in food and raw materials, a strong industrial base, an advanced technological military base, a large population (though one that is balanced by sufficient resources to sustain it), a strong national morale and homogeneous society (relatively free of debilitating internal conflicts) and, above all, a strong government. But in particular, the government must be intelligent, so that it can balance resources against commitments (as in Gilpin), as well as evaluate the FPs of other states and successfully emulate the leading powers. Both of these tasks, Morgenthau argues, are extremely difficult to achieve, as becomes more obvious when we come to examine his theory of the balance of power. In his first systemic (adaptive) theory of the state and of the balance of power, he emphasises the need for states to minimise the relative power gap through intelligent adaptation (demystification, bluffing, evaluation and emulation), as well as through balancing (top half of figure 2.8). However, he has a second theory of the balance of power which is based on his second theory of the state (the bottom half of figure 2.8), to which we now turn.

Morgenthau's major (second) 'non-systemic' theory of the state: the state as the determining agent of international politics
Turning to the bottom half of figure 2.8, Morgenthau's second theory of the state focuses on varying degrees of state agential power, autonomy and norms as the basis of international politics. In contrast to Waltz, Morgenthau – somewhat contradictorily – also argued that the balance of power would not automatically occur as states followed their adaptive survival strategies, because of the 'inadequacy' of the balance of power

(Morgenthau 1948/1978: 221–44). Rather than being self-sustaining, the balance of power had to be *intentionally constructed by states*. This could best be achieved when states' domestic agential power was high. Here, Morgenthau also brings in the importance of norms, which comprise the fundamental ingredients of the maintenance, and indeed success, of the balance of power (leading him into a 'practical realism'). The balance of power is nested or embedded within social norms that operate across international society (where Morgenthau draws close to Hedley Bull as well as to constructivism more generally). These international norms are enabled under conditions of high domestic state agential power.

Morgenthau traces two historical periods: first, the balance under the 'aristocratic international' (the classical heyday of the seventeenth–nineteenth centuries) and, secondly, the balance in the age of 'nationalistic universalism' (the twentieth century). The balance led to peace in the former period but war in the latter. Why? The key to the success of the balance occurs when states' domestic agential power is high, which in turn leads to a high degree of international state agential power to overcome inter-state competition. Under *monarchical sovereignty*, the state was well insulated (i.e. had high domestic autonomy) from the masses. This enabled noble monarchs to determine international politics and create a relatively peaceful international sphere (i.e. through high international agential state power). It was the specific set of aristocratic international norms that was vital. Thus,

the fuel for the European (17th to 19th century) balance of power was the intellectual and moral foundation of Western civilisation. These men [monarchs] knew Europe as 'one great republic' with common standards of 'politeness and cultivation' and a common 'system of arts, and laws, and manners'. The common awareness of these common standards restrained their ambitions 'by the mutual influence of fear and shame', imposed 'moderation' upon their actions, and instilled in all of them 'some sense of honour and justice'. (Morgenthau 1948/1978: 225–6)

The 'morals' of the noble monarchs led to the development of international norms (the 'aristocratic international'), which enabled a moral consensus between states 'without which its [the balance of power's] operation is not possible' (Morgenthau 1948/1978: 221). It is worth extending this citation further:

Before establishing the balance of power states had first to restrain themselves by accepting the system of the balance as the common framework of their endeavours. It is this consensus . . . of common moral standards and a common civilisation as well as of common interests – that kept in check the limitless desire for power . . . Where such a consensus no longer exists or has become weak and is no longer sure of itself . . . the balance of power is incapable of fulfilling its functions for international stability and national independence. (Morgenthau 1948/1978: 226–7)

The expansion of the moral boundary to the international level was possible only when states' domestic agential power was high. However, this phase ended with the nationalist and democratic revolutions of the late eighteenth and nineteenth centuries, which led to a reduction of domestic state agential power. The masses now had a direct role in the shaping of foreign policy. 'When in the course of the nineteenth century democratic selection and responsibility of government officials replaced government by the aristocracy, the structure of international society and, with it, of international morality underwent a fundamental change' (Morgenthau 1948/1978: 252). Thus, in distinct contrast to neorealism, changes in the nature of the units (i.e. a reduction of domestic state agential power) directly led on to fundamental changes in the structure of IP. As domestic agential power declined, so too did international agential power, which led on to a contraction of the moral boundary from the international to the national level. International aristocratic morality was replaced by a nationalistic ethic of 'Right or wrong – my country' (Morgenthau 1948/1978: 253). State restraint was replaced by a crusading 'nationalistic universalism' in which national states looked to impose their own ethics on all others. Accordingly, restraint was replaced by endemic international conflict (a 'war of all against all'). It should not escape notice that this is a type of inverted Kantian position: modern national states are more conflictual than their aristocratic ancien regime predecessors.

It is this emergence of a new form of national unit, based on extended citizenship rights rather than international anarchy, that has rendered all international efforts to contain the new era of unmitigated conflict operationally useless. Concurring with Carr (1939), all twentieth-century international institutions (e.g. the League of Nations and the United Nations) must fail to secure peace because their success requires a supranational basis of loyalty, which is precluded not by anarchy but by the predominance of nationalistic universalism. Ultimately national sovereignty is not divisible: it cannot be shared with international institutions (Morgenthau 1948/1978: 328–34). Most importantly, the current 'war of all against all' is not a function of anarchy nor the 'dysfunctional' nature of international institutions, but the direct product of the nationalistic form of unit that was based on a mass franchise and low domestic agential state power. In sum, although domestic agential state power varies through time, nevertheless at all times the state has international agency to shape the international structure. International agential power was very high under the 'aristocratic international' and enabled the state to create a relatively peaceful international system, but was moderate under 'nationalistic universalism' (where states created a conflictual international system).

High international agential state power, moral norms and the construction of eternal peace

Morgenthau is commonly thought of as a realist who sought to distance himself from so-called 'liberal utopianism' on the grounds that the struggle for power between states would last forever and therefore, that peace is viewed as a chimera or a product of liberal wishful thinking. But in the final chapter of *Politics Among Nations*, Morgenthau returns to his 'practical realist' strand, arguing that the 'moral intelligence' of the state's compensatory moral diplomacy could help bring about an end to structural conflict and a more peaceful world. As noted above, when a state's domestic agential power is low, so too is its international agential power to mitigate inter-state competition, and international conflict becomes endemic (as under twentieth-century nationalistic universalism). This suggests that if such conflict is to be mitigated, the state needs to regain high levels of domestic agential power. It is the regaining of this domestic autonomy that is crucial to the effective functioning of what Morgenthau calls 'compensatory diplomacy'. Eternal peace will be possible only when a world-state can command supranational loyalty. The means to the creation of such a pre-requisite is that of 'compensatory diplomacy', which must follow nine rules (Morgenthau 1948/1978: 551–9). The first three require that:

(1) diplomacy must detach itself from crusading nationalistic universalism

(2) in the atomic age national security must be ensured not at the *expense* of other states but in such a way that all states can be made secure

(3) diplomats must relate at an intersubjective level, putting themselves in the shoes of 'opponents' and must be willing to compromise on secondary issues.

Morgenthau stipulates six further conditions that need to be met, perhaps the most important being the need for the state to lead public opinion rather than be its slave (point (9)). All of this suggests that diplomats must reject defining the national interest in terms of 'power' and should promote an interdependent web of 'shared convictions and common values' between states which enables 'a moral consensus within which a peace-preserving diplomacy will have a chance to grow' (Morgenthau 1948/1978: 552).

Martin Griffiths (1992) has perceptively labelled Morgenthau a 'nostalgic idealist' on the grounds that his prescriptions for eternal peace could be achieved by initially returning to the conditions that prevailed under the 'aristocratic international'. The key to the success of the balance of power and of self-restraint under the aristocratic international (seventeenth–nineteenth centuries) was the state's high domestic agency which enabled a high degree of international agential power to overcome inter-state competition. Morgenthau transposes the key ingredient of monarchical sovereignty into late twentieth-century compensatory diplomacy: the need to regain state autonomy from the masses. This is the ultimate Bonapartist balancing act, between maintaining popular support while at the same time restraining its militaristic influence. Supranational government cannot be set up overnight, but can be achieved only through gradual day-to-day diplomatic accommodations (Morgenthau 1948/1978: 558–9): an argument that parallels Mitrany's argument in form (though not, of course, in content). In this way, super-intelligent diplomacy can create supranational loyalties, in turn enabling a future world-state that would be 'more in keeping with the technical potentialities and the moral requirements of the contemporary world' (Morgenthau 1948/1978: 10).

In sum, the bulk of Morgenthau's analysis is based not on systemic anarchy but on fundamental unit-force variables. High domestic agential state power enables high international agential power to mitigate anarchy (as in the aristocratic international); conversely, low domestic agential power leads to moderate international agential power and the creation of a conflictual international system. Here, the units and the specific relationship of the state to society form the determining base of IP (a second-image approach). That is, IP reflects changes in the units, rather than the other way round (as in neorealism). It is interesting to note how this approach differs from Morgenthau's sixth principle of political realism (for which he is more famous): that 'the political realist maintains the autonomy of the political sphere just as the economist, the lawyer, the moralist maintain theirs' (Morgenthau 1948/1978: 11), which implies that the state is always absolutely autonomous from society. But his non-systemic theory of the state fundamentally denies this claim, where the state's autonomy from society varies.

There are, then, two theories of the state and two theories of IP discernible in Morgenthau: a systemic and a non-systemic. Nevertheless, the non-systemic approach is given far greater weighting throughout *Politics Among Nations*. This approach reflects a rich, historical theory of IP that clearly transcends neorealism's static parsimony (principle (1), figure 2.1, p. 18). It also specifies the state as *the* determining agent of IP (principles (2)–(6), figure 2.1; see also figure

2.7). This 'dynamic' approach, I would suggest, provides an alternative interpretation to conventional understanding, which suggests that the summary statements for which Morgenthau is famous could be revised as follows: that 'the struggle for power is *not* universal in time and space' (cf. Morgenthau 1948/1978: 36); and that, 'All history show[s] that nations are [*not*] always preparing for . . . (*nor*) actually involved in . . . (*nor* are) recovering, from organised violence in the form of war (cf. Morgenthau 1948/1978: 42, emphases mine). Moreover, if the problem of war is a product not of anarchy but of the specific form of state, then if such a state can be reformed (through an increase in autonomy and super-intelligent diplomacy), eternal peace becomes a possibility. Unfortunately, we cannot end our summary here. This is because Morgenthau's systemic approach to the state and IP is also evident, as is clear in his first theory of the balance of power and his first systemic theory of the 'adaptive state'. The overwhelming problem here is that these two approaches cannot be easily reconciled, since they are mutually exclusive. This suggests, as Ashley (1981) and Walker (1987: 65) argue, that there are considerable tensions in Morgenthau's overall approach. I suggest that Carr's work abolishes the systemic approach in favour of a non-systemic theory, and therefore manages to resolve this contradiction.

The 'socialised nation' – the highest stage of sovereignty? Carr's 'critical' break from neorealism

As with Morgenthau, conventional understanding assumes that Carr was most definitely in the 'systemic–realist' or neorealist camp (e.g. Smith 1986), where Carr is thought to be radically opposed to liberal and moral or 'utopian' thinking. Such a view stems from IR scholars' reading of his famous text *The Twenty Years' Crisis* (Carr 1939). Burchill's summary of Carr is typical: '[f]or Carr, as for all realists, conflict between states was inevitable in an international system without an overarching authority regulating relations between them' (Burchill 1996: 72). While this reading is not without some merit (with respect to *The Twenty Years' Crisis*, at least), I argue that it fails to reflect the more substantive arguments made by Carr in his other more important works, in which he advanced a *non-systemic* theory of IP that clearly differentiates him from neorealism. If Morgenthau's theory of the state and of IP was part systemic and mostly non-systemic, Carr's was decidedly non-systemic. Morgenthau's work thus provides a bridge or 'via media' between Waltzian neorealism and Carr's classical realism. Moreover, my interpretation is reinforced by a series of recent publications, which suggest that Carr leaned towards a non-systemic or emancipatory critical theory approach (Cox 1986: 206, 211; Booth 1991: 530–2; Howe 1994; Linklater 1998: 159–68; Jones 1998), or what Dunne aptly labels a 'postmodern realist' approach (Dunne 1998: 37).

Standing Waltz on his head: social-citizenship adaptation, norms and the agential powers of the state as the fundamental core of IP

In contrast to *The Twenty Years' Crisis*, in *Nationalism and After* (1945) and *The New Society* (1951), Carr provides a much more complete theory of the state, and of international politics more generally (both of which are in fact missing in *The Twenty Years' Crisis*). *The Twenty Years' Crisis* was more concerned with producing a fundamental critique of liberal internationalism which, Carr argued, had produced the crisis between 1919 and 1939. However, these later texts put this crisis into historical perspective and in the process, radically transformed the argument of *The Twenty Years' Crisis*. In contrast to neorealism, Carr argues that there have been four different periods of IR that are informed not by the influence of anarchy or changes in the distribution of capabilities, but by *fundamental changes in the units* – specifically, changes in the domestic agential power or autonomy of the state (which led on to changes in the international agential power of states), as well as changing configurations of norms (see figure 2.9).

The first period covered roughly 1648–1792/1815, and was dominated by the 'monarchical nation' (congruent with Morgenthau's 'monarchical sovereignty'). Here, the nation was equated with the monarch (though in Eastern Europe with the nobility as well). This gave rise to the 'monarchical international' (congruent with Morgenthau's 'aristocratic international'). International law was basically respected and order was broadly kept in place because of the norms of international society: common moral values, shared language (French) and common obligations which were based on monarchs honouring their word. As with Morgenthau's second non-systemic theory of the state, the key here was the high domestic agential power of the state. The monarchical state was largely insulated from the masses, which enhanced its international agential power such that it was able to construct a relatively peaceful international system based on aristocratic norms. Thus in the monarchic international, the moral boundary extended to the international, and states were accordingly relatively peaceful. As this period closed with the onset of the French Revolution and its diffusion into international society, a second one emerged by 1815 that lasted until 1919, but began to unravel after 1870.

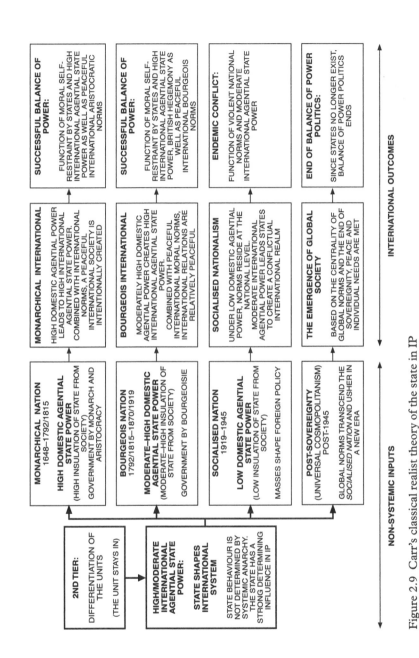

Figure 2.9 Carr's classical realist theory of the state in IP

The long nineteenth century (1792–1919) was the most peaceful in modern history. This was in part because of the emergence of the 'bourgeois nation' or, more accurately, the 'bourgeois state', which entailed a broadening of citizenship rights to the dominant capitalist class. Through a series of compromises, the growing economic demands of the bourgeois nation could remain consistent with internationalism. The bourgeois nation still retained considerable institutional autonomy from the masses, which in turn enabled high international agential power to mitigate anarchy and the maintenance of international norms, leading to a relatively peaceful international order. Here Carr also emphasised the importance of British hegemony, which not only actively promoted the development of the world economy, but was successful because it managed to promote the illusion that economics was impersonal and divorced from power politics (Carr 1945: 13–17). But precisely because the economy's freedom was in fact bound up firmly within what Carr calls the 'autocratic management' of the world economy by British hegemony, the peaceful system would sooner or later inevitably unravel.

The transition from the bourgeois state to the 'socialised nation' was informed *not* by the 'first tier' of anarchy (as in Waltzian neorealism), nor changes in the third tier – i.e. changes in the distribution of power from British hegemonic unipolarity to multipolarity (as in HST) – but to a fundamental change in the nature of the units (the second tier). This change comprised the domestic extension of citizenship rights which occurred progressively after 1870. This ushered in a third period of international politics, beginning in 1870 and crystallising fully by 1919. The rise of Germany was crucial here, *not* because it represented a change in the distribution of power as in neorealism, but because Germany was undergoing a transition to the socialised nation. It was not anarchy, nor changes in the distribution of power, nor even liberal internationalism (as Carr had originally argued in *The Twenty Years' Crisis*) that made the first half of twentieth century international politics a dangerous realm, but the rise of the 'socialised nation'. With the decline of domestic state agential power under the socialised nation, national and social policies (the 'planned economy') were now welded firmly together and the internationalism of the world economy subsequently dissolved into competing economic nationalisms. Ironically, the reduction in state agential power went hand in hand with an increase in the surveillance powers of the state, which enabled it to play a more centralised planning role at home, as well as keeping out foreign immigrants (Carr 1939: 228). Now each state came into constant struggle in order to promote the exclusive nationalist welfare interests of the masses (as in Morgenthau's 'nationalistic universalism'). The moral boundary accordingly shrank back from the international to the national level, and a 'war of all against all' ensued. Nineteenth-century laissez-faire liberalism, embodied in the 'night-watchman state' gave way to the socialised nation based on economic nationalism, embodied in the 'social service state'. The result was disaster: 'total war' occurred twice within the space of a generation (Carr 1945: 19–27). So while international law and relative peace had been respected and achieved in the first two historical eras, this was overturned in the third with the rise of the 'socialised nation'.

Thus far, we have noted that fundamental non-systemic changes in the nature of the units were responsible for concrete changes in IR. Simultaneously, international norms became salient under conditions of high domestic agential state power, as in Morgenthau's second theory of IP. The next part of Carr's argument concerns his analysis of the fourth period – the transcendence of the contradictions of the 'socialised nation' – in which global norms attain autonomy from the state and come to transcend sovereignty. It is especially here that Carr utilises a critical theory approach.

From the 'nationalistic universalism' of the socialised nation to a post-sovereign world based on universal citizenship?

It is commonly thought that the central aspect of Carr's work lies in his critique of moral thinking, which he labelled 'utopian'. Indeed the 'realism' of Carr and Morgenthau is commonly equated with anti-idealism. Whittle Johnson (1967), however, has argued that there were 'two Carrs' (which, like the 'two Morgenthaus') both contradict each other. I suggest that the common equation of Carr with Realism, as well as Johnson's claim that there are two Carrs are incorrect: there was only 'one Carr' who had much in common with critical theory. Three points above all make this clear. First, when Carr attacked 'utopian' (i.e. liberal) thinking in *The Twenty Years' Crisis*, he was not actually critiquing moral thinking *per se*, but merely the 'spurious' liberal form that it had taken between 1919 and 1939. This critical analysis was made on the basis that liberal internationalism was not a genuine moral project, but was rather a protective front for maintaining the dominance of the great powers, a critique which is congruent with critical theory's preference to unsettle ossified thought, of which early twentieth-century liberal internationalism happened to be its dominant expression (Carr 1939: 14–5, 1951: 18; cf. Howe 1994). Secondly, Carr fundamentally rejected the deterministic 'continuity' problematic of neorealism, not least because it diminishes the role of human agency to alter the pattern of events (Carr 1951: 1–18, 118–19); a point that is also made consistently throughout *The Twenty Years' Crisis*. In direct contrast to neorealism (i.e. technical realism) Carr argues that no absolute and unchanging notion of history is possible: such 'grandiose pronouncements of the judgment of history . . . sometimes provides evidence only of the bankruptcy of the [intellectual] groups [i.e. neorealists] from which they emanate' (Carr 1951: 14, 100). Thirdly, throughout *Nationalism and After* and *The New Society*, Carr subscribed to a clear and unswerving moral stance, which informs the basis for the construction of a 'new (post-sovereign) society'. This morality was based on the fundamental cosmopolitan needs of all men and women, regardless of their nationality. Moreover, this moral approach informs Carr's tracing of the changing moral boundary between the national and international realms. Critically extending Morgenthau's non-systemic analysis, Carr ascribed a full autonomy to global moral norms. This aspect of his work is applied to his analysis of the post-1945 period, in which the socialised nation is transcended by global moral norms.

For Carr, the 'socialised nation is the apex of nationalism' (Carr 1945: 31–4) or, as we have put it here, 'the highest stage of sovereignty'. In strong contrast to neorealism, Carr argues that the post-1945 period is witnessing the *decline of the sovereign state*, which had reached its most totalitarian and militaristic form in the moral bankruptcy of the socialised nation: national units 'can survive only as an anomaly and as an anachronism in a world which has moved on to . . . [new] forms of [political] organisation' (Carr 1945: 37, 1939: 229–30). Carr's normative project urged against constant state adaptation to anarchy (as in neorealism), in favour of respecting the moral requirements and the cosmopolitan needs of individuals throughout the world. Thus military and economic security for all peoples could best be achieved through the transcendence of the national form by a post-sovereign global society based on universal citizenship (as in critical theory). Carr's 'emancipatory realism' comes to the fore in part 2 of *Nationalism and After*:

What we are concerned to bring about is not the putting of Albania on an equal footing with China or Brazil, but the putting of the individual Albanian on an equal footing in respect of personal rights and opportunities, with the individual Chinese or individual Brazilian . . . The equality of individual men and women . . . is an ideal which . . . can be accepted as a constant aim of human endeavour . . . The driving force behind any future international order must be a belief . . . in the value of individual human beings irrespective of national affinities or allegiances and in a common mutual obligation to promote their well being. (Carr 1945: 43–4)

In line with postmodernists, Carr argues that peace is not possible as long as the sovereign nation-state remains the fundamental political form. Here Carr ascribes considerable autonomy to global norms for the fourth era, commencing in 1945 (just as international norms were vital in the first two eras and national norms were salient in the third period). Global moral norms, based on the non-exploitation of all individuals, required the transcendence of the socialised nation and the end of the sovereign state. The socialised nation must be disbanded in favour of a post-sovereign universal community of citizenship, since it was this morally obsolete national form (as opposed to anarchy and the distribution of power) which was ultimately the cause of international disorder; a claim that he makes constantly in the last half of the book. 'An international organisation must rest on common principles worthy of commanding the assent and loyalty of men and women *throughout the world* if it is to succeed' (Carr 1945: 61ff., emphasis mine). Thus the new international order would be fundamentally shaped by the realities of global morality rather than global power. It would, however, be wrong to assume that Carr's critical analysis existed only with the analysis of the post-1945 era, for throughout these two books his chief concern was to trace the changing configuration of the moral boundary: from its expansion to the international level after 1648 to its contraction after 1919 back to the national level, and to its subsequent expansion outwards to the global level after 1945.

It *is* the case that Carr had trouble specifying the exact political form in which the global moral boundary and the political boundary must converge. What he seems to point to is some kind of regional form, existing halfway between international and national forms of political authority. Only then can the conflictual nature of IP based on the 'socialised nation' be transcended through a superior system of overlapping and interlocking loyalties. Moreover, he was committed to a (reformist) socialist society in which workers would be motivated not by the 'economic whip' (of hunger) but by a more inclusive sense of social obligation and freedom. Only then would there be truly 'government of all and by all and for all' (Carr 1951: 111). In sum, therefore, far from being a 'realist critic of idealism', who produced a static, parsimonious, systemic and scientific approach to international politics and the state, there is good reason to conclude that Carr developed a relatively complex and rich historical–sociological theory of the state and international politics, which ultimately leaned towards an 'idealist critique' of neorealism.

Discussion questions

On Waltzian neorealism

- What is the 'continuity' problematic, and how does this lead to the state being denied international agential power? What for Waltz, is the problem with what he calls 'reductionist' theory?
- Why does the second tier of the international political structure drop out for Waltz; put differently, why are states functionally alike?
- Exactly why is the 'billiard-ball' metaphor so apt in capturing neorealism's theory of the state?
- What are the two 'adaptive' strategies that states follow, and how in the process is anarchy unintentionally reproduced?
- On what grounds do some scholars claim that Waltz endows the state with international agential power, and what are the limits, if any, of this view?

On 'modified' neorealism

- How can Gilpin bring in the theme of international change and yet reproduce Waltz's 'continuity' problematic? Is this contradictory?
- Although Gilpin opens up the 'black-box' of the state, why nevertheless does he fail to accord the state a degree of international agential power?
- How does the theory of the adaptive/maladaptive state constitute the motor of the cycle of the rise and decline of the great powers?
- Why can states not spontaneously solve the 'collective action problem'?
- Why do neorealists view regimes as much less robust than do neoliberal institutionalists?
- What is the conventional account of hegemonic decline, and why is it problematic?

On classical realism

- What is the conventional reading of classical realism and neo realism? What, if anything, is problematic with this view?
- Why does high domestic agential power lead to high international

agency in the early period, and low agential state power lead to moderate international agency in the later period?

- Why can it be claimed that Morgenthau is a quasi-constructivist and Carr a quasi-critical theorist?

- How can it be claimed that Morgenthau provides a bridge or the 'via media' between Waltz and Carr?

- What processes inform the expansion and contraction of the moral boundary since 1648 for both Carr and Morgenthau?

Suggestions for further reading

The standard place to start is Smith (1986), though this presents the conventional accounts of the key realists. Important recent analyses can also be found in Schweller and Priess (1997), Guzzini (1998) and Donnelly (2000). Perhaps the best place to start for *rethinking* realism in general are the sensitive poststructuralist readings found in Ashley (1981) and Walker (1987). Griffiths (1992) produces an alternative account to the standard reading of Morgenthau (and parallels my own), in much the same way that Booth (1991), Howe (1994), Dunne (1998), Jones (1998) and Linklater (1998: 159–68) produce alternative accounts of Carr, which also parallel my own. A good way into Waltz's work is chapter 5 of his 1979 book as well as his defence (Waltz 1986). Moreover, the critiques by Cox (1986) and Ruggie (1986) are essential (though Ruggie's piece is worthy of several revisits – see also Ruggie (1998). Once Waltz has been thoroughly absorbed, the reader would do well to visit the debate on whether Waltz's theory is structuralist or agent-centric; see Wendt (1987, 1991) for the latter position and Hollis and Smith (1991) for the former. And once this is absorbed, it is important to progress on to 'structural realism' (Buzan, Jones and Little 1993). This seeks to update Waltz in the aftermath of the Cold War, essentially by producing a much more *complex* and historical-sociological realist approach that develops a 'thick' account of the international structure. This approach has been complemented by the rise of 'neo-classical realism'; see Rose (1998) for an excellent introduction. Finally, the best introductions to HST and neorealist IPE theory are found in Gilpin (1987: 72–80, 123–42, 343–63) and for a critical introduction, see Guzzini (1998: chapter 10).

3   Liberalism

I argue that it is possible to discern five basic variants of liberalism which are situated within two categories: *individual-centric liberalism*, comprising classical liberalism, new liberalism and functionalism; and *state-centric liberalism* which comprises English school rationalism and neoliberal institutionalism. I suggest that new liberalism (though not functionalism) constitutes the 'via media' between classical liberalism and modern 'state-centric' liberalism. There are perhaps three fundamental traits that define the rational kernel or essence of the liberal theory of the state and of political institutions more generally:

(1) *The theory of the socially-adaptive state:* the prime directive of state behaviour is to meet the economic and social needs of individuals. Rather than technically conform to anarchy (as in neorealism), states must ultimately conform to the needs of individuals: states must be *socially* adaptive.

(2) *Socially adaptive states have high international agential power and can buck the logic of anarchy:* paradoxically by conforming to the economic and social requirements of individuals, states are able to buck the logic of anarchy and inter-state competition thereby creating a peaceful world. In the process, the international realm is redefined as a *realm of possibility,* which enables states to maximise global welfare and create peace. While neorealism prescribes that states should be primarily concerned to gain 'technical control' in a hostile anarchic environment, liberals prescribe that states *should pursue a 'practical' rationality, by which states come to create a peaceful, cooperative and orderly world.*

(3) *Only the 'appropriate' institutions (domestic and international) can achieve the desired ends of global welfare and peace:* inappropriate domestic and international institutions lead to diminishing global and national welfare, as well as war.

With respect to the two main attributes of the state – *international agential power* (the ability to make foreign policy and to shape the international realm free of international constraints), and *domestic agen-*

tial state power (i.e. the ability to determine domestic or foreign policy and shape the domestic realm free of domestic non-state actor influence), liberalism prescribes not only a very different formula to that of neorealism but also demonstrates considerable internal differences across its variants. If Waltzian neorealism presents the paradox of high domestic agential power and no international agential state power, classical liberalism embraces the paradox of 'low domestic agential power and high international agential state power'; new liberalism prescribes 'moderate domestic agential power and high international agential state power'; rationalism and neoliberal institutionalism (i.e. state-centric liberalism) prescribe 'high domestic agential power and high international agential state power'. Functionalism, however, ultimately views the sovereign state as a blockage to the realisation of the economic needs of individuals, and accords it moderate rather than high international agential power. In sum, compared to neorealism, liberalism for the most part endows the state with less domestic agential power to over-ride domestic interests, but much higher degrees of international agential power to reconstitute and shape the international structure.

The conventional view, derived from the distorted lens of the first state debate, suggests that liberalism under-estimates the state while neorealism exaggerates it. But viewed through the lens of the second state debate, I suggest that neorealism *under-estimates* the agential powers of the state in IP, while liberalism grants the state considerable agency to determine IP and overcome inter-state competition.

'Individual-centric' liberalism: the socially-adaptive state

Classical liberalism

There are three fundamental paradoxes in the classical liberal theory of the state:

(1) *the existence of the state is essential for economic growth; the state, however, is the source of man-made economic decline* (North 1981: 20)

(2) *in remaining socially neutral, the state demonstrates a modicum of institutional autonomy, but such autonomy is necessary to ensure a minimalist laissez-faire stance by the state.*

(3) *in performing a laissez-faire 'minimalist' role, the state is able to generate high international agential power to mitigate anarchy and inter-state competition.*

Understanding these three paradoxes takes us to the heart of classical liberalism and its theory of the state.

Adam Smith's *magnum opus, An Inquiry into the Nature and Causes of The Wealth of Nations* (1776/1937), systematised a highly parsimonious and economistic approach to the state. Smith's primary concern was to analyse the origins of national 'opulence' (i.e. the productive wealth of 'nations') which, in strict contrast to the 'realist' mercantilist school, prescribed the *autonomous self-constituting economy* as the secret of national wealth accumulation. That is, the economy functions optimally when it is allowed to operate free from state or political intervention. The individual, which is the basic unit of analysis, will ensure the optimal allocation of societal resources when he is allowed to freely choose which industry or area of activity to engage in (women are omitted). At bottom is Smith's view of human nature which constitutes 'the propensity to truck, barter and exchange one thing for another' (1776/1937: 13). Above all, it is *not* 'benevolent cooperation' that ensures the betterment of society, but the selfish actions of the individual, which through 'an invisible hand' promotes 'an end which was no part of his intention' (1776/1937: 423, 421), that end being the economic progress of the whole society. 'It is not from the benevolence of the butcher, the brewer or the baker, that we expect our dinner, but from their regard to their own interest' (1776/1973: 14).

This argument rests upon what I call the 'spontaneity thesis', which stipulates that the economy will self-generate if it is left free from political intervention. Thus the statesman, 'who should attempt to direct private people in what manner they ought to employ their capitals', would very quickly undermine the 'opulence' of the country (1776/1937: 422–3). That is, the self-regulating hand of the economy is cut off when the state undertakes a positive interventionist role. 'Great nations are never impoverished by private misconduct but by public [i.e. state] misconduct, where much of the annual revenue [i.e. GNP] is employed in maintaining unproductive hands' (1776/1937: 325ff). In short, the positive interventionist state is the problem – the minimalist state the solution.

'Maladaptive state interventionism' and 'moderate international agential state power' as the problem

Beginning with the top half of figure 3.1, classical liberalism argues that the central problem of political economy lies with the distorting effects of state interventionism, in which the maladaptive state fails to adapt or conform to the requirements of individual economic needs. Nowhere is this argument clearer than in Smith's discussion in book IV of the 'evils' of tariff protectionism (1776/1937: 397–652). Tariff protection might well promote the private interests of a particular industry in the short

THE PROBLEM: *POSITIVE MALADAPTIVE STATE INTERVENTION*

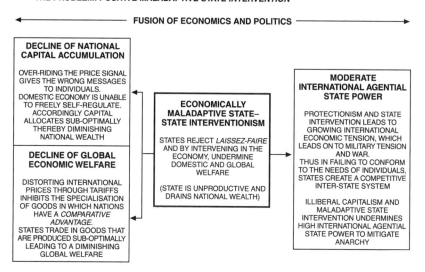

◀──────── FUSION OF ECONOMICS AND POLITICS ────────▶

DECLINE OF NATIONAL CAPITAL ACCUMULATION

OVER-RIDING THE PRICE SIGNAL GIVES THE WRONG MESSAGES TO INDIVIDUALS. DOMESTIC ECONOMY IS UNABLE TO FREELY SELF-REGULATE. ACCORDINGLY CAPITAL ALLOCATES SUB-OPTIMALLY THEREBY DIMINISHING NATIONAL WEALTH

DECLINE OF GLOBAL ECONOMIC WELFARE

DISTORTING INTERNATIONAL PRICES THROUGH TARIFFS INHIBITS THE SPECIALISATION OF GOODS IN WHICH NATIONS HAVE A *COMPARATIVE ADVANTAGE*. STATES TRADE IN GOODS THAT ARE PRODUCED SUB-OPTIMALLY LEADING TO A DIMINISHING GLOBAL WELFARE

ECONOMICALLY MALADAPTIVE STATE– STATE INTERVENTIONISM

STATES REJECT *LAISSEZ-FAIRE* AND BY INTERVENING IN THE ECONOMY, UNDERMINE DOMESTIC AND GLOBAL WELFARE

(STATE IS UNPRODUCTIVE AND DRAINS NATIONAL WEALTH)

MODERATE INTERNATIONAL AGENTIAL STATE POWER

PROTECTIONISM AND STATE INTERVENTION LEADS TO GROWING INTERNATIONAL ECONOMIC TENSION, WHICH LEADS ON TO MILITARY TENSION AND WAR. THUS IN FAILING TO CONFORM TO THE NEEDS OF INDIVIDUALS, STATES CREATE A COMPETITIVE INTER-STATE SYSTEM

ILLIBERAL CAPITALISM AND MALADAPTIVE STATE INTERVENTION UNDERMINES HIGH INTERNATIONAL AGENTIAL STATE POWER TO MITIGATE ANARCHY

THE SOLUTION: *LAISSEZ-FAIRE AND THE ADAPTIVE STATE*

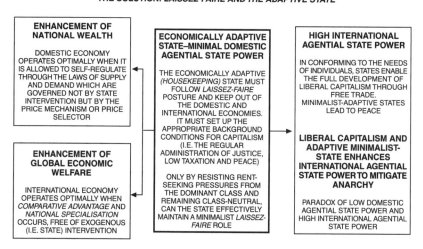

ENHANCEMENT OF NATIONAL WEALTH

DOMESTIC ECONOMY OPERATES OPTIMALLY WHEN IT IS ALLOWED TO SELF-REGULATE THROUGH THE LAWS OF SUPPLY AND DEMAND WHICH ARE GOVERNED NOT BY STATE INTERVENTION BUT BY THE PRICE MECHANISM OR PRICE SELECTOR

ENHANCEMENT OF GLOBAL ECONOMIC WELFARE

INTERNATIONAL ECONOMY OPERATES OPTIMALLY WHEN *COMPARATIVE ADVANTAGE* AND *NATIONAL SPECIALISATION* OCCURS, FREE OF EXOGENOUS (I.E. STATE) INTERVENTION

ECONOMICALLY ADAPTIVE STATE–MINIMAL DOMESTIC AGENTIAL STATE POWER

THE ECONOMICALLY ADAPTIVE *(HOUSEKEEPING)* STATE MUST FOLLOW *LAISSEZ-FAIRE* POSTURE AND KEEP OUT OF THE DOMESTIC AND INTERNATIONAL ECONOMIES. IT MUST SET UP THE APPROPRIATE BACKGROUND CONDITIONS FOR CAPITALISM (I.E. THE REGULAR ADMINISTRATION OF JUSTICE, LOW TAXATION AND PEACE)

ONLY BY RESISTING RENT-SEEKING PRESSURES FROM THE DOMINANT CLASS AND REMAINING CLASS-NEUTRAL, CAN THE STATE EFFECTIVELY MAINTAIN A MINIMALIST *LAISSEZ-FAIRE* ROLE

HIGH INTERNATIONAL AGENTIAL STATE POWER

IN CONFORMING TO THE NEEDS OF INDIVIDUALS, STATES ENABLE THE FULL DEVELOPMENT OF LIBERAL CAPITALISM THROUGH FREE TRADE. MINIMALIST-ADAPTIVE STATES LEAD TO PEACE

LIBERAL CAPITALISM AND ADAPTIVE MINIMALIST-STATE ENHANCES INTERNATIONAL AGENTIAL STATE POWER TO MITIGATE ANARCHY

PARADOX OF LOW DOMESTIC AGENTIAL STATE POWER AND HIGH INTERNATIONAL AGENTIAL STATE POWER

◀──────── SEPARATION OF ECONOMICS AND POLITICS ────────▶

Figure 3.1 The classical liberal theory of the 'socially-adaptive' *minimalist* state

term, but it will harm the national economy in the long run. Tariffs raise the domestic price of a particular good, and in creating a 'monopoly rent' for one specific area of industry divert resources from the areas of production in which the economy has a *natural advantage* (1776/1937: 421).

David Ricardo in his famous book, *The Principles of Political Economy and Taxation* (1817/1969) systematised this in his theory of *comparative advantage*. In a particular example, Ricardo argues that England had a comparative advantage in producing cloth which might, for argument's sake, take up the employment of 100 men per year. If England tried to produce wine, in which it does not have a comparative or natural advantage, it might take the employment of 120 men (to produce the equivalent value). Thus a tariff on wine diverts capital away from the sphere of natural advantage (i.e. cloth production), in turn leading to a reduction in national wealth. Taxes on international trade are harmful because they distort the 'natural price' of a commodity, and accordingly prevent the optimal allocation of capital 'which is never so well regulated as when every commodity is freely allowed to settle at its natural price, unfettered by artificial restraints' (Ricardo 1817/1969: 98; Smith 1776/1937: 848–9). The 'natural price' of a commodity is determined by the amount required to pay the various factors of production the rewards for their employment: that is, the amount to pay the rent of the land, the wages of the labourer and the returns to capital, which are employed in the production of that good (Smith 1776/1937: 55). The 'market' price of a commodity is regulated by supply and demand through the *price mechanism*, such that when demand exceeds supply, the market price will consequently rise above the 'natural' price. This attracts more investment of land, labour and capital in order to expand production so as to take advantage of the higher market price. But as supply increases so an eventual decline in the price ensues as supply comes to equal demand. When eventually supply exceeds demand, the market price drops below that of the natural price, leading to an exodus of producers in that commodity, once again leading to a new equilibrium and a restoration of the market price to that of the natural price. Thus the price mechanism is the 'signal' or the 'selector' of the optimal allocation of resources in production. 'The natural price therefore is, as it were, the central price, to which the prices of all commodities are continually gravitating' (Smith 1776/1937: 58).

State interventionism is bad because, by distorting prices, it prevents the price mechanism from optimally allocating resources. Thus a tax or tariff on a particular good affords a 'monopoly rent' to the producers of that good, which by according those protected producers a permanent advantage undermines the ability of the price mechanism to spontaneously restore the market price back to its natural price. This creates an artificial incentive for producers to move into this area away from one in which comparative advantage might have existed. Speaking of customs taxes (tariffs), Ricardo argued that they 'divert a portion of capital to an employment which it would not naturally seek . . . it is the worst species of taxation' (1817/1969: 211; Smith 1776/1937: 420–522, 821ff.). Thus state intervention which interferes with the price signal will ultimately undermine the developmental prospects of the national economy. But tariffs are bad not just because they reallocate capital to sub-optimal activities. Tariffs are also a form of taxation which, if raised to high levels, chokes the 'supply side' of the economy. High taxes 'crowd out' (i.e. reduce) the amount of savings that individuals choose to raise which, because savings are the tap root of investment, necessarily undermines economic growth: '[t]here are no taxes which have not a tendency to lessen the power to accumulate' (Ricardo 1817/1969: 97). The base of this argument hinges on Smith's distinction between *productive* and *unproductive* labour (book II). Productive labour adds to the capital stock (i.e. manufacturing production), while unproductive labour does not add value and constitutes a drain on resources. Unproductive labour takes the form of 'services' such as opera singers, dress-makers and teachers, though Smith singled out the state as particularly unproductive. Speaking of the king and his ministers he wrote: '[t]hey are themselves always, and without exception, the greatest spendthrifts in . . . society' (Smith 1776/1937: 329). Moreover, 'their service . . . produces nothing for which an equal quantity of service can afterwards be procured . . . the effect of their labour this year, will not purchase . . . protection, security and defence for the year to come' (1776/1937: 315).

This argument formed the basis of *commercial liberalism* – later developed by Richard Cobden, Herbert Spencer and Joseph Schumpeter – as well as the *republican liberalism* of Immanuel Kant (1795/1914). In essence, interventionist (authoritarian or despotic) states had a natural propensity towards tariff protectionism which, in undermining international interdependence, exacerbated tensions and jealousies between states, which led on to tariff wars and eventually military conflict. Moreover, unlike liberal states, authoritarian states had a penchant for warfare, which in turn undermined economic growth owing to their tendency to divert savings into taxes and debt in order to pay for unproductive military expenses. In sum, the positive interventionist state had moderate rather than high international agential power. That is, the state—society complex autonomously shaped the international system (i.e. moderate agency), but had insufficient agential power to overcome inter-state competition.

The 'economically adaptive minimalist state' and 'high international agential power' as the solution

Moving to the bottom half of figure 3.1, classical liberals advocate a non-interventionist laissez-faire state posture, so that the whole society can benefit, which in turn enhances the state's international agential power to overcome inter-state competition. Returning to Ricardo's example, England had a comparative advantage in cloth production (employing 100 men per year) over wine production (which took 120 men). However, Portugal might have to employ only eighty men to produce the same amount of wine. Accordingly, it would be in Portugal's interest to switch from production of cloth to wine-making and export it through free trade in exchange for England's cloth. Simultaneously, England would be better off in switching production from wine to cloth and freely exchanging it for Portuguese wine (Ricardo 1817/ 1969: 82–3). 'If a foreign country can supply us with a commodity cheaper than we can make it, better buy it of them with the fruits of our own industry, employed in a way that we have some advantage' (Smith 1776/1937: 424).

Classical liberalism insists that national economies should *specialise* in their areas of comparative advantage, the fruits of which can then be traded for foreign goods that are not produced domestically. In this way, through free trade and specialisation, all countries gain optimally, although neoclassical liberal economists fully recognise that the gains from free trade are not always equal. Nevertheless, this poses no problem because minimalist liberal states are not envious of each other (that is, they are not sensitive to unequal gains), and seek merely to enhance their interests through cooperative trading arrangements. More importantly still, this process diffuses a 'general benefit, and binds together, by one common tie of interest and intercourse, the universal society of nations throughout the civilised world' (Ricardo 1817/1969: 81). This led on to the theory of *commercial liberalism*, the essence of which was the 'spontaneity thesis' which posits that unfettered capitalism is inherently pacific. A further version was developed by Immanuel Kant, which would later come to be known as *republican liberalism*.

In his 1795 treatise *Eternal Peace* (or *Perpetual Peace and other International Essays*) Kant called for a *confederation of republican states* which would ensure peace. In contrast to Bull and in agreement with Waltz and Rousseau, Kant stated that the international state of nature is a state of war. Unlike Waltz, he argued that states must not conform to anarchy, but must transcend it. Kant's principal focus was on the form of state: war was a function of high domestic agential state power, found especially in autocratic states, whereas peace could be achieved through the low domestic agential power of the republican/liberal state. According to his first 'definitive article' a republican constitution enables peace because it is founded upon the consent of its members who are naturally averse to war (1795/1914: 76–81). This is because the costs of war outweigh the benefits. These involve the constant increase in the national debt, the loss of life that war entails and the physical and material devastation that war creates. By contrast, authoritarian states frequently resort to war because the masses have no say in foreign policy. That is, high domestic agential power is a fundamental cause of war. Because the monarch faces none of the personal costs incurred by the people under a republican form of government, he can 'resolve for war from insignificant reasons, as if it were but a hunting expedition' (1795/1914: 78).

Kant's second 'definitive article' stipulates that 'the law of nations shall be founded on a federation of free states' (1795/1914: 81–6). Rejecting an international state, he argues that perpetual peace can be secured by a pacific federation of free states; 'instead of the positive idea of a universal republic – if all is not to be lost – we shall have as a result only the negative surrogate of a federation of the states averting war, subsisting in an eternal union' (1795/1914: 86, also 81, 97–8; but see Hurrell 1990). Thus by conforming to the political needs of individuals, the state gained considerable international agential power to mitigate the conflictual aspects of anarchy.

The three paradoxes of the classical liberal theory of the state
Adapting North's paradox, we note that:
(1) *The minimalist state is essential to economic growth; the positive interventionist state is the source of man-made economic decline*: As John Locke and Thomas Hobbes originally argued, the state is required in the first instance to ensure sufficient order or pacification, without which capitalism cannot exist. To borrow Margaret Thatcher's phraseology, the state must act as a 'housekeeper': it must provide only the necessary background conditions for capitalism to develop. These essentially comprise the creation of private property rights, a conducive system of law and company law, a police force and an army/navy to ensure order and security. These institutions effectively create 'confidence', without which the smooth running of the economy will be impossible. In addition, the state must keep taxes as low as possible, especially customs taxes. As Smith put it,

'Commerce and manufactures can seldom flourish long in any state which does not enjoy a regular administration of justice, in which the people do not feel themselves secure in the possession of their property, in which the faith of contracts is not supported by law, and in which the authority of the state is not supposed to be regularly employed in enforcing (high taxes)' (1776/1937: 862). Or, as Smith's biographer Dugald Stewart put it, 'most of the state regulations for the promotion of public prosperity are unnecessary, and a nation in order to be transformed from the lowest state of barbarism into a state of the highest possible prosperity needs nothing but bearable taxation, fair administration of justice, and peace' (cited in List 1841/1885: 120). However, if the state steps beyond this minimalist laissez-faire role and intervenes positively, it very quickly undermines the economy by cutting off its self-regulating hand. The economy can perhaps be understood through the metaphor of the 'spinning top'. Like a top, it spins perfectly when free of external (state) intervention. As soon as the visible hand of the state intervenes, the top, as if it were touched very gently by a human finger, would spin out of its equilibrium and work suboptimally, or even crash (as in the case of interventionist socialist states). The appropriate role for the state is to create a perfect, frictionless environment upon which the top can spin freely. But beyond this minimal role, the state must not tread.

(2) *In remaining neutral, the state demonstrates a modicum of institutional autonomy, but such autonomy is necessary to ensure a minimalist laissez-faire stance by the state*: Conventional wisdom assumes that classical liberalism grants the state no institutional autonomy and ends the discussion here. But the paradox of the liberal position here is that a minimalist state requires a modicum of institutional autonomy. This is because Smith fully recognised, and devoted considerable analysis to the point, that strong producer groups often push for monopoly rents such as tariff protection as well as rules which limit competition (1776/1937: 118–43). In modern public choice theory, this behaviour by private groups is termed 'rent-seeking' (see e.g. Ekelund and Tollison 1981). Thus the state must have sufficient domestic agential power to resist rent-seeking pressures from strong economic interest groups, so that the economy can self-regulate in the absence of monopoly distortions. This notion of state autonomy, however, is not equivalent to state interventionism. Rather, it is a 'negative' form of power in that it requires the state to resist private groups from appropriating monopoly rents.

Thus while the state can resist the demands of the dominant

producer groups, nevertheless, such autonomy is functionally required if the state is to maintain a minimalist laissez-faire role – the pre-requisite for a smooth running economy. It is the economy that dictates a minimalist state posture: hence the state is explained by, or reduced to the 'primitive' structure of the market. Thus, analogous to Waltz's formulation, the state is required to *adapt or conform to the logic of the market*, or suffer the consequences (recession, economic decline and warfare).

This leads on to the third paradox of classical liberalism's theory of the state

(3) *In performing a laissez-faire 'minimalist' role, the state is able to enhance its international agential power to mitigate anarchy*: Unlike Waltz, classical liberalism implicitly invested the state with the agential power to buck or mitigate the logic of anarchy. Thus by enabling an autonomous self-constituting economy, states would naturally come to cooperate internationally, thereby securing both global welfare and international peace (the 'spontaneity thesis').

Here, the second and third paradoxes entwine: low domestic agential power finds its paradoxical corollary in a high degree of international agential state power to mitigate anarchy. In sum, when the state successfully conforms or adapts to the economic needs of individuals, it gains very high international agential capacity to overcome inter-state competition and thereby secure peace.

Thus the institutional definition of the state found in classical liberalism might be summarised as follows: *the minimalist adaptive state, armed with a modicum of domestic agential power adapts through conforming to the logic of the free market and individual economic needs, which in the process enhances the state's international agential power to enable global welfare maximisation and international peace. In short, the minimalist state acts as a factor of economic and political cohesion or stability.*

Liberal institutionalism

Commercial liberalism – and, indeed, classical liberal internationalism – reached their apogee in the pre-First World War years, at a time when international interdependence was high; so much so that Norman Angell (1912) famously predicted that interdependence had finally rendered warfare obsolete. For the 'new liberals', the first world war rendered classical liberal internationalism obsolete. Anarchy could not be mitigated by minimalist states and free trade. Positive state interventionism was required, not just at the national level but above all at the international level, if peace and global welfare were to achieved.

New liberalism

John Atkinson Hobson was perhaps the ideal representative of the 'new liberal' school. For the most part, IR scholars have tended to treat Hobson's complex theory in one-dimensional terms in two key respects: firstly, as a purely *domestic* (second-image) theory of international relations, and secondly as an international theory that deals exclusively with imperialism (e.g. Waltz 1979: chapter 2; Gabriel 1994: 59–65). I suggest that this is a distorted view which most likely emanates from the exaggerated emphasis IR scholars all too often pay to Hobson's classic book *Imperialism: A Study* (1902/1968), to the detriment of many other equally important books. Hobson's theory of the state and IR went beyond crude second-image theory (invoking a 'weak first-image approach'), in which domestic forces are primary, but international institutions are added in as intervening variables. Hobson's work stood at the interface between two main areas of IR. It represented a 'new liberal' *political economy* approach going beyond Smith and Ricardo by giving the state a positive role within the domestic arena – an idea that was later developed (and explicitly acknowledged) by John Maynard Keynes. It also represented a 'new liberal internationalism' – as Long (1996) dubs it – or what Hobson called 'constructive internationalism', in which states set up international government in order to secure international cooperation and peace. I argue here that Hobson was the 'via media' between classical liberal internationalism and neoliberal institutionalism (cf. Long 1996: chapter 9, 173–4).

The principal innovation that Hobson brought that transformed classical liberal internationalism into its more modern guise stemmed from his rejection of the 'spontaneity thesis'. Capitalism is not self-constituting such that it can self-regulate, but has to be propped up by positive political intervention at both the domestic and international levels. As he proclaimed: 'the whole conception of the State disclosed by [new liberalism] . . . as an instrument for the active adaptation of the economic and moral environment to the new needs of individual and social life, by securing full opportunities of self-development and social service for all citizens, was foreign to the [classical] liberalism of the last generation . . . The old liberalism is dead' (1909: 3).

Comparing figures 3.1 and 3.2, it is clear that Hobson inverts the traditional problem and solution: now the minimalist state is the problem, the positive state the solution.

SEPARATION OF ECONOMICS AND POLITICS

MINIMALIST-MALADAPTIVE STATE: MODERATE INTERNATIONAL AGENTIAL POWER

ALTHOUGH STATE-SOCIETY RELATIONS DETERMINE IP (MODERATE INTERNATIONAL AGENCY), NEVERTHELESS THE MALADAPTIVE STATE HAS INSUFFICIENT AGENTIAL CAPACITY TO CREATE INTERNATIONAL GOVERNMENT

MINIMALIST-MALADAPTIVE STATE: LOW DOMESTIC AGENTIAL POWER

THE STATE FAILS TO OVERCOME THE CRISIS OF UNDER-CONSUMPTION AND IS UNABLE TO RAISE AGGREGATE DEMAND

THE STATE GRANTS THE DOMINANT CLASS MONOPOLY TRADE RENTS AND TAX RELIEF THROUGH REGRESSIVE INDIRECT TAXATION (I.E. TARIFF PROTECTIONISM)

CRISIS OF UNDER-CONSUMPTION

MALDISTRIBUTION OF INCOME AND UNTAXED UNEARNED INCOME (VIA REGRESSIVE TAXES AND TARIFFS) LEADS TO OVER-SAVING AND REDUCTION IN AGGREGATE DEMAND

RENT-SEEKING AMONG PRIVILEGED GROUPS

PRIVATE DOMESTIC GROUPS PUSH FOR AND GAIN FROM THE STATE TARIFF PROTECTIONISM TO SHORE UP THEIR TRADING AND PERSONAL TAXATION POSITIONS

IMPERIALISM AND WAR

BECAUSE OF OVER-SAVING, LACK OF PROGRESSIVE TAXATION OF UNEARNED INCOME AND UNDER-CONSUMPTION, CAPITALISTS LOOK TO OVERSEAS COLONIES AS OUTLETS FOR INVESTING THEIR SURPLUS INCOME. COMPETITION BETWEEN RIVAL NATIONAL CAPITALIST CLASSES LEADS TO POLITICAL TENSION AND EVENTUALLY WAR

THE SOLUTION – ECONOMICALLY-ADAPTIVE STATE WITH HIGH INTERNATIONAL AGENTIAL POWER

POSITIVE-ADAPTIVE STATE: HIGH INTERNATIONAL AGENTIAL STATE POWER

STATES COLLABORATE THROUGH CONSTRUCTING INTERNATIONAL GOVERNMENT, WHICH PERFORMS THREE PRIMARY FUNCTIONS

POSITIVE-ADAPTIVE STATE: MODERATE–HIGH DOMESTIC AGENTIAL POWER

STATE ACQUIRES SUFFICIENT DOMESTIC AGENTIAL POWER TO INTERVENE AGAINST THE INTERESTS OF THE DOMINANT CLASSES BY REDISTRIBUTING INCOME VIA TAXATION AND WELFARE REFORMISM

IRONING OUT THE BUSINESS CYCLE

WITH REDISTRIBUTION OF INCOME, AGGREGATE DEMAND IS RAISED, RESTORING ALL FACTORS OF PRODUCTION TO FULL EMPLOYMENT

FREE TRADE

STATE HELPS PROMOTE GLOBAL WELFARE MAXIMISATION AND COOPERATIVE INTERNATIONAL COMMERCIAL RELATIONS

END OF IMPERIALISM

WITH THE END OF OVER-SAVING AND UNDER-CONSUMPTION, CAPITALISTS CAN NOW INVEST THEIR MONEY AT HOME RATHER THAN ABROAD

END OF WAR

DESTROYING THE TAP-ROOT OF WAR (I.E. IMPERIALISM) ENABLES PEACE AMONG NATION STATES

POSITIVE INTERNATIONAL GOVERNMENT–(1) ENHANCES DOMESTIC AGENTIAL POWER OF STATES

ENHANCES THE STATE'S DOMESTIC ABILITY TO GO AGAINST THE INTERESTS OF PRIVILEGED PRODUCER GROUPS IN ORDER TO END UNEQUAL DISTRIBUTION OF WEALTH

POSITIVE INTERNATIONAL GOVERNMENT–(2) ENABLES INTERNATIONAL FREE TRADE

(1) MONITORING STATES' ADHERENCE TO RULES OF FREE TRADE
(2) INSTILLING CERTAINTY AND STABILITY IN WORLD ECONOMY AND DISSEMINATING INFORMATION

POSITIVE INTERNATIONAL GOVERNMENT–(3) ENHANCES INTERNATIONAL AGENTIAL STATE POWER TO MITIGATE ANARCHY BY REQUIRING STATES TO:

(1) COLLECTIVELY AGREE AND SUBMIT TO THE WILL OF THE ARBITRATION COURT
(2) AGREE TO MILITARILY COLLABORATE SO AS TO DEFEAT AGGRESSORS, AND ENFORCE THE COURTS DECISIONS

FUSION OF ECONOMICS AND POLITICS

Figure 3.2 John A. Hobson's 'new liberal' theory of the 'socially-adaptive' *interventionist* state

The maladaptive-minimalist state and moderate international
agential power as the problem

Beginning with the top half of figure 3.2, we note a chain of events: a weak minimalist 'laissez-faire' state, armed with moderate international agential power, is unable to prevent the maldistribution of income which leads to a crisis of under-consumption, which in turn leads on to imperialism – the 'tap-root' of war. Rejecting classical liberalism, Hobson argued that the economy was not governed by a self-regulating set of laws of supply and demand, because the economy's effective functioning was constantly distorted by privileged elites – especially the landowners and capitalist interests.

What was missing in classical liberalism was the theory of *unproductive surplus* and the *maldistribution of income*. These phenomena derive from *unearned income* which, in turn, derive from those areas in which there is a natural or legal monopoly. Unearned income derives from such areas as land which enjoys rental increases and value increases, which come about not through the hard work and savings of landowners, but rather through the level of general prosperity generated by the whole community. Distribution does not naturally occur as in classical liberalism, where through self-help all individuals would be fairly remunerated for their efforts, but is distorted by the 'forced gains' and superior bargaining power of elites compared to the masses (Hobson 1900: 295–361, 1909: 162–75). This unearned income or surplus constitutes excess profit which is neither spent nor reinvested, but merely saved. This 'over-saving' by the wealthy classes is the tap-root of under-consumption and unemployment. As income accrues disproportionately to the wealthy, the majority of the population have less and less income, which in turn constrains the ability of the masses to purchase goods produced (the problem of decreasing 'overall' or *aggregate* demand). Accordingly, maldistribution of income and unproductive surplus lead to economic depression because of the inherent tendency for demand to fall, resulting in a structural inability of the economy to absorb the goods that are produced (Hobson 1896: 88–93, 98–111).

This over-saving by elites can be invested in one of two places: either domestically or abroad. But with under-consumption at home, capitalists and landowners seek to invest their money abroad (i.e. imperialism), in order to obtain a better return. In turn imperialism, Hobson argued, was the source or 'tap-root' of war. This obtained because as national capitalist classes searched for monopolistic investment outlets, so they came into competition with other national capitalist classes. This eventually spilled over into warfare as the various national states were called upon by their respective imperial elites to defend their monopoly interests

(1902/1968: chapter 7). Whether right or wrong, the argument – written in 1902 – proved uncannily prophetic! Imperialism is self-reinforcing, because imperial elites are able to secure further advantages which exacerbate under-consumption at home (1902/1968: chapter 7). First, imperialism leads to huge military expenditures which crowd out welfare expenditures, in order to defend investment outlets. With low welfare expenditures, one of the means to redistribute income is cut off. As Hobson put it '[t]he vast expenditure on armaments, the costly wars . . . the check upon political and social reforms within Britain, though fraught with great injury to the nation, have served well the present business interests of certain industries and professions' (1902/1968: 46). Secondly, to pay for these unproductive military expenditures, elites persuade governments to rely on regressive indirect taxes, especially tariff protectionism, which penalise the lower-income groups to the relative advantage of the wealthy. These two aspects of imperialism are especially damaging because they fundamentally cut off the means to redistribute income to the working classes through progressive taxation, thereby exacerbating the problem of under-consumption. Thus Hobson's theory of under-consumption is complex and can be summarised as:

Under-consumption = Minimalist maladaptive state + (Unearned income + Forced gains + Over-saving) + Indirect taxation + Tariff protectionism + Military expenditure.

In short, the maladaptive state, in failing to conform to the economic needs of all individuals, gains only a moderate degree of international agential capacity and accordingly creates a competitive and conflictual inter-state system.

The 'interventionist-adaptive state' and positive international governmental intervention as the solution

Moving to the bottom half of figure 3.2, Hobson argued that the solution to this problem requires the implementation of a complex set of positive policies by the state at the domestic and international level. If all investment could be absorbed domestically, there would be no need for investment abroad and the tap-root of imperialism would be cut (1902/1968: 85–9). This could be achieved, he argued, by abandoning laissez-faire and endowing the state with a positive interventionist or moderate domestic agential power as well as an interventionist or high international agential state power. Such positive intervention must in the first instance be implemented by the 'social-democratic' state.

Specifically, in the domestic sphere, this required the state to intervene and tax progressively all *unearned surplus* income. Through redistribution to the poorer classes via progressive taxation and welfare spending, consumption can be enhanced so as to improve aggregate demand, thereby enabling an ironing out of the business cycle (1896: 88–92, 98–111). Most commentators assume that Hobson singled out only the financial classes as the basis of imperialism: he did not. All classes that enjoy unearned income, especially the landowners, are culpable because it is this broader constellation of elite interests that effectively promotes under-consumption (1902/1968: 48ff., 97) – the tap-root of imperialism. It is interesting to note that across the spectrum of his extensive writings, the Lords came in for special and constant attack (see especially Hobson 1909: chapters 1–2) – which explains why he turned down a knighthood. It was not for nothing that Hobson favourably cited John Stuart Mill's famous dictum that colonialism constituted 'a vast system of outdoor relief for the upper classes' (1902/ 1968: 51). He therefore prescribed land taxes, death duties and progressive income taxation to restore the harmony of the economy by eradicating unproductive surplus and over-saving. At this point, new liberalism stands radically opposed to its classical predecessor. For Smith and Ricardo, progressive taxation was an evil almost as bad as customs taxation, which served only to undermine savings and therefore crowd out investment and economic growth.

The long-term solution would be for the state to positively intervene, first through progressive taxation and secondly through welfare reformism which, by redistributing income from the rich to the poor, would restore aggregate demand, thereby undermining domestic under-consumption. While Adam Smith did allow for a modicum of institutional state autonomy, Hobson took this much further, insisting that the state must consistently go against the broad fiscal interests of the dominant classes and actively promote working-class interests through redistribution in order to shore up the economy. The economy for Hobson has a 'non-homeostatic' tendency: it is prone to break down if left to its own devices. Moderately high domestic agential power is the base of the adaptive social-democratic state, which is in turn the pre-requisite for the economy's successful reproduction. It *is* the case that Hobson envisaged that laissez-faire state policy could be diverted to shoring up the interests of the dominant classes, implying a more class-sensitive theory of the state to that developed by classical liberalism. But Hobson granted the state more domestic agential power than did Lenin or Marx. He also granted much higher levels of international agential power to mitigate anarchy – in contrast to Marxism in all its variants. Hobson's fundamental claim was that the state had significant, though not completely sufficient, domestic agential power or autonomy to intervene

against the interests of the dominant classes on behalf of the working classes.
The state for Lenin had no such ability because it was structurally
constrained by capital. So, for Hobson, capitalism could be reformed by
the state – a position which retains the fundamental aspects of liberalism
in strict contrast to Marxism–Leninism. Ironically, though, his theory of
the state was not dissimilar to neo-Marxism's notion of 'relative
autonomy' in which the state goes against the short-term interests of the
capitalist class in order to shore up the long-term requirements of the
economy. But there are two key differences. First, Hobson granted
greater domestic agential power or autonomy to the state because he
argued that it could ultimately reconcile the struggle between classes – a
position which the Marxist 'relative autonomy' approach in the last
instance falls short of. And, secondly, Hobson fundamentally parted
company from Marxism and neo-Marxism by arguing that the high
international agential power of the social-democratic state could bring
about international peace, precisely because it could reconcile the
struggle between classes.

A new 'constructive internationalism'

The conventional interpretation of Hobson's theory ends with the policy
prescription of domestic social-democratic state interventionism in
order to effect a redistribution of income so as to cut off the tap-root of
imperialism and war (e.g. Waltz 1979: chapter 2; Gabriel 1994). But,
thus far, we have covered only a part of Hobson's overall argument. And
the careful reader will have picked up the point made earlier: that the
social-democratic state did not have *sufficient* domestic agential power or
autonomy to intervene *against the interests of the dominant classes on behalf
of the working classes.* Such autonomy needed to be enhanced by
international government – the second part of his overall theory of the
state and international relations.

Hobson's theory of 'constructive internationalism' – or what Long
(1996) aptly dubs the 'new liberal internationalism' – was outlined in a
number of works, not least, *Towards International Government* (1915),
and *The Morals of Economic Internationalism* (1920). International government would play three fundamental roles (see bottom of figure 3.2):
(1) to enhance the domestic agential power of the state to go against the
    interests of social elites; this was derived from the second and third
    roles:
(2) to bring about universal free trade
(3) to bring about universal peace.
Because the first role derives from the second and third, it makes sense
to begin with these latter functions.

In *The Morals of Economic Internationalism*, Hobson embraced Cobden's belief in international free trade as enabling international peace and global welfare maximisation (Hobson 1920: 14). But free trade would not naturally come about through minimalist states following the theory of comparative advantage, because 'the suspicions, jealousies and hostilities of nations are inspired more by the tendency of groups of producers to misrepresent their private interests as the good of their respective countries [i.e. national interests] than by any other single circumstance' (Hobson 1920: 14–15). Hobson argued that while international free trade was a necessity for peace, it would not naturally occur: it had to be forged or engineered by a 'pincer movement' of domestic state interventionism and positive international government. In this respect, Hobson's theory of free trade developed what John Ruggie (1998: 62–84) would later call 'the compromise of embedded liberalism' (Long 1996: 142–3), and echoed Karl Polanyi's famous argument that the path to free trade could be secured only by the active interventionism of the state.

Hobson envisaged two roles for international economic authority, both of which pre-empted Keohane's (1984) theory of regimes. First, it would maintain and monitor states' adherence to the rules of free trade. It would deal with matters such as freedom of access to trade routes and equal opportunities for investors. Secondly, it would instil certainty and stability in the world economy and would disseminate information to states, thereby reducing their temptation to defect from cooperation. Individual states alone could not bring about international free trade because of the problem of *global under-consumption*. Because all advanced states were undergoing under-consumption (global under-consumption), imperialist rivalry between nations ensued. Even if the British state unilaterally reformed imperialism out of existence, other less democratic states (especially Germany and Russia) would maintain imperialism, and so war would continue. To solve this international problem required not just domestic reform (as most commentators on Hobson incorrectly conclude) but above all international reform (see also Long 1996: chapter 6). In fact, universal free trade could be brought about only by positive international government.

This second role was complemented by the third: the ability to mitigate anarchy. In *Towards International Government* (1915), Hobson rejected collective disarmament, because if one state defected from such an arrangement, the problem of war would remain (Hobson 1915: 19–23). He in effect prescribed collective security stipulating a league or confederation of states, with as wide a membership as possible. If each member pledged to join together to repel or deter an aggressive

power, peace could be forged. Moreover, moral sanction is not sufficient; the Powers must be prepared to submit to an international
arbitration Court or commission any conflicts or grievances they might
have. And, in particular, they must be prepared to accept the will and
decisions of the commission (1915: chapter 2). Moreover, in any
instances in which one state refused to abide by a particular ruling, all
other states must be prepared to enforce international law. The second
and third roles enabled the first. Thus by binding themselves to international free trade and peace agreements, states enhanced their domestic agential capacity to implement reforms against elite interests, not
least to block moves towards protectionism, indirect taxation and
militarism.

Finally, although Hobson's approach grants the state considerable
domestic agential power, nevertheless state autonomy remained, as in
classical liberalism, an *intervening variable*. The reproduction of the
economy requires moderately high state interventionism in much the
same way that for classical liberalism, the economy requires a minimalist
state. Domestic state agential power is therefore, reduced to the 'primitive' structure of individual needs. Nevertheless, this promoted very
high levels of international agential state power to mitigate the logic of
anarchy. Accordingly, in contrast to neorealism, states are not the
passive victims of anarchy but have sufficient international power and
agency to create a peaceful world. In sum, Hobson's prescription of the
state involves 'moderate domestic agential power and high international
agential power'.

Functionalism

The theme of the positive state and positive international institutions
was given a unique twist in the functionalist writings of David Mitrany
prior to and during the Second World War. There are two main aspects
to Mitrany's work on international relations; first, a 'functionalist'
normative project outlined in his classic text *A Working Peace System*
(1943/1966), for which he is famous. However, this treatise said little or
nothing about the state. Moreover, it produced only an 'approach' to
IR, as opposed to a full theory (Taylor and Groom 1975: 1; Tooze
1977). But there was a second, lesser-known aspect to Mitrany's work,
outlined in *The Progress of International Government* (1933) and in
various articles, in which he developed a historical–sociological theory
of the state and international relations. An examination of these other
works does not undermine conventional readings of Mitrany, but serves
to bring into focus vital aspects of his work that have been ignored or

neglected. These historical–sociological aspects help us understand more fully his specific calls for a 'working peace system': indeed they crucially contextualise his specific 'political' project.

Basic historical concepts

Though he never actually used these labels, I suggest that there are three implicit categories that inform Mitrany's historical and normative approaches. For want of better terms, these might be called: *mode of inclusion/exclusion*, *economic/social processes* and *dialectical evolutionism*.

Political institutions as modes of inclusion/exclusion   Political institutions are implicitly conceptualised as 'inclusionary' or 'exclusionary'. The more inclusive a political institution, the greater its adaptive ability is to meet the economic and social needs of individuals, and the higher its international agential power becomes. Through time, political institutions adapt to rising economic individual needs, which were initially submerged but were 'brought to the surface' through the enabling hand of economic processes. Nevertheless Mitrany ultimately grants the state moderate international agential power where states shape the inter-state system, but have insufficient agential capacity to overcome the competitive logic of anarchy.

Economic/social processes   These comprise 'economic interdependence', especially through the development of global technologies, as well as changes in citizenship rights within states. As history progresses, these processes have an 'enabling effect', pressurising states and international institutions to conform to the needs of individuals.

Dialectical evolutionism   Implicitly, there is a notion that history progresses through a dialectical process. Thus those historical political institutions that act as 'fetters' to the realisation of individual human needs are through time replaced by higher less exclusionary or more inclusionary adaptive forms. Institutional forms adapt through historical time as 'enabling processes' develop. More specifically, Mitrany's historical approach presents a five-stage 'dialectical–evolutionary' model in which institutions begin as exclusionary, but through time become increasingly inclusive. Progress ends with the emergence of a global society that fully satisfies the economic and social needs of all humanity (Mitrany 1933: 52). Mitrany effectively examines the shifting boundary or 'interaction cleavage' between political institutions (modes of inclusion/exclusion) on the one hand, and the economic and social needs of individuals which are enabled through the 'processes' of global interdependence and domestic citizenship rights extensions, on the other. Institutional change gradually adapts or evolves towards realising underlying economic individual needs (1933: 48).

The normative (functionalist) project complements this historical project by specifying the 'appropriate' institutional forms of the present period (the fifth and final stage) that can bring about the full satisfaction of global human economic and social needs. As Mitrany puts it, for today '[w]e have reached a point where the material forces at our disposal threaten to escape our control and to warp the very civilisation which they are meant to enhance. To discover how we can make the elements serve the needs of the human race, without allowing their use to be distorted by political frontiers or political notions, is therefore an urgent task of political science' (1933: 17). But this can be understood only through a prior discussion of Mitrany's historical–sociological theory.

The historical-sociological approach

Mitrany argues that since the end of the Roman Empire (fifth century AD), the world has progressed through five stages, in which individual economic and social needs are the underlying logic which are initially submerged and unfulfilled, but are gradually forced to the surface as history progresses. *Through history the international agential powers of the state increase, but ultimately stop short of high power to mitigate anarchy.*

1st stage – medieval unity   Beginning at the bottom of figure 3.3, the first stage covered the fifth century to c. 1648. This comprised medieval feudal institutions which constituted a maladaptive *mode of exclusion*, in which individual needs went unrealised. Although European international society was held in place by the supra-'national' institutions of the Papacy and the Holy Roman Empire, nevertheless such unity was precarious owing to the constant conflict between these two institutions. The emergence of the Reformation and Renaissance dissolved this fragile unity, and unleashed a new system of individualistic (sovereign) competing states (1933: 20–5).

2nd stage – absolutist sovereignty   The weak domestic political institutions of feudalism were replaced with the sovereign absolutist state, which was also a maladaptive exclusionary mode. There was a two-fold problem here: sovereignty created a fragmented multi-state system in which sovereign state rights and the balance of power took precedence over individual human needs. In this phase, realism could aptly characterise international politics. 'To the succeeding centuries one could

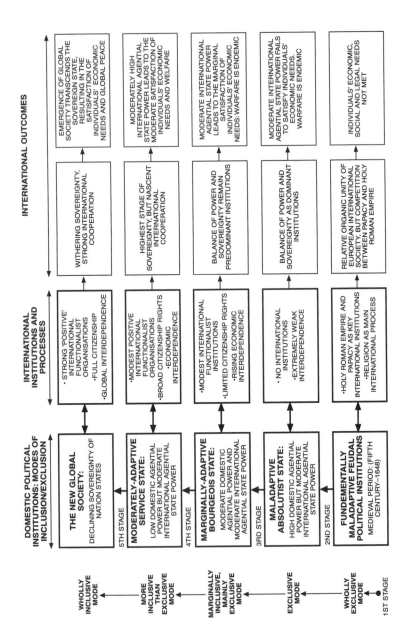

Figure 3.3 Mitrany's historical–sociological model of the 'socially-adaptive' state in international change

apply without injustice Hobbes's dictum that man is a wolf to man . . . [that there was] a state of anarchy without order or principle' (1933: 23). The works of Machiavelli and Bodin served to provide legitimacy for the absolutist sovereign state. The second problem was that the regime form was despotic. The state's high domestic agential power and autonomy fundamentally blocked the realisation of human economic needs, not least by keeping the masses out of the political realm, thereby depriving the state of sufficient international agency to mitigate inter-state conflict.

3rd stage – constitutional/bourgeois sovereignty   Following the French Revolution, the economic, social and political needs of the bourgeoisie led to a change in the form of the state away from absolutism to the constitutional or bourgeois state. Even though domestic agential state power or autonomy remained moderately high and international agential power moderate, there was some progress. The bourgeois state was marginally inclusive, in that it ushered in individualism. The progressive function of individualism took three key forms. First, 'negative rights' were crucial in that the prime political objective was to ensure freedom from arbitrary interference by an absolutist state form (i.e. laissez-faire political economy). Secondly, the bourgeois state also made tentative overtures to international notions of democracy. And, thirdly, it served to unleash creative individual energy that had previously been suppressed. Internationally, the bourgeois state was embedded in a larger international economic system in which the process of rising economic interdependence pressed the state to adapt and conform to economic needs. In this respect, states could no longer live in 'splendid isolation'. The need for cooperation led to international institutions, and some 900 treaties were established between 1874 and 1883. Progress was made in terms of setting up international functional organisations – e.g. the International Postal Union. This helped create a rudimentary organic unity – an international society. By the turn of the century, as represented in the two Hague Conferences, interdependence had brought humanity 'to the threshold of a genuine international society' (1933: 45).

However, individualism also took on two negative or exclusionary aspects that ultimately outweighed the benefits. First, although a laissez-faire political economy had a mildly positive function as mentioned above, it also had a negative function because it blocked *positive domestic participation*. Secondly, it reaffirmed political individualism between states (i.e. preserving external sovereignty) in the international sphere (1933: 19, 35). While the bourgeois state was more inclusive and adaptive than its absolutist predecessor, it still basically served to block the realisation of individual needs, and thus the state's international agential power remained only moderate.

4th stage – the service state as the highest stage of sovereignty The bourgeois state gave way to the planned state or *service state*, or what he later called the 'comprehensive' state (Mitrany 1975). It was a clear advance upon its predecessor, being more adaptive to social individual needs although, paradoxically, it simultaneously represented the highest stage of sovereignty (the negative blocking aspect). It drew economic needs to the surface in three key ways. First, it promoted a common social outlook between states based on individual welfare rights. Secondly, it brought about a common functional or administrative structure across international society, through which economic needs could start to be met. Thirdly, it was beneficial because it eroded the negative function of the separation of the economic and political realms that was imposed under the bourgeois laissez-faire state. Here the extension of citizenship rights was crucial (1933: 47). Paradoxically, the state's role for the first time in history became 'positive'; paradoxically, because it had to lose a large degree of domestic agential power or autonomy to become 'positive'. The comprehensive state represented a watershed or a threshold in which the role of the state was fundamentally transformed. 'No longer does the state enshrine the nature of society; it is the social current that determines in perpetual adjustment, the make-up of the governmental system . . . in the last resort the form of government and its laws and institutions are shaped and reshaped by the restless flux of the community's social pressures' (1975: 26–7). The service state is the most advanced – i.e. the most inclusive – in terms of adapting to individual social needs, and has the highest degree of international agential capacity of any state form in the last 1,500 years (though the lowest degree of domestic agential power or autonomy).

Despite all this, the state was deprived of the necessary degree of international agential capacity to overcome anarchy and satisfy individual economic needs, given that there were two central contradictions of the service state operating at the domestic and international levels. Domestically, although the state had become much more inclusive than previous political formations, there remained clear vestiges of exclusiveness. The service state ultimately diluted popular participation because it sought too rigid a control of its population (through strong 'surveillance' powers); hence Mitrany's alternative term was later used – 'the comprehensive state'. 'All the aims of political democracy were to control government; all the aims of social democracy end in control by government' (1975: 31). The comprehensive state could not sufficiently meet individual needs because of its inability to harmonise with the policies of other states which sometimes offset a particular state's domestic ability to meet social needs. This occurred in part because of the second fundamental contradiction of the service state

The second, and perhaps *the* fundamental contradiction of the service state was that while there was a definite decline in domestic agential power, international agential state power to mitigate anarchy was stymied. That is, the comprehensive state served to release old economic nationalist/mercantilist tendencies, which reproduced state individualism (i.e. the maintenance of external sovereignty), making inter-state conflict inevitable. The nation-state, even in its moderately progressive 'social-service' manifestation, is ultimately 'un-natural': it represented the highest stage, or 'last gasp' of sovereignty. What was required was a less rigid and politically inclusive political container within which the economic, social and legal rights of individuals could be fully realised. This was further reinforced by the prevailing set of international institutions – the League of Nations – which by reaffirming sovereignty constituted a 'blocking' or negative function (1933: 47). Rather than instituting positive rights, it provided negative rights – rights of a 'thou shalt not' kind.

But despite the schizophrenic nature of the comprehensive state, it was embedded within a global society based on economic interdependence and new global technologies, which served to undermine the negative exclusionary function of the state. 'If the present time is likely to prove a historical turning point [it will be] because of such dramatic changes in the scientific–technological field . . . but especially because every new invention . . . is now apt to breed problems which, for the first time in history, are global in their very nature and in their scale' (1975: 30). These global technologies and global processes (e.g. satellites, epidemics, nuclear power, exploration of the seabed and so on), require technical or functional solutions at the global level. They require new international organisations which are shaped 'not by any theory as to the political self-determination of the parties but by the technical self-determination of each of the matters involved' (1975: 30). To deal with these technologies, a vast body of international law developed, which in turn sought to transcend the old 'diplomatic law', replacing it with a 'true development of international government' (1975: 30). In this way, economic processes demanded new forms of international governance.

5th and final stage – international functionalism and the withering away of sovereignty   As with Carr (1951), so for Mitrany, the 'comprehensive'

or 'service' state represented the 'highest stage of sovereignty'. At this point, Mitrany's normative (functionalist) political project came to the fore. In order to meet individuals' economic, social and legal needs, both the service state and the League of Nations – understood ultimately as 'blocking' institutions – must be overcome by functionalist international organisation, thereby ushering in a fifth and final stage of human progress. This normative/functionalist aspect of Mitrany's work is well known; it is in fact what he is famous for, and was fully outlined in *A Working Peace System* (Mitrany 1943/1966). He fundamentally rejected formal international government, whether in the form of a league of nations, or a regional, continental union. He also rejected all radical political projects. Here, the principal difference with Marxism becomes apparent. The objective was to downgrade 'politics' and 'political ideology' as far as possible so as to minimise friction between states as well as with the sovereign state itself. But it would be wrong to argue that Mitrany's technical approach is free of political ideology: it rested fundamentally on a liberal ideology that sought to promote and satisfy individual needs (Tooze 1977). Moreover, he leaned more to the reformist politics of John A. Hobson, who also argued that positive international institutions were vital if human needs were to be properly satisfied. But, unlike Hobson, Mitrany rejected the role of formal international government, preferring a more informal set of functional international organisations/institutions. And in further contrast, he argued that the sovereign state ultimately constituted a blockage or fetter to the development of global society. Accordingly, he argued that as international functional organisation developed so the sovereign state would gradually wither away.

A clear approach to the state (and of IR) emerges from Mitrany's historical–sociological theory. First, states must have relatively low domestic agential power in that they must conform to the needs of individuals. Nevertheless, the state even in its social-service guise cannot fully satisfy human needs. Through time, Mitrany's implicit 'dialectical–historical' approach demonstrates how the domestic agential power of the state recedes, and how international functionalist institutions gradually overcome the sovereignty of the state, resulting in the gradual removal of the impediments or institutional fetters to the full realisation of human needs. Nevertheless, for much of human history the state has had moderate international agential power, in that it creates a conflictual international realm. The service or comprehensive state, however, has the highest degree of international agential power of any state in history, insofar as it sets up international functionalist organisations which can create a peaceful and cooperative global society. Nevertheless, Mitrany fails to ascribe the state high international agential power (as in Keohane, Bull and Hobson) because the state ultimately constitutes an impediment or fetter to the creation of a fully peaceful world.

State-centric liberalism

English school rationalism

The liberal theory of 'rationalism' was developed by the 'English school', and was headed by Martin Wight, Hedley Bull, Charles Manning, Adam Watson and John Vincent. This section discusses perhaps the most famous and important book of this genre: Hedley Bull's *The Anarchical Society* (1977). While IR scholars frequently characterise Bull as a 'realist', this section will show why Bull was clearly non-realist, and why rationalism more generally should be treated as a liberal theory (but see Dunne 1998 and Wheeler 2000 for more constructivist readings of the English school). Bull began, as did Wight, by differentiating the rationalist from the realist, as well as the cosmopolitan, perspectives: rationalism, in Wight's words, occupies a 'via media' between realism and revolutionism or cosmopolitanism (i.e. Kantian liberalism).

In strong contrast to the liberal institutionalism of Mitrany, Bull produced a fundamentally *state-centric* liberal theory: '[t]he starting point of IR is the existence of states, or independent political communities, each of which possess a government that asserts sovereignty' (Bull 1977: 8, 24–6). Bull fundamentally rejected the radical cosmopolitan belief that order can be achieved only by the transcendence or overthrow of the system of sovereign states. This is not necessary because sovereign states can form a cooperative international society, which ensures that order is achieved and maintained over time. Like neorealists, Bull provides a very strong normative defence of the sovereign state. And like neorealists, Bull essentially 'black-boxes' the state, granting it high domestic agential power or autonomy such that it is unaffected by non-state actors. But the key point is that, in strict contrast to neorealism, Bull defends the sovereign state on socially *progressive* grounds: that it constitutes the most appropriate political institution to create international order; and that, above all, the state has a high degree of international agential power to buck the logic of anarchy. Thus the key differences between neorealism and rationalism are two-fold: first that rationalism invests the state with considerable international agential power to shape the international system as well as to mitigate anarchy. Secondly, rationalism implicitly conceptualises anarchy differently, viewing the international realm as one of *possibility* rather than one of *pure necessity*. Through long-term cooperation, states can come to forge an 'international society' under anarchy; hence Bull's famous quote, that '[a] society of states (or international society) exists when a group of states, conscious of certain common interests and common values, form a society in the sense that they conceive themselves to be bound by common sets of rules . . . and share in the working of common institutions' (1977: 13).

Bull rejects the neorealist 'domestic analogy' which draws on Thomas Hobbes, whereby international anarchy entails a 'war of all against all'. The fundamental basis of Hobbes's theory (and thus neorealism) is the view that order is possible only when a state or higher authority exists which can make laws which are enforced though coercive power. In short, no coercive (higher) authority – no order. Against this coercive thesis, Bull argues that '[i]t is not fear of a supreme authority that is the source of order within the modern state . . . individuals are capable of order because they value it' (1977: 48). In contrast to neorealism's 'Hobbesian domestic analogy', rationalism invokes a type of 'Lockean domestic analogy' which stipulates that in the international state of nature, basic or primary order can exist in much the same way that primary order allegedly existed within the state of nature found in primitive stateless societies (see Suganami 1986). In turn, order in the state of nature is enabled by rules even if these are not made or enforced by a state. Such rules tend to take the form of norms and conventions which are based on morality, custom and religion (Bull 1977: 53–60). Important here is the role of the fundamental 'constitutional' rules or *norms* (1977: 4–5, 17–8), which enable basic or primary order in three respects, to ensure:

(1) that life is secure from violence (security)
(2) that agreements will be honoured (contract)
(3) that the possession of things is relatively stable (property rights).

These are attained ultimately because of the value that states attach to order, without which state behaviour would be severely constrained to do anything other than look out for its own individual security (1977: 8, 47–8). Here Bull precisely inverts Waltz. For Waltz, states passively adapt to the dictates of anarchy, thereby unintentionally reproducing the anarchic state system. For Bull, states have high international agential power to promote primary international order, thereby intentionally reproducing the international society of states (a position which overlaps with Morgenthau's notion of the 'aristocratic international' and Carr's 'monarchical international').

High international agential state power and international institutions as the providers of international order

Bull ascribes the sovereign state as the central institution that could provide for international order (1977: 71–4) (see figure 3.4). A world state is not required because states act as the guardians of international order. And, like Hobson, Bull rejected classical liberalism's belief in the 'spontaneity thesis' on the grounds that primary order could be creatively and intentionally engineered only through the construction of four international normative constitutional institutions. These comprise:

(1) *The balance of power/systemic warfare:* in contrast to Waltz, the balance is consciously maintained by states in order to preserve international society. It does not spontaneously and unintentionally emerge as a function of the short-term adaptive survival needs of states. While the balance of power was not inevitable for Bull (unlike Waltz), it is nevertheless vital for the maintenance of international society. Thus European international society has been largely preserved by the balance, for on the occasions when an aspiring imperial power attempted to destroy the multi-state system in favour of an imperial hierarchy (e.g. the Habsburgs, Louis XIV, Napoleon Bonaparte, Adolf Hitler), the other states ganged up against it so as to maintain the survival of the multi-state system or international society. The balance goes hand-in-hand with the positive role of systemic warfare, which paradoxically plays an important role in maintaining an orderly international society of states. It is functional to order because it ensures that aspiring imperialists can be suppressed, thereby retaining the integrity of the multi-state system. To the balance of power and systemic warfare, Bull adds the role of nuclear deterrence which, he argues, has played an important role in securing peace and order after 1945 (Bull 1977: chapters 5, 8).

(2)*Diplomacy:* diplomacy is functional for order not least because it enhances communication between states, facilitates agreement and minimises friction (Bull 1977: chapter 7).

(3) *Great power management:* Bull argues that inequality between states is functional to preserving international society, because 'it is difficult to see how, apart from resort to alliances that may introduce a contrived element of inequality, international conflicts could ever be settled and laid to rest' (1977: 205–6). Great powers are important in that they help to preserve the balance of power, seek to avoid crises and wars between each other and are able to contain conflicts within their respective alliances (1977: 208–29).

(4) *States and international law:* while neorealists denounce international law as ineffective because it is not enforced by a world state,

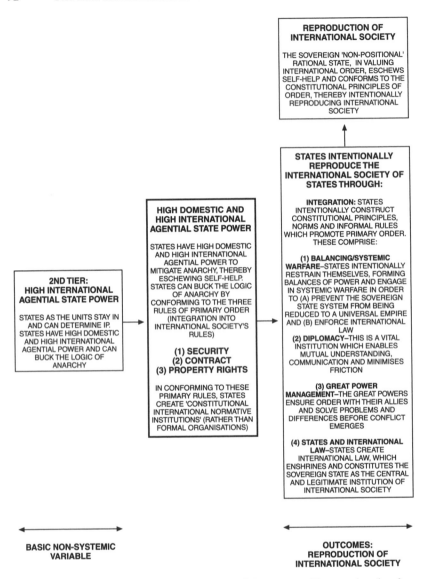

Figure 3.4 Bull's rationalist theory of the state and international order

Bull insists that law is nevertheless backed up by the coercive power of the individual states themselves. States enforce international law through war and reprisals (1977: 129–32). Thus the pursuit of war against international law-breakers is not a symptom of anarchy (as neorealists assume), but is rather a sign that international society is functioning effectively. The key point, though, is that law is respected not simply because it is backed up by force, but because states voluntarily prefer to conform to international law. Echoing Louis Henken, Bull argues that, '[i]f it were possible . . . to conduct a quantitative study of obedience to the rules of international law, it might be expected to show that most states obey most agreed rules of international law most of the time' (1977: 137). International law is especially valued by states because it enshrines sovereignty by *prescribing states as the central actors in IP*, and continues to do so even at the end of the twentieth century (1977: 139–61).

The rationalist theory of the state in IR

Bull's theory (see figure 3.4) is best differentiated with Waltz's (see figure 2.2, p. 25). As chapter 2 showed, for Waltz anarchy is primary and the state is secondary. For Bull the state is primary: it has high international agential power and intentionally seeks through self-re-straint to create order and preserve the society of states. Although both Bull and Waltz prescribe the state with high domestic agential power or institutional autonomy, nevertheless, Bull invests the state with high international agential power to mitigate anarchy (unlike Waltz). For neorealism, states are completely free of external or internal actors' preferences but have no international agential power, being heavily circumscribed by the invisible hand of anarchy. In rationalism, states constantly restrain themselves, which paradoxically enhances international agential power to mitigate anarchy. Thus Bull prescribes 'high domestic and high international agential state power'.

Implicitly attacking Waltz, Bull rejects the neorealist 'functionalist' or structuralist framework, which stipulates that the anarchical system is self-constituting, and prescribes state behaviour as functional to the maintenance of anarchy. 'International society does not display the kind of [systemic] wholeness or unity that would point to such . . . functionalist explanations' (1977: 75). In contrast to Waltz's 'top-down' approach, Bull effectively invokes a 'bottom-up' approach which begins with the intentions of states, as the fundamental agents of international society. Bull goes beyond Waltz in a number of key ways. First, states are not reducible to anarchy, but can actively avoid conforming to its constraining logic. They do this by creating normative international or constitutional institutions. These institutions are not autonomous of states; they have only a 'relative autonomy' since they are ultimately determined by states and for states. As in neoliberal institutionalism (informal) international constitutional institutions push states away from short-term (adaptive) 'self-help' towards long-term 'collective-help'. Although these constitutional institutions are not autonomous of states, they are, however, autonomous of anarchy and the distribution of power. In short, Bull downgrades the importance of structure and places prime focus on the international agential power of the state.

Borrowing from Ashley (1981), this difference between rationalism and neorealism is equivalent to the difference between 'practical rationalism' and 'technical neorealism'. Thus for rationalism, states are practically committed to develop consensus and order through communication and shared understanding. This 'practical rationalism' has direct consequences for the problematic predicament that states find themselves in the late twentieth century, as various global crises batter the inter-state system. Neorealism is frequently taken to task for what Ashley (1981) calls the 'impossibility theorem', whereby geniune cooperation between sovereign states is impossible, rendering the sovereign state impotent to overcome global challenges. But rationalism posits that sovereign states can escape the 'impossibility theorem'. They can overcome the collective action problem and create a functionally efficient and orderly world. Thus sovereignty does not confound cooperation; it is *the* constitutive institution that makes cooperation possible in the first place. This suggests that a radical transcendence of international society and the sovereign state is not necessary in order to solve global crises (Bull 1977: 233–320).

In sum, the rationalist theory of the state can be summarised as: *the sovereign state, armed with high domestic and high international agential power intentionally creates informal normative or constitutional international institutions to promote long-term primary order, which in turn leads to the development and reproduction of an international society of states, thereby enabling the state to avoid conforming to the short-term adaptive or technical requirements of international anarchy.*

The emergence of international regime theory

The second strand of state-centric liberalism is found in neoliberal institutionalism. Paradoxically, the origins of the theory began with neorealist hegemonic stability theory (HST); 'paradoxically' because HST was developed precisely to undermine liberalism and interdependence theory (within the first state debate). Krasner originally pointed to various problems with HST, most notably that its prediction of the demise of the post-1970 free trade regime had failed to materialise. Initially, in order to try to explain this anomaly, Krasner invoked the lagged effect of domestic policy interests which continued to favour free trade (Krasner 1979: 342–3). But this was confounded when US domestic interests turned towards favouring protectionism. By 1983, Krasner turned to a new 'lagged' variable in his pioneering edited volume *International Regimes* (1983a): that of the trade regime itself. Nevertheless, he endowed the regime with only a *relative autonomy* from anarchy and the distribution of power, thereby retaining the integrity of neorealism (see the discussion of the tectonic plate metaphor in Krasner 1983b: 357–8). Thus the regime could 'lag' or hobble on for a short while. But, unprotected by hegemony, the regime was rendered highly vulnerable to a random external shock. Nevertheless the problem remained: that the freer trade regime persisted. While neorealism could not explain this, neoliberal institutionalism was created to fill this void.

Neoliberal institutionalism and the theory of international regimes

Perhaps the most significant writer here has been Robert Keohane, whose pioneering book, *After Hegemony* (1984), brought the neoliberal institutionalist theory to the forefront of the IR research agenda. Through a 'creative dialogue' with neorealism, Keohane sought to go beyond liberal institutionalism (hence *neo*liberal), by synthesising it with neorealism in order to develop a non-realist theory of cooperation in world politics. Recognising that neorealists could dismiss liberal institutionalism by simply rejecting the premises of state actions that the approach posited, Keohane sought to close this avenue off from realist attack (Keohane 1984: 66–7). To achieve this, he explicitly borrowed three basic assumptions of state behaviour from neorealism.

First in contrast to 'liberal institutionalism' he argued that states are *not* motivated by self-abnegation and 'other-regarding' idealist motivations, but are *rational egoists* which generally seek to maximise their utility gains. Though he later relaxed this assumption in his chapter 7 (see the discussion of 'bounded rationality'), the crucial point that he sought to establish was that regimes were effective even under conditions of utility-maximising rationality. Secondly, he sought to further expunge the idealistic and normative basis of liberal institutionalism by insisting that world politics is not dominated by harmony and cooperation, but that discord frequently prevails, as neorealists insist. In fact, discord is extremely important in his theory because it is this that creates the need for regimes in the first place. 'Without the specter of conflict, there is no need to cooperate' (1984: 54). Thirdly, Keohane supposedly adopted a 'systemic' approach and 'black-boxed' (i.e. held constant) the state, such that domestic state–society relations and non-state actors were excluded from the explanatory model, given his premise that non-state actors 'continue to be subordinate to states' (1989: 8). This led him to develop a 'state-centric' approach, in which sovereign states are the principal actors in world politics. Thus, in sum, he claimed that by 'starting with similar premises about motivations, I seek to show that [neo]realism's pessimism about welfare-maximising cooperation is exaggerated' (1984: 29, 67).

The rational choice/functionalist theory of regimes and cooperation
Having allegedly borrowed neorealism's premises of state rationality (to be critically reviewed later), Keohane proceeded to make three basic amendments to neorealism (figure 3.5). In the process he rejected classical liberalism's 'spontaneity thesis' by arguing that cooperation would not naturally occur – it had to be creatively engineered through the construction of international regimes.

(1) *Regimes are absolutely autonomous of anarchy and the distribution of power, but only relatively autonomous from states*   Fundamental to neorealism is the 'collective action problem', where anarchy ensures that states eschew or defect from cooperation in favour of adaptive competitive self-help. HST argues that the collective action problem can be overcome by hegemony, though only in the short run. Neorealism retains the integrity of its assumption that states do not voluntarily and spontaneously cooperate, because it is only the pressure and coercion of a powerful hegemon that can promote regimes and enforce cooperation among states. Thus cooperation is never spontaneous but is always imposed (cf. Young 1983: 100–1). Nor does cooperation last long. For as hegemony inevitably declines so, too, do regimes. That is, regimes do not have a full autonomy from the distribution of power (i.e. from hegemonic unipolarity).

In contrast, Keohane argues that while hegemony and a unipolar distribution of power can be important in initially setting up international regimes and institutions, it is *not a sufficient* variable. States as agents can negotiate or voluntarily agree to set up and maintain institutions, because they value the long run gains that such regimes provide (see also Young 1983). In turn, regimes empower states to overcome the collective action problem under anarchy. The key move here is to endow regimes with a full autonomy from anarchy and the distribution of power, and to thereby conceptually delink regimes from hegemony. This

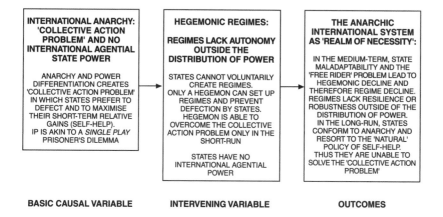

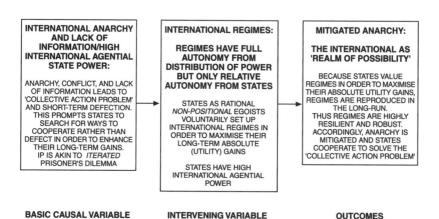

Figure 3.5 Neoliberal and neorealist theories of states and international regimes

has two fundamental consequences: first, that neoliberalism is able – unlike neorealism – to explain the persistence of regimes *after US hegemony*. And secondly, regimes are much more 'resilient' or 'robust' for neoliberals than for neorealists (Hasenclever, Mayer and Rittberger 1997: 86–7). By conceptually delinking regimes from hegemony and embedding them in state power, neoliberals are able to ascribe much greater 'resilience' to regimes.

However, as we note later, regimes do not have a full autonomy from states. Regimes have only a *relative autonomy* from states, since it is states that intentionally create regimes in order to avoid conforming to the logic of short-term relative gains (associated with anarchy), so that they can enhance their long-term absolute gains. In this crucial respect, regimes are only intervening variables that lie between states (the basic causal variable) on the one hand and international outcomes on the other (even though regimes have considerably more power than that granted by neorealism).

(2) *Cooperation is fundamental to the long-term utility-maximising interests of states*   A fundamental aspect to neoliberalism is its use of the *prisoner's dilemma* (PD), in which two actors can either cooperate or 'defect' (i.e. go it alone). In a single-play PD, as neorealists argue, the dominant strategy among rational egoists is to defect and dob in the other – hence cooperation is avoided. But the key point is that in *repeated* PD games (termed 'iterated' games) through tit-for-tat, the two players *learn* to cooperate since this provides greater long run pay-offs than defecting (Axelrod 1984). Against neorealism, Keohane argues that world politics is better characterised by *iterated* PD games, because over time states constantly come into reciprocal contact with each other. Accordingly, cooperation ensues not because of morality or idealistic motivations, but because it satisfies the long-term interests of power-maximising rational egoistic states (Keohane 1984: chapter 5).

Regimes or institutions prevent defection and cheating by lengthening the 'shadow of the future' (Axelrod and Keohane 1993). This is achieved in a number of ways. First, the process of retaliation and reciprocity, or 'tit-for-tat', provides a major disincentive to defect. The essence of iterated PD games is that, through time, both players learn to cooperate. That is, they learn that defection is punished with retaliation, and cooperation rewarded with reciprocity. This leads states to think in terms of future (absolute) cooperative gains rather than following short-term relative gains through defection. The 'more future pay-offs are valued relative to current pay-offs, the less the incentives to defect today, since the other side is likely to retaliate tomorrow' (Axelrod and

Keohane 1993: 91; Axelrod 1984). Paradoxically, the possibility of future 'retaliation' is crucial to the effective functioning of regimes; 'paradoxically', because it is retaliation that provides the basic reasoning behind neorealism's rejection of the efficacy of international regimes in the first place.

Secondly, the notion of 'issue-linkage' also prevents defection. Regimes are 'nested' or embedded within a multitude of policy arenas – in security, trade, finance, etc. (Keohane 1984: 89). Thus under the post-1945 liberal trade regime, a state might come under pressure from a domestic manufacturer to impose import quotas. But the state might resist such domestic rent-seeking pressures because of the negative consequences that this might have for other areas of trade (in which the state favours free trade), or because it does not wish to face foreign retaliation from other governments. In short, as with J.A. Hobson, regimes enhance the domestic agential power of the state *vis-à-vis* domestic actors. Moreover, by complying in trade, states are able to maintain gains in other non-trading arenas such as security or finance. Thirdly, states wish to establish and maintain a 'good reputation', which requires that they avoid defection and enter into long-term cooperation. Having a poor reputation jeopardises the maximisation of a state's long-term gains (1984: 103–6). All this rests upon one fundamental assumption: that states are better off by following long-term (optimal) cooperative gains than following short-term defection (sub-optimal) strategies.

(3) *Defining anarchy in term of an assymetrical distribution of information*   Keohane accepts that anarchy promotes uncertainty as to whether states will keep their commitments. But, for Keohane, anarchy gives rise to the collective action problem not because of the unequal distribution of power (as in neorealism) but because of the asymmetrical distribution of information, or the lack of information. It is this that promotes defection and cheating because states do not know, and therefore do not trust, the intentions of others. Accordingly, states create international regimes in order to enhance the density and spread of information, which reduces the tendency for defection and cheating (1984: chapter 6). In this way, regimes can reduce the 'transaction costs of agreements', since they reduce the need for states to monitor whether agreements are complied with by others, thereby promoting trust and cooperation. As we shall see, this position sees international anarchy as highly malleable.

The neoliberal/neorealist debate in the 'second state debate'
Many IR commentators often describe Keohane as a neorealist – or, more accurately, as a 'modified neorealist'. This section shows why this

view is fundamentally flawed. The design of Keohane's project was *potentially* ingenious. By using realist premises about state motivations, he hoped to insulate himself from neorealist attack. But the problem here is that he failed actually to adopt neorealist premises in the first place. I argue here that Keohane produced a non-realist theory of the state which was encapsulated within a non-systemic approach.

As the neorealist Joseph Grieco has pointed out, neorealists do not in fact view the state as a *rational egoist that seeks to maximise its absolute gains interests under systemic anarchy*. States are 'defensive positionalists' that seek to *maintain* their relative position – that is, they privilege short-term *relative gains* over long-term absolute cooperative gains (Grieco 1993a, 1993b; see also Waltz 1979: 105–6; Mastanduno 1991; Krasner 1993). Moreover, some neorealists go even further and argue that states seek to *maximise* their relative gains over others: that states are *offensive* as well as 'defensive' positionalists (Gilpin 1975: 23, 34–6, 85–92; Mearsheimer 1995: 11–12). For neorealists, states are highly 'sensitive' to the distribution of gains under cooperation. It is not a lack of information and uncertainty, nor cheating or defection that constitutes the problem for cooperation. Rather, the problem lies with 'incentives' for cooperation in the first place. Thus state *A* will gladly forgo any gains that it might have accrued through cooperating with state *B* if *B*'s relative gains exceed those of *A*, since *B* might subsequently turn around and use its enhanced power to militarily undermine A. Prudent statesmanship dictates envy. Thus, under anarchy, states cannot afford to be indifferent or insensitive to others' gains (Grieco 1993a: 128–31). As Krasner put it: while neoliberals emphasise that states are interested in getting to the 'Pareto Frontier' – the point at which all states maximise their gains through cooperation – the problem for neorealists is 'not how to get to the Pareto Frontier but which point along the frontier will be chosen' (Krasner 1993: 237–8, 235). For neoliberalism, precisely because of anarchy, states cooperate to maximise absolute cooperative gains and are indifferent or insensitive to the unequal distribution of gains between states. Thus *A* will gladly cooperate with *B* so long as *A* is better off, even if *B*'s gains outweigh *A*'s. The difference is that power is defined in relative terms for neorealists but in absolute terms for neoliberals. This leads to a non-systemic and non-neorealist theory of international agential state power.

A non-systemic/non-neorealist approach to the state and IR   Keohane did not in fact adopt a purely systemic theory, as many have assumed (see, for example, Keohane 1984: 26–9; 1993: 294). A 'pure systemic' approach would derive the state from the requirements of the system

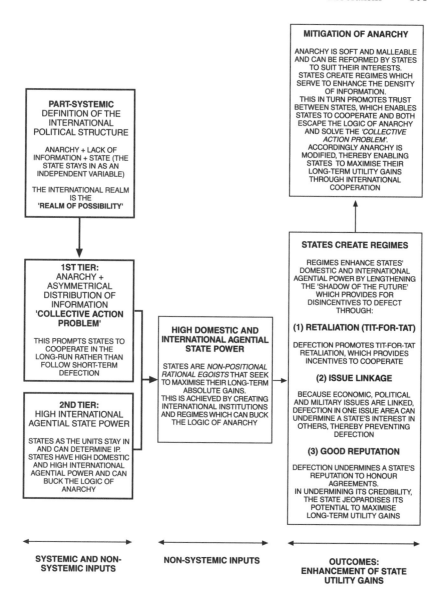

MITIGATION OF ANARCHY

ANARCHY IS SOFT AND MALLEABLE AND CAN BE REFORMED BY STATES TO SUIT THEIR INTERESTS. STATES CREATE REGIMES WHICH SERVE TO ENHANCE THE DENSITY OF INFORMATION. THIS IN TURN PROMOTES TRUST BETWEEN STATES, WHICH ENABLES STATES TO COOPERATE AND BOTH ESCAPE THE LOGIC OF ANARCHY AND SOLVE THE *'COLLECTIVE ACTION PROBLEM'*. ACCORDINGLY ANARCHY IS MODIFIED, THEREBY ENABLING STATES TO MAXIMISE THEIR LONG-TERM UTILITY GAINS THROUGH INTERNATIONAL COOPERATION

PART-SYSTEMIC DEFINITION OF THE INTERNATIONAL POLITICAL STRUCTURE

ANARCHY + LACK OF INFORMATION + STATE (THE STATE STAYS IN AS AN INDEPENDENT VARIABLE)

THE INTERNATIONAL REALM IS THE **'REALM OF POSSIBILITY'**

1ST TIER: ANARCHY + ASYMMETRICAL DISTRIBUTION OF INFORMATION **'COLLECTIVE ACTION PROBLEM'**

THIS PROMPTS STATES TO COOPERATE IN THE LONG-RUN RATHER THAN FOLLOW SHORT-TERM DEFECTION

2ND TIER: HIGH INTERNATIONAL AGENTIAL STATE POWER

STATES AS THE UNITS STAY IN AND CAN DETERMINE IP. STATES HAVE HIGH DOMESTIC AND HIGH INTERNATIONAL AGENTIAL POWER AND CAN BUCK THE LOGIC OF ANARCHY

HIGH DOMESTIC AND INTERNATIONAL AGENTIAL STATE POWER

STATES ARE *NON-POSITIONAL RATIONAL EGOISTS* THAT SEEK TO MAXIMISE THEIR LONG-TERM ABSOLUTE GAINS. THIS IS ACHIEVED BY CREATING INTERNATIONAL INSTITUTIONS AND REGIMES WHICH CAN BUCK THE LOGIC OF ANARCHY

STATES CREATE REGIMES

REGIMES ENHANCE STATES' DOMESTIC AND INTERNATIONAL AGENTIAL STATE POWER BY LENGTHENING THE 'SHADOW OF THE FUTURE' WHICH PROVIDES FOR DISINCENTIVES TO DEFECT THROUGH:

(1) RETALIATION (TIT-FOR-TAT)

DEFECTION PROMOTES TIT-FOR-TAT RETALIATION, WHICH PROVIDES INCENTIVES TO COOPERATE

(2) ISSUE LINKAGE

BECAUSE ECONOMIC, POLITICAL AND MILITARY ISSUES ARE LINKED, DEFECTION IN ONE ISSUE AREA CAN UNDERMINE A STATE'S INTEREST IN OTHERS, THEREBY PREVENTING DEFECTION

(3) GOOD REPUTATION

DEFECTION UNDERMINES A STATE'S REPUTATION TO HONOUR AGREEMENTS. IN UNDERMINING ITS CREDIBILITY, THE STATE JEOPARDISES ITS POTENTIAL TO MAXIMISE LONG-TERM UTILITY GAINS

SYSTEMIC AND NON-SYSTEMIC INPUTS

NON-SYSTEMIC INPUTS

OUTCOMES: ENHANCEMENT OF STATE UTILITY GAINS

Figure 3.6 Keohane's theory of the state and international regimes

and would argue that states *must* conform to international requirements; failure to do so would result in punishment by the system. In strong contrast to Waltz's systemic view of the international as the 'realm of necessity', Keohane sees it as a *realm of possibility*. Keohane shows not only that states can buck the logic of the system, but more importantly, that they can reform and reshape the international system in order to suit their interests *without being punished by the system*: a position that fundamentally contradicts Waltz's structuralist approach (see pp. 26–7). Rather than conceptualise anarchy as hard and unchanging, Keohane implicitly views it as soft and malleable. By enhancing the density and distribution of information at the international level through international institutions, states are able to modify anarchy to suit their interests. Thus while both Waltz and Keohane ascribe high domestic agential power to the state, in strict contrast to Waltz, Keohane endows the state with high international agential capacity to overcome the collective action problem. Accordingly, states are no longer condemned to *technically* conform to an exogenous anarchic environment, but can *practically insulate* themselves from it, and even escape its requirements. Paradoxically, cooperation through institutions does not make states more vulnerable as it does for neorealism, but makes them stronger. Regimes enable states to maximise their interests by *preventing* them from entering the 'defection avenue' of short-term relative gains preferences (the sub-optimal power strategy) and by pushing them to enhance their long-run gains (the optimal power-maximisation strategy). Thus, for neoliberalism, the 'second level' of the international system – the units (i.e. states) – does not drop out but stays in, which in turn leads to a clearly non-systemic and non-realist theory of world politics. As with Bull, Keohane upgrades the international agential power of the state and significantly downgrades the importance of international structure.

The neorealist critique of neoliberalism focuses on denouncing the autonomy of international institutions over states and insists that states are prior to institutions and that states have more power. This angle is one that very much derives from the first state debate. But we can reconfigure this understanding by applying the interpretative strictures of the 'second state debate'. From this angle, we can see that the neorealist critique of neoliberalism seriously misconstrues the neoliberal argument, a misconception that is found even within non-realist discussions of neoliberalism. For neoliberals, regimes are created by and for autonomous states in order to enhance their power under anarchy (Keohane 1993: 273–4): 'Institutions are necessary . . . in order to achieve *state* purposes' (Keohane 1984: 245, emphasis in the original); and, 'institutions *empower* governments rather than shackling them'

(1984: 13, emphasis in the original). Regimes do not limit state behaviour/autonomy *per se*: they merely limit *sub-optimal* short-term state behaviour (i.e. defection), thereby enabling states to optimally realise long-term utility gains. I suggest that states for neoliberals are conceptually equivalent to the neo-Marxist conception of the dominant class, which has in effect a 'collective action problem'; it is internally fragmented and prone to short-term defection from long-term cooperation (Poulantzas 1973; Offe 1974). For Poulantzas and Offe, the bourgeoisie requires and creates an 'ideal collective capitalist' state. Armed with a *relative autonomy* from the short-term interests of capital, the state functions to stretch the short-term conflictual outlook of the bourgeoisie into a long-term collaborative and unified position (in the face of the proletariat) *precisely so as to enhance the power of capital*. Likewise for neoliberals, states are prone to short-term defection and accordingly create 'ideal collective institutions' (i.e. regimes) which, armed with a 'relative autonomy' from states, can convert their short-term defection tendencies into long-term collaboration *precisely so as to maximise state power*. Indeed, as with J.A. Hobson's new liberal theory, Keohane argues that international institutions enhance the domestic agential power of the state, enabling it to resist vested interest groups who, for example, might call for protectionism for their particular industry. Accordingly, international institutions are, for Keohane, only intervening variables (Keohane 1984: 64). Thus although neoliberals argue that regimes have full autonomy from anarchy and the distribution of power, they have only a *relative autonomy* from the state, insofar as regimes go against the short-term (defection) actions of states in order to shore up their long-term interests.

In contrast to the neorealist reading, neoliberals do *not* exaggerate the autonomy of institutions over states; they in fact *analytically reduce* institutions to state utility-maximising interests. Regimes are fundamentally embedded in high international agential state power. Paradoxically, states create regimes precisely so as to enhance their agential power to buck the logic of anarchy; a position which ironically grants far greater international agential power to the state than is accorded under neorealism. This suggests that the neorealist critique of neoliberalism should not focus on neoliberalism's conception of regimes, and set up a sterile first state debate between 'state-centredness' versus 'international society-centredness'. Rather, the key difference lies with the high degree of international agential power granted by neoliberals, compared to the passive theory of the state found in neorealism. Thus in locating this debate within the framework of the second state debate, it becomes clear that it is neoliberalism that attributes very high international agential capacity to the state, while neorealism paradoxically marginalises the 'power' of the state. In sum, the assumption of rational egoism that Keohane employs leads not only to a different theory about cooperation but, above all, to a radically different theory of the state and IR.

We are now in a position to compare the neorealist and neoliberal theories of the state. The neorealist theory of the state can be defined as: *the sovereign 'positional'-adaptive state, armed with high domestic agential power maximises its short-term survival interests by minimising its relative power gap with other states (or even enhancing its relative power over others), but has no international agential power and must accordingly conform to the adaptive requirements of anarchy.*

In contrast, neoliberalism posits that: *the sovereign 'rational egoistic' state, armed with high domestic agential power maximises its long-term interests by creating 'relatively autonomous' international regimes which, in acting as an 'ideal collective state', enhance international agential state power thereby enabling states to buck, or* avoid conforming *to the short term (suboptimal) adaptive requirements of international anarchy.*

Some of the key figures in this debate have called for a 'grand synthesis' of the two theories (e.g. Keohane 1984: 135, 1993: 273, 291–3; Grieco 1993b: 328–35; Powell 1993; Hasenclever, Mayer and Rittberger 1997: 59–68, 134–5). Despite his original claim that neorealism and neoliberalism are distinct schools of thought (Keohane 1989: 8), Keohane has more recently gone so far as saying that the neoliberal/neorealist debate is not about incommensurable paradigms: '[w]e agree on 90 per cent and the remainder is essentially an empirical problem' (cited in Wæver 1996: 166). But synthesising these two approaches is problematic, not least because their theories of anarchy and the state are radically different. In according states high international agential power, neoliberals ontologically downgrade international structure; conversely, in focusing exclusively on anarchy, neorealists fail to accord the state with any international agential power. It *is*, however, entirely possible to synthesise many of the insights of both theories, but it is vital to note that the end product will necessarily be radically different from both of the original theories (see chapter 7, pp. 223–35, for an outline of what such a theory might look like). And given that many observers are increasingly viewing the neoliberal/neorealist debate as sterile and exhausted (e.g. Wæver 1996; Moravscik 1997), I suggest that relocating and reconciling it within the second state debate provides a promising way forward, not only for this specific debate but for IR theory more generally.

Discussion questions

- Why do all liberal approaches (apart from functionalism and pluralism) consign high amounts of international agential power to the state? How do they vary in the levels of domestic agential power assigned to the state?

- Why for classical liberals is state intervention in the economy bad?

- Why for new liberals is free trade good but minimalist state intervention in the domestic economy bad?

- Why for new liberals is the social-democratic state endowed with moderate domestic agential power a necessary but not sufficient factor in the promotion of global peace?

- What are the similarities and differences between J.A. Hobson's and Marxism's theory of the state?

- What are the similarities and differences between Mitrany's and Marx's theories of history?

- Why, for Mitrany, is the modern 'service' state the highest form of state in history but ultimately a fetter to the development of a peaceful global society?

- Although both Bull and Waltz produce state-centric approaches to IR, how are they differentiated in terms of the international agential power accorded the state?

- What is problematic with the view that Keohane's neoliberal institutionalist theory is equivalent to a modified form of neorealism? On what grounds is it claimed in this volume that it is problematic to reconcile neoliberalism and neorealism?

Suggestions for further reading

On classical liberalism, a good place to start is David Ricardo's (1817/ 1969) relatively short treatise (given that Smith's book, *The Wealth of Nations*, though highly readable, is extremely long). The classic statement of liberal international political theory is found in Kant's (1795/ 1914) short and readable text. Excellent introductions to liberal international relations theory can be found in Zacher and Matthew (1995) and Dunne (1997). The best introduction to J.A. Hobson's theory of IR is Long (1996) – Gabriel (1994) produces the conventional reading. While Hobson's *Imperialism* (1902/1968) constitutes the conventional starting point, his shorter books on international relations are essential for understanding his overall approach to IR (Hobson 1915, 1920). While Mitrany's classic text *A Working Peace System* (1943/1966) remains an essential text on functionalism, nevertheless his full theory is presented in *The Progess of International Government* (1933); his (1975) article is also helpful, as is the edited volume by Groom and Taylor (1975). An excellent introduction to inter-war liberal institutionalism is Long and Wilson (1995). On the English school, seee especially Bull (1977), Wight (1977) and Vincent (1986); while the best secondary introduction is Dunne (1998). The classic statement of neoliberal institutionalism is found in Keohane (1984), but see also Axelrod and Keohane (1993) for a good summary. The key text for the neorealist/ neoliberal debate is Baldwin (1993), which contains all the major contributions.

Part 2

Recent sociological theories of the state
and international relations

4   Marxism

Introduction

Though Marxism is clearly not a 'recent' theory, it has only recently been integrated into IR theory (though mainly within IPE). Like its realist and liberal counterparts, Marxism is far from a monolithic body of thought, and embodies a wide number of variants. Nevertheless, with respect to the state's agential power (see pp. 5–8 for full definitions) I suggest that there are three broad positions in the Marxist theory of the state:

(1) a theory of low domestic agential state power but moderate international agential state power found in classical Marxism
(2) a theory of moderate domestic agential state power and moderate international agential state power, also found in parts of classical Marxism but most especially in 'orthodox' neo-Marxism
(3) a theory of low-moderate domestic agential state power but no international agential state power, found in world systems theory (WST).

Classical Marxism

Marxists often argue that Karl Marx never developed a finished theory of the state – a task that was supposedly reserved for his projected sixth volume of *Capital*. The prominent neo-Marxist state theorist Bob Jessop even goes so far as arguing that the construction of a 'finished' Marxist theory of the state is not even possible (Jessop 1984: 29, 211–13). However, Marx did succeed in formulating a theory of the state, even though at times it was ambiguous and, arguably, it would be surprising if his projected sixth volume would have added much more to what he had already produced in his extensive writings between 1843 and his death in 1883. Perhaps there is no theorist in the social sciences who evokes such fundamentally different interpretations among scholars than Karl Marx. On the one hand are the majority of neo-Marxists, who insist that Marx developed a non-reductionist theory of the state while, conversely, many of Marx's critics argue that his theory of the state was economically reductionist or determinist. In what follows I argue that there are two shades to Marx's theory of the state: a *dominant* approach which accords the state low domestic agential power (i.e. low autonomy) and a *minority* version which accords a moderate autonomy to the state (cf. Held 1987: 113–21). Marx's basic claim was that the modern 'liberal' state does not represent the general interest of all people in society, but acts to support the interests of a small privileged class. Before we can explain this, however, we must first begin with a discussion of Marx's overall or general theory of history.

Marx's dialectical–materialist theory of the state and history

There are three key aspects or concepts in Marx's general approach: a dialectical method, the mode of production and a 'dialectical–materialist' theory of history.

The 'dialectical' method

The dialectical method provides the essence of Marx's 'scientific' approach, in which Marx made a fundamental distinction between 'appearances' and 'material reality'. Marx argues that we are confronted with, or bedazzled by, a world that *appears* extremely complex. The trick is to trace or reveal the essence that underlies this complexity. This is achieved through Marx's dialectical or 'scientific' method of *class analysis*, in which the everyday appearance of things and events is reduced to, or explained by, the contradictory relationship between classes that lies at the very base of society (i.e. 'class struggle'). As he put it in *Capital* (vol. 3), 'all science would be superfluous if the outward appearance and the essence of things directly coincided' (1867/1959: 817).

The key point here is that to fail to 'scientifically' trace the class origins of 'things' is to necessarily fall into the *bourgeois* trap of 'fetishism' – a concept that plays a central organising principle of Marx's 'mature' work in *Capital*. Marx took classical liberal political economy to task for equating the world of appearances with 'reality'. Thus such 'bourgeois' theorists incorrectly assumed that the commodity, for example, inherently possessed its own value or power. Gold has a higher natural value than silver because it is in higher demand. But the value of a particular commodity according to Marx is not intrinsic to it, but is rather determined by the average number of hours of the exploitation of labour that it takes to produce it: 'As values, all commodities are only definite masses of congealed labour-time' (Marx 1867/1954: 47). Thus 'commodity fetishism', for example, occurs when the observer mistakenly assumes that commodities have their own inherent power or value and, therefore, fails to uncover the underlying social relations of exploitation that actually inscribe a particular commodity's value. Thus in liberal political economy, 'a definite social relation between men . . . assumes a fantastic [illusory] form of a relation between things' (Marx 1867/1954: 77, 54–88).

Two key points emerge from this. First, fetishism is dangerous because it obscures the contradictory struggle between classes, which in turn produces the illusion that capitalism is natural, harmonious and eternal. But, like any other system or 'mode' of production, capitalism is destined to be overthrown through class struggle; something which only becomes apparent once we reveal the dialectical class contradictions upon which capitalism is founded. Secondly, fetishism applies to everything, not least the state. Thus the dialectical method shows that the state does not exist independently of society with its own autonomous powers and interests: it is fundamentally determined by class power. This is formalised in Marx's famous 'base–superstructure' model which claims that class relations within the 'mode of production' form the base or causal essence upon which is derived the superstructure, of which the state is a part (Marx 1859/1969). But before we can understand Marx's theory of the superstructure in general and the state in particular, we must first understand the 'base', or what Marx called the 'mode of production' (MOP).

The mode of production as the essence of social and political change/development

The complex world of appearances can be understood only through the concept of the MOP. The MOP consists of two phenomena:

(1) *The forces of production*: these are the technologies or tools or 'means' through which production is carried on (e.g. the machine in capitalism, or the plough and windmill in feudalism).

(2) *The relations of production*: these refer to the contradictory or dialectical relationship between the subordinate class (or the 'producer class') and the superordinate/dominant class (or the 'non-producer' class). In any MOP, the latter extracts a surplus from the former through 'exploitation' (to be discussed shortly). These contradictory relations are *irreconcilable* such that the two classes are engaged in a zero-sum struggle for power, where the dominant class gains economically at the expense of the subordinate class. It is this concept of class struggle that provides the crux of Marx's whole theory, as revealed explicitly in the opening line of *The Communist*

Manifesto: 'The history of all hitherto existing society is the history of class struggles' (Marx and Engels 1848/1977: 79). Marx combined his concept of the MOP with his 'dialectical method' to produce a dialectical or 'historical–materialist' conception of historical development.

Dialectical materialism (historical materialism)

In place of Hegel's 'dialectical idealism', which posited that historical development is generated by the contradictory interplay of ideas, Marx substituted material reality for ideas. Now it is the contradictory relationship between the producer and non-producer classes that generates the development of history (Marx in Marx and Engels 1859/1969: 503). For Hegel, an initial 'idea' (the thesis) is negated or contradicted by an 'opposing idea' (the antithesis), leading on to an eventual 'synthesis' which occupies a higher plane of development. By 'standing Hegel on his head', Marx sought to show that ideas are secondary to material production (Marx 1867/1954: 29). Thus in each mode of production, the thesis (the non-producer class) is negated by its antithesis (the producer class) with an eventual synthesis (a revolutionary overthrow of the MOP) leading to a new and more developed MOP. To undermine Hegel's idealism, Marx insisted in *The German Ideology* on the primacy of 'the labour premise'. That is, before mankind can think and before ideas can be made, man must be fed, clothed and sheltered. In order to do this, mankind must be employed. Thus the employment of labour is the first and most important fact of history, while ideas are secondary, and are confined to the 'superstructure'. How did Marx apply this to theorising historical development?

Specifically, Marx argued that there were two material forms of contradiction that informed the movement of history and politics: first what might be called the *social contradiction* between classes within the MOP; second, what might be called *social fetters*. How do these inform historical development? There have been four successive MOPs in history, each with its own 'laws of motion' (or laws of development). History began with *primitive communalism*, where all individuals were equal and where there was no struggle between classes. In time, however, a small minority managed to subject the majority to slavery. This is the point at which the first MOP – the ancient mode of classical Greece and Rome – came into being. Here, the producer class was the slave, the non-producer or exploiting class the slaveowner. At this point, the first generic type of contradiction, the 'social contradiction' emerged, with the resulting exploitative relations leading to a constant class struggle. As exploitation increased through time, so the class struggle intensified until eventually the MOP was overthrown by the subordinate class through revolution. This pattern was repeated in each successive MOP. Thus the ancient mode gave way to feudalism. The class struggle between the noble and peasant was eventually resolved with the emergence of capitalism, where the struggle between the capitalist (bourgeoisie) and worker (proletarian) eventually led on to the socialist MOP. And through the 'dictatorship of the proletariat', bourgeois society is to be dismantled, until the state eventually withers away to enable the rise of communism. Communism represents the 'end of history', given that classes have ceased to exist. This historical development is also informed by the 'social fetters' contradiction, where through time the development of a MOP reaches the point at which the social relations of production come into contradiction with the forces of production. That is, a given set of social relations eventually becomes a fetter to the continued development of the productive/technological forces. For example, feudal social relations are incompatible with capitalist technologies. At this point, the social fetters 'burst asunder' and, through revolution, a new MOP emerges, within which the productive forces continue their progressive development anew (Marx and Engels 1848/1977: 85).

But to understand this general theory it is vital to examine more closely the laws of motion of a particular MOP. Marx's most detailed analysis of the laws of motion was reserved for the capitalist MOP, and was fully developed in his 'mature' work – *Capital*.

The 'laws of motion' of the capitalist MOP

Marx opens his classic text, *Capital*, vol. 1, by stating that 'it is the ultimate aim of this work, to lay bare the economic law[s] of motion of modern society' which, he sometimes claimed, 'work with iron necessity towards inevitable results' (Marx 1867/1954: 19, 20). What, then, are these laws? Marx begins with the assumption that in capitalism, workers own nothing but their 'labour-power' since, in contrast to feudalism, it is the dominant class that controls the means of production. Marx referred to the 'dull compulsion of capitalist social relations' or 'wage slavery', such that the worker had no choice but to go to work for the bourgeoisie who owned and controlled the means of production (the factory, machines, etc.). What happens once the worker is employed within the capitalist enterprise? Employers are centrally concerned to make profits, so that their firms can remain competitive. How are these profits derived? The capitalist derives profit from exploiting labour-power, which under capitalism becomes 'commodified' – that is, labour (the proletarian) is treated merely as an object of the bourgeoisie in its progressively desperate pursuit of profits. This Marx explains through the *labour theory of value*, which states that profits are derived solely through the exploitation of labour-power. Machines cannot be exploited, only workers. How is this achieved?

Marx refers to the working day as split up roughly into two time periods (1867/1954: 222–3). The first half of the day involves what he termed *socially necessary labour time*, where the worker receives full remuneration for the time spent working. The second half of the day involves the extraction of a surplus or 'surplus-value' (known as 'surplus labour time'), where the worker receives no remuneration. This surplus is the root of profit, and is in turn used for reinvestment in machinery. But, through time, the extraction of profits leads to the central contradiction of capitalism.

The specific contradiction of capitalism

Through time, capitalists face a falling rate of profit. Why? The key here is the *long-run tendency for the organic composition of capital to rise*. The organic composition of capital is expressed in a simple ratio between 'fixed' capital (FC) (i.e. machinery) and 'variable' capital (VC) (i.e. the workers), namely $FC:VC$. Through time, the capitalist sheds labour in order to cut short-term costs. Thus labour is displaced by machinery which leads to a rise in FC and a decrease in VC: hence the organic composition of capital rises (at the expense of variable capital). Upon this development rests the central contradiction of capitalism, because by disposing of labour, the capitalist undermines his long-run profit rate (given that labour is the source of profit). Thus the increase in the organic composition of capital logically implies the tendency for the rate of profit to fall through time (Marx 1867/1959: 211–31). In the short run, capitalists try and offset this by employing 'counteracting-influences' or counter-tendencies, which seek to raise the rate of exploitation either by lengthening the working day (*absolute* surplus-value), or reducing the socially necessary labour time (*relative* surplus-value) (see Marx 1867/1954: 299, 173–500, 1867/1959: 232–6). But these are only short-term palliatives. And, moreover, they help only to further alienate the working class, thereby hastening the day of reckoning (i.e. socialist revolution).

So what are the implications of all this for Marx's theory of the state? Two key points emerge: first, in his general theory, the laws of motion of capitalism and of history are determined by what goes on *exclusively within the MOP.* The state is not directly implicated in historical development: it is a second-order or derivative 'entity'. Second, having analysed in some detail what the base is and how it operates, we are now in a position to understand the core of Marx's approach to the state, as expressed in his famous 'base–superstructure model'.

Marx's dominant theory of the state: the class-adaptive state

The 'dominant' (i.e. economistic) reading of Marx was formalised in the Preface to *A Contribution to the Critique of Political Economy* (1969), in which he forwarded his famous 'base–superstructure' model. It is necessary to cite the relevant passage in full:

The general result at which I arrived and which, once won, served as a guiding thread for my studies, can be briefly stated as follows: In the social production of their life, men enter into definite relations that are indispensable and independent of their will, relations of production which correspond to a definite stage of development of their material productive forces. *The sum total of these relations of production constitute the economic structure of society, the real foundation, on which rises a legal and political superstructure and to which correspond definite forms of social consciousness.* The mode of production of material life conditions the social, political, and intellectual life process in general . . . With the change of the economic foundation [i.e. the base] the entire immense superstructure [including the state] is more or less rapidly transformed. In considering such transformations a distinction should *always be made* between the material transformation of the economic conditions of production [i.e. the base] which can be determined with the precision of natural science, and the legal, political [i.e. the state], religious, aesthetic, or philosophic [i.e. the overall super-structure] – in short, ideological forms in which men become conscious of this conflict and fight it out. (Marx 1859/1969: 503–4, emphasis mine)

Scholars who see the 'base–superstructure' model as central to Marx's whole approach make this claim on the grounds that it emerges from his 'dialectical method', in which the world of appearances (the superstructure) must be penetrated or 'reduced' to the social relations of production and class struggle (the base). Thus all phenomena – their existence and function – are determined by the class struggle within the MOP. Functionally, the superstructure exists to maintain the power of the dominant economic class over the subordinate class. Most importantly, Marx's scientific or dialectical approach denies that the state can have a power that is independent of the social relations of production that produced it – to assume otherwise is to fall into the 'bourgeois' trap of 'statist fetishism' in which the theorist is seduced by the illusory appearance of state autonomy. It was this that led him to critique Hegel's political realism. If Hegel saw the state as 'the realm of external necessity' to which society must conform (see Marx 1967: 153, 153–64), Marx viewed the state as 'impotent' (Marx 1967: 349). The appearance of the state as sovereign, autonomous and unitary is an illusion – a product of 'bourgeois fetishism' (Marx 1967: 164–77). Thus Marx inverted Hegel and argued that it is the realm of private interests within civil society that is the 'realm of necessity', to which the state must adapt or conform. Accordingly, the state is granted only low domestic agential capacity or institutional autonomy (from class power). As he stated in *Capital*, vol. 3, '[i]t is always the direct relationship of the owners of the conditions of production to the direct producers . . . which reveals the innermost secret, the hidden basis of the entire social structure, and with it the political form of the relation of sovereignty and dependence, in short, the corresponding specific form of the state' (Marx 1867/1959: 791).

We can at last turn to Marx's formal definition of the state, expressed most famously in *The Communist Manifesto*: that 'the bourgeoisie has at last . . . conquered for itself, in the modern representative State, exclusive political sway. *The executive of the modern State is but a committee for managing the affairs of the whole bourgeoisie*' (Marx and Engels 1848/1977: 82, emphasis mine; see also Marx 1845/1967: 470). The prime focus here is not on the *form* of state (i.e. its institutional and territorial aspects which change through time), but on the state's *function* – namely, to act as the representative of the dominant economic class (cf. Lenin 1917/ 1932). While I have argued that Marx's principal theory of the state involved granting it only low domestic agential power (i.e. limited ability to conduct policy free of domestic constraint), nevertheless I argue that classical Marxism attributed a *moderate* international agential power to the state (i.e. the ability to conduct policy free of international constraint). And, perhaps surprisingly, I argue that although classical Marxism accords the state less domestic agential power than that found in neorealism and first-wave neo-Weberianism, nevertheless classical Marxism attributes to the state greater international agential power.

Classical Marxist theory of international relations

Karl Marx was not an IR theorist as such and wrote very little on the subject, and what he did write was confined to short and fragmentary statements. Indeed, Friedrich Engels approached IR in a much more sustained way, most notably in his important work, 'The Role of Force in History' (in Marx and Engels 1970: 377–428). Nevertheless, it would be wrong to assume that Marx's writings were irrelevant for understanding IR (and indeed they were faithfully applied by Engels in his text cited above). Marx's general theory was in any case a 'theory of everything', and could therefore be readily applied to IR. Marx's emphasis on the MOP as the organising principle of IR was revealed in occasional remarks, most notably in *The German Ideology*, in which he argued that: 'The relations of various nations with one another depend upon the extent to which each of them has developed its productive forces, the division of labour and domestic commerce . . . [T]he relation of one nation to others . . . depends on the stage of development achieved by its production' (Marx 1845/1967: 410). This suggests a strong second-image approach in which domestic economic or class forces are the key determinants of IR. This insight was faithfully applied by Vladimir Lenin in his theory of international relations.

Vladimir Lenin's theory of war and imperialism

In his classic pamphlet originally entitled *Imperialism as the Highest Stage of Capitalism* (1916/1933), Vladimir Lenin sought to produce an *economic* account of war and imperialism, and implicitly, in contrast to neorealism and Marxian WST, he developed a strong second-image explanation of IR. Lenin, following Hilferding, argued that it was the rise of 'monopoly capitalism' in general, and the domination of 'finance capital' in particular, that was the ultimate tap-root of imperialism or colonialism. And following Marx's dialectical-materialist approach, it was the basic laws of motion of the capitalist MOP that made the rise of monopoly capitalism inevitable. While the phase of free market or 'freely competitive capitalism' (which lasted until 1880) was based on the export of goods and free trade, the subsequent monopoly phase was based on the 'concentration' of production into monopoly combines and the domination of 'finance capital'. Lenin defines 'finance capital' as the fusion of industrial monopolies with bank/financial monopoly capital. Once formed, finance capital of necessity exports capital, which in turn leads to the territorial division of the world by the imperial powers, and eventually war between them. Colonies are little more than monopoly outlets for this export of capital. The crucial question, then, is why did this occur?

The key sentence reads as follows: 'The necessity for exporting capital arises from the fact that in a few countries capitalism has become "over-ripe" and, owing to the backward stage of agriculture and the impoverishment of the masses, capital lacks opportunities for profitable investment' (1916/1933: 58). What does Lenin mean by this? I follow the orthodox interpretation here and suggest that Lenin was focusing on the problematic economic conditions that existed within the advanced capitalist countries as the cause of the export of capital (see also Roxborough 1979: 55–7; Gilpin 1987: 37–4). In turn, it would seem that 'over-ripe' refers to the decline in the rate of profit and the rise in

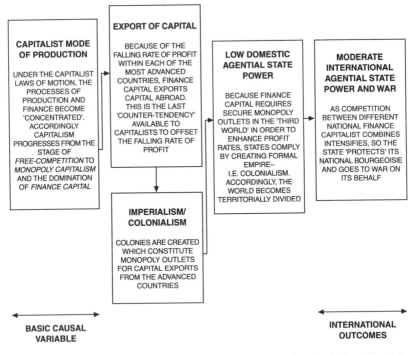

Figure 4.1 Classical Marxist theory of international relations (Lenin)

the organic composition of capital; factors which would have necessitated the export of capital. Lenin seeks to show that finance capital has no choice but to export capital if it is to remain profitable, since the domestic economy no longer provides an immediately profitable environment whereas, by contrast, the profit rates in the backward countries are high because capital is scarce (Lenin 1916/1933: 58). For Hobson, this occurred because the state had been insufficiently pro-active, and because it had allowed the level of aggregate domestic demand to fall, so capitalists looked to colonial policy as a means of maintaining their preferred rate of profit. Lenin, however, sought to show that the export of capital (imperialism) was not ultimately a misguided policy of the state (that could be corrected through the appropriate interventionist policies of the social-democratic state), but was rather an inevitable outcome of the capitalist MOP. In contrast to J.A. Hobson, it seems that for Lenin the masses were impoverished because of the structural and *non-reversible* effects of the rise in the organic composition of capital. And the accompanying fall in the rate of profit could not be corrected through enlightened state interventionist policies of raising the level of aggregate demand, precisely because the state is structurally required to follow the interests of finance capital, which unequivocally chose imperialism over domestic reform.

Perhaps the crucial point is that imperialism is the last available 'counter-tendency' that capital could employ so as to offset the falling rate of profit, given that the rate of exploitation had reached its highest point in the advanced economies. It was an inevitable product of the capitalist MOP in its highest or final stage. Nevertheless, echoing Hobson, Lenin was intent on showing that imperialism was 'ultimately' a fetter to the continued development of capitalism at home. Lenin referred to this as 'parasitism'. But, unlike Hobson, Lenin emphasised that imperialism constitutes not simply the highest stage of capitalism, but capitalism's 'last gasp'. In his words, 'imperialism is "dying" capitalism' (Lenin 1916/1933: 114). For Lenin, imperialism served only to bring the contradictions of capitalism to the fore, thereby bringing closer the day of reckoning (the revolutionary transition to socialism). Moreover, one of the underlying themes of the pamphlet was Lenin's vitriolic critique of the 'social-democratic' theory of so-called *ultra-imperialism* – a condition in which the imperial powers cooperate to exploit the rest of the world, which would in turn necessarily abolish warfare between these imperial powers. For Lenin, imperialism and warfare are utterly inextricable. Once the world has been fully divided up into colonies by the leading capitalist powers (completed by 1913), so competition between the different national finance capitalist combines intensifies until eventually war breaks out: 'the war of 1914–1918 was on both sides imperialist (i.e. an annexationist, predatory, plunderous war), a war for the partition of the world, for the distribution and redistribution of colonies, of "spheres of influence" of finance capital, etc.' (Lenin 1916/1933: 9, 9–14). And the spoils of imperialism or what Lenin calls the 'booty', are 'shared by two or three world-dominating pirates armed to the teeth . . . who embroil the whole world in *their* war over the division of *their* booty' (Lenin 1916/1933: 11, emphases in the original). In short, states go to war as they seek to protect the class interests of finance capital, given that they must support the interests of the dominant economic class. In sum, therefore, it seems clear that Lenin forwards an orthodox Marxist 'second-image' approach to the analysis of IR. It is second-image because it is the fundamental contradictions of the capitalist MOP within each of the advanced economies that is the ultimate tap-root of capital exports, imperialism and war.

Kenneth Waltz's neorealist approach attempted to refute Lenin by pointing out that imperialism is not in fact unique to late capitalism but existed in virulent form in classical Greece and Rome and that, this being so, capitalism could not have constituted the 'tap-root' of late nineteenth-century imperialism (Waltz 1979: chapter 2). Lenin however, pre-empted this point by arguing that modern imperialism is qualitatively different to classical imperialism not only in form but also by virtue of the fact that, by 1914, the whole world had been territorially divided up by capital (compared to the only partial division of the globe in previous imperialisms) (Lenin 1916/1933: 75). Thus it was not international systemic forces that lay at base of imperialism and war, as Waltz claimed, but socio–class forces residing within the national territory of the advanced capitalist countries.

Lenin's theory of the state and IR

Lenin perfectly reproduces Marx's dominant theory of the low domestic agential power of the state. States went to war as they conformed to the economic requirements of finance capital or the imperatives of late monopoly capitalism. As he put it, the 'non-economic superstructure [i.e. the state] . . . grows up on the basis of finance capital' (Lenin 1916/ 1933: 77). Thus states and state policy are fundamentally determined by the social dictates of capital. But this also implies that the state has moderate agential power in the international system. Why?

We noted in chapter 3 that in classical liberalism, states have only low domestic agential power but have high agential power in the international realm. Thus by conforming to the social requirements of individuals within society, states come to create an interdependent and peaceful world. For Lenin as well as Marx, by conforming not to the general interests of the masses but to the particular interests of the dominant economic classes, the state creates a world that is premised upon inter-state conflict, imperialist rivalry and militarism. This represents only a moderate level of international agential state power, as opposed to the high levels found in liberalism because, for classical Marxism, states will of necessity create a conflictual world as they respond to the exploitative needs of the domestic dominant economic class. States cannot create a peaceful world, because this would require them to overcome or reconcile domestic class struggle (since it is domestic class struggles that spill over and cause international conflict). This is logically not possible because it would mean that class power does not lie at the base of states and state policy. Recall that, for Marx, the state was not the resolver of social struggles, but a reflection of them. And on this fundamental point, Lenin was unequivocal. In *State and Revolution*, Lenin argued that '[t]he state is the product and the manifestation of the *irreconcilability* of class antagonisms. The state arises when, where, and to the extent that the class antagonisms *cannot* be objectively reconciled. And conversely, the existence of the state proves that class antagonisms *are* irreconcilable' (Lenin 1917/1932: 8, emphases in the original. This reinforces the low domestic agential power of the state approach of Marx, while also illustrating the point that the state has only moderate rather than high agential power in the international system. Nevertheless, this degree of international agential state power is considerably higher than that attributed by neorealism and first-wave neo-Weberianism, which wholly ignore domestic forces in the determination of IR.

Orthodox neo-Marxism

While Marx was mainly concerned to show that the state has only low domestic agential power or autonomy from the dominant economic class, neo-Marxist theorists of the state have primarily sought to overcome 'economic reductionism', and to show that the state cannot be simply reduced to class power. Why? Neo-Marxists generally react strongly to the charge of economic or 'class reductionism', levelled most frequently by their critics. Given that the charge of reductionism has done much to discredit Marxism, at least within academic circles, most neo-Marxists have counter-attacked by developing arguments which demonstrate that the state does in fact have some autonomy or domestic power; a claim which in turn enables them to defend Marxism as a whole from the reductionist charge. The search for a non-reductionist theory of the state is also 'politically' important for neo-Marxists, because it enables them to exorcise the politically unacceptable face of Stalinism, which embodied a purely economistic approach to theorising history. Thus for Marxists there is a great deal at stake in showing that the state does in fact have some domestic autonomy or agential power.

The quest for a non-reductionist Marxist theory of the state by neo-Marxists has entailed three fundamental tasks: first, to draw out those aspects of Marx's approach that are in some way amenable to, or suggestive of, a non-reductionist approach to the state; second, to develop in their own writings the basis for a non-reductionist Marxist theory in general; and third, to develop a non-reductionist theory of the state in particular. There are many sub-variants of neo-Marxism which have sought to do this; they vary from neo-Gramscian Marxism (e.g. Hall and Jacques 1984; Cox 1986, 1987, 1996; Gill 1990, 1993; Murphy 1994; Rupert 1995), to 'political Marxism' (e.g. Mooers 1991; Brenner 1982; Rosenberg 1994; Wood 1995), to Althusserian or 'structural' Marxism (e.g. Althusser 1969; Poulantzas 1973), and many others, all of which draw upon elements from a wide variety of sources (e.g. Anderson 1974; Trimberger 1978; Mouzelis 1986; Block 1987; Jessop 1990). Here, I shall examine how 'orthodox' neo-Marxists have advanced these three specific tasks, before proceeding to analyse their concept of the relative autonomy of the state.

The 'moderate domestic agential power' or 'relative autonomy of the state' approach in Marx and Engels

Neo-Marxists' first task has been to draw out those areas of the works of Marx and Engels that are suggestive of a non-reductionist theory of the state. While neo-Marxists often seize upon various statements that Marx on occasion made, clearly the most common element that almost all neo-Marxists point to here is the notion of the 'Bonapartist' state (see e.g. Althusser 1969: chapter 3; Poulantzas 1973; Perez-Diaz 1978). The crux of the argument, found in Marx's *The Eighteenth Brumaire of Louis Bonaparte*, was that in 1848 the French bourgeoisie was weak and disorganised in the face of a severe proletarian challenge. To solve this crisis, the bourgeoisie had to 'abdicate' their direct hold of the state apparatus and defer to the strong man, Louis Bonaparte – see Perez-Diaz (1978) and Elster (1985: 411–22) for a full discussion. As Marx put it, 'Only under the second Bonaparte does the state seem to have made itself completely independent' (1852/1969: 478). Marx depicts the relationship of the state and bourgeoisie as riddled with tension, in turn suggesting that his instrumentalist or reductionist definition of the state – found especially in *The Communist Manifesto* – is in need of revision. According to neo-Marxists, Marx was clearly aware that the state is no simple reflection of the needs of the dominant economic class. But – and this point needs emphasising – nor was the state wholly independent of the bourgeoisie (see also McLellan 1983: 148). As Marx put it: 'Under Napoleon, bureaucracy was the only means of preparing the class rule of the bourgeoisie. Under Louis Philippe [the state] . . . was the instrument of the ruling class however much it strove for power of its own' (Marx 1852/1969: 477–8). This position succeeds in according a 'relative autonomy' to the state but ultimately retains Marxist integrity. Thus although the state might well conflict with the bourgeoisie in the short term, nevertheless ultimately the state would function to support the dominant class.

This argument is taken further elsewhere. Friedrich Engels made famous a preliminary theory of the 'relatively autonomous' state in his 'class-equilibrium' theory, found in *The Origins of the Family, Private*

Property and the State. Here he argued that 'By way of exception, however, periods occur in which the warring classes balance each other so nearly that the state power, as ostensible mediator, acquires, for the moment, a certain degree of independence of both' (Engels in Marx and Engels 1970: 328). For Engels, such autonomy is 'exceptional' and occurs only in unique moments of class-equilibrium – notably in those transitionary periods in which the old MOP gives way to a new one (e.g. under absolutism, the Bonapartism of the first and second French empires and in Bismarckian Germany).

In a rarely cited passage in *Capital*, vol. 1, Marx laid down his most developed argument for a certain autonomy of the state, which in fact constitutes *the* proximate version of the subsequent neo-Marxist theory of 'relative autonomy'. This argument was found in the passage concerning the class struggles in mid-nineteenth century England for the shortening of the working day to ten hours (i.e. the Ten Hours Act) (Marx 1867/1954: 226–81). The passing of the Ten Hours Act was met with severe resistance by the capitalist class. *Inter alia*, the capitalists sought to challenge this ruling in the courts, a 'revolt of capital' which was finally crowned victorious in 1850 when the Court of Exchequer abolished the Act. But the victory of capital was short-lived. The crucial point is that in the face of working-class resistance, the state's factory inspectors 'urgently warned the Government that the antagonism of classes had arrived at an incredible tension. Some of the masters themselves murmured: "On account [of the Court's decision] a condition of things altogether abnormal and anarchical obtains"' (Marx 1867/1954: 276). As a result, the original legislation was brought back by the state, albeit with some compromises, much to the disgust of the bourgeoisie. In other words, the state was prepared to go *against* the immediate profit-making interests of capital so as to avoid social revolution, thereby ensuring the continued or long-term reproduction of the capitalist MOP. This implies a 'certain' autonomy of the state in its short-term relations with the dominant economic class (albeit under exceptional conditions) even if the state was ultimately constrained by the long-term requirements of the MOP – an argument that was raised into a general principle by neo-Marxists.

The 'non-reductionist methodology' of neo-Marxism

The second task for neo-Marxists has been to produce a non-reductionist theory of history in general. However, the rejection of economism within a Marxist framework is no easy or small task, not least because it requires confronting some of the economistic pillars of Marx's theoretical edifice and subjecting them to substantial revision. The basic position is the neo-Marxist insistence that there is no 'one-to-one correspondence' between the economic (the MOP) and the political (the state); and that the political cannot be simply 'read off' from the economic. To make this claim requires a substantial revision of Marx's 'base-superstructure model'. In providing a legitimate or authoritative basis for tampering with the base–superstructure model, many neo-Marxists cite a specific passage in Engels' letter to J. Bloch:

According to the materialist conception of history, the *ultimately* determining element in history is the production and reproduction of real life. More than this neither Marx nor I have ever asserted. Hence if somebody twists this into saying that the economic element is the *only* determining one, he transforms that proposition into a . . . senseless phrase. The economic situation is the basis, but the various elements of the superstructure . . . also exercise their influence upon the course of the historical struggles and in many cases preponderate in determining their *form*. (Engels in Marx and Engels 1970: 487, emphases in the original)

Following this, neo-Marxists have pursued two basic strategies: first, to argue that there are two Marx's: an 'early' Marx who was reductionist and a 'mature' Marx who absolved himself of this simplistic or 'vulgar' economism, as was most famously argued by Louis Althusser (1969; also Jessop 1984: chapter 1). This leads to the second and perhaps the most common revisionist method employed by neo-Marxists: the attempt to do away with Marx's base–superstructure model altogether. Neo-Marxists' frustration with the economistic straightjacket that the base–superstructure model imposes is aptly conveyed in the words of one prominent Marxist: 'The base/superstructure model has always been more trouble than it is worth. Although Marx himself used it very rarely . . . it has been made to bear a theoretical weight far beyond its limited capacities' (Wood 1995: 49; but see Cohen, 1978: 216–48, for an alternative view). The second revisionist strategy has effectively involved collapsing the 'superstructure' into the mode of production. Perry Anderson typically wrote, that all

previous [pre-capitalist] modes of exploitation operate through extra-economic sanction – kin, customary, religious, legal or political. It is therefore, in principle, always impossible to read them off from economic relations as such. The superstructure of kinship, religion, law or the state necessarily enters in to the constitutive structure of the mode of production in pre-capitalist social formations. (Anderson 1974: 403)

Cohen aptly summarises this approach: 'if the economic structure is constituted of property . . . relations, how can it be distinct from the *legal* superstructure which it is supposed to explain? (Cohen 1978: 217–18, emphasis in the original).

Althusser and his associates (Balibar and Poulantzas) argued that the MOP is more than simply the social relations of production: it comprises three levels or regions – the economic, the political and the ideological (e.g. Poulantzas 1973: 13–18). In essence they argued that in any particular MOP, the economic level 'assigns' the other levels certain functions or powers. Drawing on Marx's discussion in *Capital*, vol. 3 (1867/1959: 790–3), they argue that in feudalism, for example, the economic level assigns 'dominance' to the political level, in the sense that the political is the dominant force that is responsible for the extraction of a surplus from the producer class. Accordingly, they argue that the state can attain a certain power or autonomy. But the general point is that the social relations of production are not self-constituting and do not exist independently of the political or ideological levels. These arguments have also been integrated into 'political Marxism', and are also utilised in part by Gramscian Marxism, even if there are some crucial areas of divergence between these schools.

However, there is an obvious problem here. Marx's basic claim was that the MOP *is* 'self-constituting': that is, it does not require the intervention of non-economic forms of power for its own reproduction. Put differently, if the MOP cannot be separated out from the super-structure, then Marx's dialectical method is negated, which necessarily returns us to 'bourgeois theory'. In order to retain or save Marxist integrity, structural Marxism added in a key phrase: 'the determination by the economic *in the last instance*' (Althusser 1969: 110–28). This is perhaps *the* crucial aspect of the 'relative autonomy' of the state. This can all be put another way. If at one extreme lies 'vulgar' Marxism, which emphasises only one autonomous variable – the mode of produc-tion – and at the other lies Mann's neo-Weberian theory, which empha-sises four autonomous variables – ideology, economic, military and political power (the IEMP model) – then neo-Marxism seeks to occupy a middle ground. Rather than grant equal weighting to each of these four variables as do neo-Weberians, neo-Marxists produce a hierarchy in which the economic (class relations) stands atop with full autonomy, while the military, ideological and political variables imbued with relative autonomy rest beneath (i.e. an E_{IMP} model).

Neo-Marxism and the 'relative autonomy' of the state

While for neo-Marxists there can be no 'one-to-one correspondence' between the economic and political, equally there can be no perfect 'non-correspondence' between the two. The striking of this extremely delicate balancing act between the MOP and the state in particular, and between Marxist and bourgeois theory in general, has been *the* task that has preoccupied neo-Marxist theorists of the state. The solution to this problem is the concept of the 'relative autonomy' of the state and 'determination by the economic in the last instance'. The classic statement is contained in Poulantzas' *Political Power and Social Classes* (1973: 255–321). The essential formula runs as follows. Because the members of the capitalist class are preoccupied with everyday competitive struggles between themselves and have a collective action problem, so the class-as-a-whole inevitably becomes disunited. As such, this renders it incapable of maintaining unity in the face of proletarian challenges. The role of the state is to act as an 'ideal collective capitalist' and to ensure that the capitalist class as a whole can survive in the long run. Being removed from the daily process of surplus-value extraction, and armed with a 'relative autonomy' from the dominant class, the state can ignore or go against the short-term needs of the bourgeoisie in order to secure the long-term reproduction of the MOP. Therefore, 'in the last instance' (i.e. in the long run) the economic is determinant such that the state must conform to the long-term survival requirements of the MOP. Thus by stopping short of ascribing a full autonomy to the state, Poulantzas is able to retain Marxist integrity by arguing that ultimately, or in the last instance, the MOP or class power is determinant. How does the state go against the short-term interests of the dominant class?

One of the most common examples of the way in which the state goes against the short-term interests of the bourgeoisie is through welfare policy. Thus, for example, capitalists might vehemently resist increases in personal income taxation which is necessary to pay for welfare expenditures for the working class. But by undertaking such reforms, the state is able to pacify the working class and prevent it from attaining revolutionary consciousness, thereby securing the long-term reproduction of capitalism in general. And, as noted above, an excellent example of this kind of approach is found in Marx's discussion of the introduction of the Ten Hours Act in England. Underlying this relative autonomy approach is the notion of the state's *legitimacy*. The state must appear as a neutral power that acts in the interests of the population in general, even if in reality it is not (e.g. Offe 1974). This finds its greatest expression in Gramsci's (1971) concept of *hegemony*. A dominant economic class is 'hegemonic' to the extent that its economic power over the working class is accepted as legitimate. This can best be secured when the state grants reforms to the working class which thereby stymie the development of a proletarian revolutionary consciousness. Of course, this treads perilously close to arguing that the state can reconcile the class struggle; something which Marx, and especially Lenin, expressly warned against. Nevertheless, Marxist integrity is preserved by the fact that such reconciliation of the class struggle is only temporary and cannot ultimately prevent the working class from pushing for socialism in the long run.

While Althusserianism has been subsequently discredited within Marxist circles, mainly because of its 'anti-historicism' and 'anti-humanism' (see Thompson 1978), nevertheless, the basic theory of the 'relative autonomy' of the state has remained. Indeed, it has become a fundamental aspect of the social-democratic or 'Eurocommunist' political movement – associated most strongly with Gramscian Marxism. And despite the 'heat' of the Miliband–Poulantzas debate of the 1970s, the concept of the relative autonomy of the state has provided a remarkable degree of unity and consensus among neo-Marxist theorists of the state (e.g. Miliband 1973; Poulantzas 1973; Anderson 1974; Offe 1974: 46–54; Perez-Diaz 1978; Trimberger 1978; Brenner 1982; Hall 1984; Block 1987; Mooers 1991; Wood 1995). Moreover, even those few neo-Marxists who are critical of this approach (e.g. the *Staatsableitung* or 'capital–logic' school) end up by going a long way to confirming it, not least because they argue that the state is an 'ideal collective capitalist' which must secure the reproduction not of particular capitalists but capital-in-general (Hirsch 1978: 66; Holloway and Picciotto 1978a). In sum, it would seem clear that neo-Marxists have pushed the boundary of the 'autonomy of the state' as far as possible within a Marxist discourse. But in stopping short of attributing a full autonomy to the state, they have managed to save themselves from tripping over the boundary into so-called 'bourgeois' theory.

At this point, it is worth noting that statist and neo-Weberian critics argue that the 'relative autonomy' approach does not go far enough in attributing the state with autonomy or domestic agential power (e.g. Krasner 1978; Parkin 1979; Mann 1993). Neo-Marxists have countered by arguing, quite correctly, that many neo-Weberians, statists and neorealists have reified the autonomy of the state and have failed to examine its social origins (e.g. Cammack 1989; Jessop 1990: 283–8). Nevertheless, I argue in chapter 6 below that recent neo-Weberian analyses – found in the 'second-wave' approaches of Mann and Hobson – insist that a state's domestic autonomy is embedded within social groupings in society. Thus while many neo-Marxists now concede that states have some autonomy, and neo-Weberians increasingly concede that states are embedded in society, we can conclude that the traditional 'great divide' between Marxism and Weberianism has considerably narrowed.

Orthodox neo-Marxist theory of international relations

Only now are we in a position to finally turn to 'orthodox' neo-Marxist theories of IR. One of the most important examples of this approach is found in the emergence of the 'neo-Gramscian' school of IR (e.g. Van der Pijl 1984; Cox 1986, 1987, 1996; Gill 1990; Augelli and Murphy 1993; Gill and Law 1993; Murphy 1994; Rupert 1995). In this section I shall focus mainly on Robert Cox's works, most notably his *Production, Power and World Order* (1987) to illustrate this theory.

We must begin by noting a crucial distinction that Cox makes, between 'critical theory' and 'problem-solving' theory. Problem-solving theory (of which neorealism is the outstanding representative), is conservative because it takes the world as it is, and in so doing seeks to find ways of solving problems in order to manage the international system as smoothly as possible. By contrast, critical theory does not take existing institutions for granted but problematises them by examining their origins, their limitations and contradictions, in order to reveal the processes which can transcend them and propel humanity to a higher stage of progress. This produces a particularly powerful critique of neorealism in many ways, not least because it reveals it as 'value-laden' rather than 'value-free' – given that neorealism accepts the anarchic state system and the sovereign state as natural, inevitable and eternal. By applying a *critical* approach, Cox goes beyond 'problem-solving theory' (Cox 1986: 207–17). The specific means by which this is achieved is through applying or transposing Gramsci's concepts of domestic society to the international sphere. It thus makes sense to begin with a discussion of Gramsci's key concepts.

Antonio Gramsci (1971) argued that there are two principal forms of domestic social order: 'hegemonic' and 'non-hegemonic'. As noted above, a hegemonic order is one in which the 'economic rule' of the dominant economic class is accepted as legitimate by the subordinate classes – that is, where there is a degree of 'relative consensus' for the bourgeoisie's rule. The key point is that hegemonic rule is an ideological cloak that hides the exploitative power of capital. How is this exploitation cloaked? Hegemony is achieved first, by the passing on of relative welfare 'concessions' to the subordinate classes through the 'relatively autonomous' state (see above); and, second, through the normative processes that are disseminated by key social institutions in civil society – the family, church, educational system, the press and so on – which serve to socialise and integrate the working classes into capitalism. For Gramsci, these social institutions form part of the state (or what Althusser called the 'ideological state apparatus'). As such the state is more than simply a set of governmental and bureaucratic institutions. This is contrasted with *non-hegemonic* orders, where the bourgeoisie's rule is not accepted as legitimate by the lower orders. Under such conditions, the bourgeoisie's rule is much weaker and precarious. Accordingly the bourgeoisie comes to rely on 'force', which is wielded by a coercive state, in order to shore up its weakened power base. In such societies, the state gains yet more relative autonomy, where state 'power' is generally exercised by a 'caesarist' strong man (Cox 1987: 236–44). But the key point is that bourgeois rule is most effectively maintained when it is exercised through relative consent (hegemonic leadership), as opposed to coercive domination.

While the key concept for Marx was the MOP, for Cox (following Gramsci) the 'historic bloc' is central. This is particularly significant for Cox because it enables him to produce a relatively non-reductionist theory of IR. The 'historic bloc' refers to the complex relationship between the political, ideological and economic spheres. 'The juxtaposition and reciprocal relationships of the political, ethical and ideological spheres of activity with the economic sphere avoid reductionism. It avoids reducing everything either to economics (economism) or to ideas (idealism) . . . ideas and material conditions are always bound together, mutually influencing one another, and not reducible one to the other' (Cox 1996: 131). As he puts it elsewhere: 'The sense of a reciprocal relationship between structure (economic relations) and superstructure (the ethico–political sphere) in Gramsci's thinking contains the potential for considering state/society complexes [historic blocs] as the constituent entities of a world order' (Cox 1986: 216).

While it should not escape notice that this is similar to the Althusserian method (where the superstructure is effectively collapsed into the base), it is however vital to note that Cox fundamentally rejects the general Althusserian approach. In particular, he constantly distances himself from Althusser's commitment to 'anti-historicism' and 'structural-functionalism'. Althusserianism is problematic because it embodies a rigid historical- and structural-determinism which denies the role of agency. As Edward Thompson famously argued, individuals are viewed as mere *Träger* – that is, as passive bearers (or victims) of structures. Thus in abolishing voluntarism, individuals become powerless to transcend the social order (Thompson 1978). So in contrast to Althusser (as well as Waltz) Cox's Gramscian concepts, which are embedded within a 'flexible' historicist and non-structuralist problematic, are then transposed to the international realm in order to produce a Gramscian theory of IR. How is this achieved?

The functions and social basis of hegemony

At the global level, Cox applies Gramsci's concept of hegemony to a particular type of leading state and world order. Cox's approach is best contrasted with Gilpin's neorealist theory of hegemonic stability (see figure 4.2). For Gilpin, a hegemon uses its power and dominance to construct a hegemonic world order. Paradoxically, it does this by sacrificing its own interests for the greater good of all other states. Accordingly, rival states enjoy a free ride, which *in part* enables them to catch up with the hegemon. By contrast for Cox, a hegemon constructs a hegemonic world order so as to maximise its own interests – or, more specifically, the economic interests of its bourgeoisie. Hegemony is an ideological cloaking device, or a set of consensual norms, that enable the leading state to successfully maximise its power. In particular, the various international institutions and organisations constitute the 'hegemonic state apparatus', in that they act to disseminate 'hegemonic norms'. How is this achieved?

While Gilpin assumes (in paradoxical liberal fashion) that liberal international regimes benefit all states, Cox sees them as the means through which the hegemon extends the power of its bourgeoisie. Thus, for example, in paradoxical realist fashion – as in Friedrich List (1885) and Carr (1939) – Cox argues that free trade does not benefit all economies but is the policy of the strongest. It enables the leading economy to penetrate the markets of all other countries in order to maximise its profits at the expense of others. But the key point is that free trade is a hegemonic norm or ideology because it creates the 'appearance' of neutrality and fairness, given that it *purports* to be a fair deal for all states. Nevertheless, it would be incorrect to assume that only a hegemonic economy benefits. This is because hegemony is also accepted by the various national bourgeoisies throughout the world, since it enables them to enhance their power over their own proletariats. Accordingly, there develops a transnational alliance of bourgeois interests – an argument that Kees Van der Pijl (1984) elevated into the concept of a 'transatlantic ruling class'. Thus an 'international historic bloc' emerges (Gill 1990; Augelli and Murphy 1993: 133; Gill and Law 1993: 96–7).

The social motor of the rise and decline of world hegemony

Like Gilpin, Cox divides the last 200 years into the rise and decline of hegemonies. There have been four periods: (1) British hegemony (1845–75); (2) the end of British hegemony and the era of rival imperialisms (1875–1945); (3) US hegemony (1945–65); (4) the end of US hegemony (1965 to the present). The key question is: what are the origins or the motor of development that informs this process?

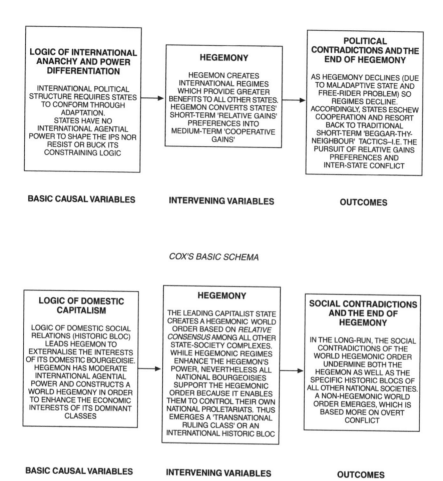

NEOREALISM'S BASIC SCHEMA

LOGIC OF INTERNATIONAL ANARCHY AND POWER DIFFERENTIATION	HEGEMONY	POLITICAL CONTRADICTIONS AND THE END OF HEGEMONY
INTERNATIONAL POLITICAL STRUCTURE REQUIRES STATES TO CONFORM THROUGH ADAPTATION. STATES HAVE NO INTERNATIONAL AGENTIAL POWER TO SHAPE THE IPS NOR RESIST OR BUCK ITS CONSTRAINING LOGIC	HEGEMON CREATES INTERNATIONAL REGIMES WHICH PROVIDE GREATER BENEFITS TO ALL OTHER STATES. HEGEMON CONVERTS STATES' SHORT-TERM 'RELATIVE GAINS' PREFERENCES INTO MEDIUM-TERM 'COOPERATIVE GAINS'	AS HEGEMONY DECLINES (DUE TO MALADAPTIVE STATE AND FREE-RIDER PROBLEM) SO REGIMES DECLINE. ACCORDINGLY, STATES ESCHEW COOPERATION AND RESORT BACK TO TRADITIONAL SHORT-TERM 'BEGGAR-THY-NEIGHBOUR' TACTICS–I.E. THE PURSUIT OF RELATIVE GAINS PREFERENCES AND INTER-STATE CONFLICT
BASIC CAUSAL VARIABLES	INTERVENING VARIABLES	OUTCOMES

COX'S BASIC SCHEMA

LOGIC OF DOMESTIC CAPITALISM	HEGEMONY	SOCIAL CONTRADICTIONS AND THE END OF HEGEMONY
LOGIC OF DOMESTIC SOCIAL RELATIONS (HISTORIC BLOC) LEADS HEGEMON TO EXTERNALISE THE INTERESTS OF ITS DOMESTIC BOURGEOISIE. HEGEMON HAS MODERATE INTERNATIONAL AGENTIAL POWER AND CONSTRUCTS A WORLD HEGEMONY IN ORDER TO ENHANCE THE ECONOMIC INTERESTS OF ITS DOMINANT CLASSES	THE LEADING CAPITALIST STATE CREATES A HEGEMONIC WORLD ORDER BASED ON *RELATIVE CONSENSUS* AMONG ALL OTHER STATE-SOCIETY COMPLEXES. WHILE HEGEMONIC REGIMES ENHANCE THE HEGEMON'S POWER, NEVERTHELESS ALL NATIONAL BOURGEOISIES SUPPORT THE HEGEMONIC ORDER BECAUSE IT ENABLES THEM TO CONTROL THEIR OWN NATIONAL PROLETARIATS. THUS EMERGES A 'TRANSNATIONAL RULING CLASS' OR AN INTERNATIONAL HISTORIC BLOC	IN THE LONG-RUN, THE SOCIAL CONTRADICTIONS OF THE WORLD HEGEMONIC ORDER UNDERMINE BOTH THE HEGEMON AS WELL AS THE SPECIFIC HISTORIC BLOCS OF ALL OTHER NATIONAL SOCIETIES. A NON-HEGEMONIC WORLD ORDER EMERGES, WHICH IS BASED MORE ON OVERT CONFLICT
BASIC CAUSAL VARIABLES	INTERVENING VARIABLES	OUTCOMES

Figure 4.2 Orthodox Gramscian–Marxist theory of international hegemony in the neorealist mirror

A world hegemony emerges when the social-hegemonic powers of the dominant class within the most powerful national economy 'spill over' from the domestic to the international sphere. In general '[t]he expansive energies released by a social hegemony-in-formation move outward onto the world scale at the same time as they consolidate their strength at home' (Cox 1987: 149). The hegemonic state sets up international institutions and economic regimes which serve to legitimate as well as materially advance the needs of its bourgeoisie. This leads to a relatively stable hegemonic world order, whose stability is based on various factors: first, the low level of class conflict in the first world countries (owing to the high levels of hegemony enjoyed by the national bourgeoisies); second, because the ensuing economic boom undermines revolutionary hopes; third, because a hegemonic world order links up all capitalist classes throughout the world into a kind of transnational ruling class alliance, thereby giving each national bourgeoisie a vested stake in the continuation of hegemony; and, fourth, because the hegemon is able to stabilise the world economy (1987: 147). Thus in the first hegemonic era, *Pax Britannica* was premised upon the power of the British bourgeoisie and the historic bloc based around the pure liberal state. The era of the *Pax Americana* was premised upon the power of US capital and the historic bloc of the neo-liberal or Keynesian welfare state. Like its British predecessor, it created a world hegemonic order based on liberal international regimes (based on free trade and fixed exchange rates). But the most important weapon in its arsenal was the Marshall Plan, which enabled it to restructure the historic blocs of the other advanced capitalist countries along pro-capitalist lines (1987: 214–16).

How, then, does a hegemonic world order come to an end? For neorealism, it ends as the international distribution of power shifts away from the hegemon owing to the 'free-rider problem' and the maladaptability of the hegemonic state. Cox, however, points to the economic and social contradictions of the hegemonic order that exist at the domestic and international level. First, following Polanyi and Marx, Cox argues that liberalism is 'non-homeostatic' or is prone to break down, which leads on to unemployment and economic crisis; second, that the world economy created by hegemony generates global inequalities which eventually undermine the illusion of harmony and equality. Eventually, the 'hegemon' loses its hegemony, as the dominant classes lose their position of legitimacy. Accordingly, the leading state has to resort to non-legitimate and coercive forms of dominance. Hegemonic leadership is transformed into naked domination based on strength and violence, thereby ushering in a new *non-hegemonic* world order – see also Augelli and Murphy (1993) for an application of this to first–third world relations. In sum, the fundamental cause of these processes lies with domestic class struggles within the 'historic bloc', which eventually transform the hegemonic world order into a non-hegemonic one.

Cox's theory of the state
Cox employs a 'modified parsimonious approach', in which social-class forces constitute the key causal variable but are supplemented by a

series of intervening variables. He sets out his general approach in an early essay (Cox 1986), which posits that there are three spheres of activity that are important: (1) forms of production; (2) forms of state; (3) world orders (hegemonic or non-hegemonic). While each has its own particular effectivity or relative autonomy in shaping IR, they do not have a full autonomy from social or class forces: they are 'intervening variables'. In considering forms of state, Cox argues that '[t]he principal distinguishing features of such forms are the characteristics of their historic blocs, i.e. the configurations of social forces upon which state power ultimately rests. A particular configuration of social forces defines in practice the limits or parameters of state purposes' (Cox 1987: 105). Moreover, strong or hegemonic states enjoy a *relative autonomy* from social forces: 'The autonomous state, whether in hegemonic or non-hegemonic societies, stands over . . . [the dominant] class to regulate its activity in a manner consistent with the economic project of the class as a whole, not responding to particular interests of elements of this class. The weak state that becomes the creature of particular [capitalist] interests is unable to achieve this level of disinterested regulation . . . [a situation that is] closer to the Hobbesian state of nature' (1987: 149). This relatively autonomous state forms an important aspect of Cox's general approach (see especially 1987: 124–8, 137–8, 148–9, 189–210, 219–44).

Cox not only attributes a moderate degree of domestic autonomy or agential power to the state, but also grants it a moderate international agential power to shape the international system. Thus as the state conforms to the long-term interests of capital in general, so it comes to shape the international system. However, the degree of conflict between states fluctuates (unlike in classical Marxist theories of imperialism) between 'relative international consensus' under hegemonic world orders to more overt forms of conflict under non-hegemonic world orders. Nevertheless, states are unable to create a genuinely free, peaceful and equal world because ultimately they are 'socialised' by exploitative class relations within the domestic sphere of production. In this way, what makes Cox an 'orthodox' Marxist is his second-image theory of IR, in which social contradictions at the national level are projected or transposed by states into a conflictual sphere of inter-state politics.

World-systems theory

IR scholars often assume that world-systems theory – hereafter, WST (often referred to as 'structuralism') – represents *the* Marxist theory of

IR. As we shall see, this is problematic for a number of reasons, and is why I view the basic-force WST approach as distinct from 'orthodox' Marxism. Moreover, I suggest that there are two main variants of WST: what I call 'classical' and 'neo-classical'. Because the 'pure' or fundamentalist form is found in the classical variant, I shall accord it the majority of attention.

Classical WST

Classical WST shares two major similarities with Waltzian neorealism: (1) both are strong third-image theories of IR and accordingly, therefore (2) both deny the state any agential power to shape or determine the international system. The key difference, however, is that for Wallerstein, IR and state behaviour is determined by the structure of the capitalist world-economy (CWE) rather than the structure of the inter-state political structure. Classical WST's approach to IR has three main aspects: a focus on 'dependency' within the world-economy; a historical–sociological theory of the rise of the capitalist world-economy and inter-state system; and a historical–sociological theory of the rise and decline of hegemonies, all of which are outlined below, albeit in brief form.

Wallerstein's basic theoretical schema

I propose to explain Wallerstein's basic approach by drawing on Waltz's key categories. In doing so, I do not wish to suggest that the two theories are precisely congruent; in certain respects there are significant differences. But it is perfectly possible to transpose Waltz's key theoretical categories in order to help shed light on Wallerstein's schema. Such a move is possible because Wallerstein shares with Waltz an approach that privileges 'international structure' and simultaneously downgrades 'agency'. Figure 4.3 borrows Waltz's definitional categories of the international political structure (see figure 2.2, p. 25) and applies these to understanding Wallerstein's international economic structure (i.e. the CWE). In effect, Wallerstein implicitly specifies three tiers or levels to the international economic structure (though the second drops out). The first tier, or the deep structure, is the *ordering principle* of the world economy which is capitalist, and prescribes that states must follow economic self-help and seek to enhance the economic interests of their national bourgeoisie. The third tier – the distribution of capabilities – suggests that states will be strong or weak depending on where they are situated within the CWE: strong states reside in the core, weak states in the periphery. The world-economy is separated or divided into three

Marxism   135

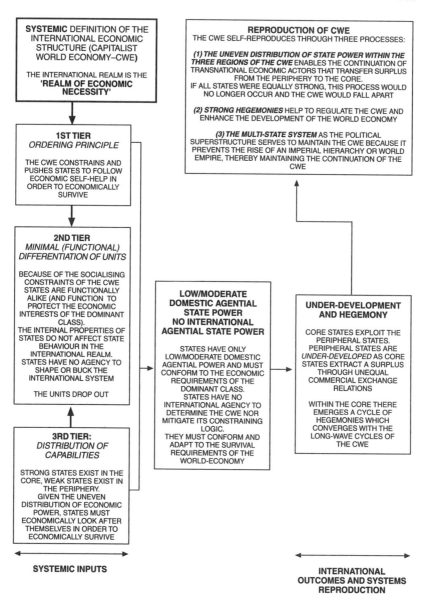

Figure 4.3 Wallerstein's systemic Marxian theory of the passive 'capitalist-adaptive' state

regions – core (the advanced first world), the periphery (the backward third world), and the semi-periphery which lies part way between the other two regions (and acts as a political buffer between the core and periphery). This is sometimes referred to as the 'layer-cake' model.

One of the key parts of Wallerstein's argument is that states within the core are strong and advanced only because they have economically undermined and exploited the third world. Thus the core extracts a surplus from the periphery through global exploitative unequal exchange relations. This point was first expounded by André Gunder Frank who, in contrast to liberal (modernisation) theorists, argued that third world countries are not backward because they are *un*-developed (implying that in time they will develop), but because they are *under*-developed through exploitation by the core (Frank 1967). A crucial point for Wallerstein, as well as Frank, is that these regions are linked up through commercial or 'exchange' relations. In contrast to 'orthodox' Marxism, what makes this a *capitalist* world-economy is *not* the extant form of domestic production or social relations, because these necessarily vary across the world system, but the fact that there is production for profit *in a world market*. Although neither Frank nor Wallerstein specified the precise ways in which the core exploits the periphery, they do supply us with a general formula: the metropolis expropriates economic surplus from its satellites through unequal exchange relations, thereby causing the under-development of the periphery (Frank 1967; Wallerstein 1979: 18–20, 1984: 15). It was subsequently left to a host of writers to specify these mechanisms (for an excellent summary, see Roxborough 1979).

Perhaps the biggest pay-off of applying Waltz's categories to explaining Wallerstein is that it gives us purchase on Wallerstein's theory of the state. This emerges from a discussion of the 'second tier'. As we noted in chapter 2, for Waltz, the second tier – the units or the states – drop out of the theoretical schema. Thus states might look quite different, and have different relations with their societies, but this does not affect their behaviour in the international system. Likewise for Wallerstein, while he recognises that the domestic social relations of production vary across states, nevertheless this does not affect the way states behave in the international economy. For Wallerstein, all states are functionally alike, in that they all serve to enhance the power of their dominant economic classes. In this respect Wallerstein's approach to the state is precisely commensurate with Waltz. Put simply, the units (national state/society) do not constitute independent variables; they have no impact upon the structure of the CWE. They *do* vary in terms of power capability, but *not* in terms of function. The structure of the

CWE is wholly distinct from national-level variables. States must conform or adapt to the exigencies of the CWE. Thus first, states have no international agential power being mere passive victims (*Träger*) of the international structure; and, secondly, the state (the second tier) drops out as an explanatory variable in IR.

Finally, one of the most important aspects of Waltz's theory is his insistence that the international system is reproduced over time through the unintended consequences of states' short-term survival behaviour. The same position is unwittingly adopted by Wallerstein. As Skocpol (1977: 1080) points out, for Wallerstein the division of the world into three core regions is vital for systems maintenance. Thus the uneven distribution of 'state power' is functional for the CWE because if states were equally strong 'they would be in the position of blocking the effective operation of transnational economic entities whose locus were in another state. It would then follow that the world division of labour would be impeded, the world economy decline, and eventually the world-system fall apart' (Wallerstein 1974: 355). But in addition, Wallerstein argues that the superstructure of the inter-state system also serves to reproduce the CWE because it impedes the possibility of a world-empire (which would transcend and destroy the world-economy). Moreover, the succession of world hegemonies (see below) all serve to reproduce the international economic structure because they regulate and enhance the developmental prospects of the CWE (Wallerstein 1996: 98–103).

World systems theory versus 'orthodox'-Marxism

Before I consider some of the central aspects of Wallerstein's historical account, it is important to explain why I differentiate WST from 'orthodox' Marxism. The key to this distinction lies with the general definition of capitalism that Wallerstein employs, as well as his explanation of the rise of the capitalist world-economy. Following the publication of the major works by Frank and Wallerstein, an important debate soon emerged within Marxist circles over the 'correct' Marxist definition of capitalism; a debate that in fact first emerged in the 1950s between Paul Sweezy and Maurice Dobb (see Holton 1985 for an excellent summary). Ernesto Laclau (1971) produced an orthodox Marxist critique of Frank's thesis. By claiming that Latin America has not been capitalist since 1600 because the form of production relations that existed in Latin America was clearly feudal, he concludes that the world-economy could *not* be described as capitalist, nor could global capitalism account for Latin America's backwardness. This was echoed by Robert Brenner (1977) in his famous 'orthodox' Marxist critique of Wallerstein.

The two central points that Brenner and Laclau made were that, first, because Wallerstein ignores the relations of production at the national level (i.e. within the mode of production), he therefore banishes the centrality of class struggle from his analysis. Thus, for Wallerstein, the fact that different forms of social relations – free wage labour in the core, unfree labour and feudal labour in the periphery – all co-exist in the CWE, is not of importance because all societies are fundamentally determined not by their extant domestic MOP but by their place within the CWE. Secondly, Wallerstein located the source of exploitation in the international sphere of *distribution* (i.e. unequal exchange relations between states), rather than in the unequal *production* relations between classes. In sum, because Wallerstein denigrates the importance of the social relations of production, he is in danger of falling into the trap of bourgeois liberal economics (Skocpol 1977: 1079). It was this that prompted Brenner to caustically label the approach as a 'neo-Smithian' Marxism (as in the 'bourgeois' theorist, Adam Smith). How then does Wallerstein utilise these definitions within his overall historical–sociological analysis?

The rise of the CWE

Wallerstein further departs from orthodox Marxism in his account of the emergence of the CWE. This system emerged by the early sixteenth century, the linchpin of which is a set of commercial linkages between regions (1974: 15). Wallerstein makes a crucial distinction between 'world-empires' and 'world-economies'. 'World-empires' refer to those systems which are dominated by one key imperial state. Prior to 1500 the world had been dominated by a succession of 'world-empires', which fundamentally stymied the development of capitalism. This occurred because the vast bureaucracy that emerged in order to control these world-empires necessarily absorbed too much of the economic surplus. By contrast, a 'world-economy' is one that is characterised by more than one political centre – i.e. in which there are a multiplicity of states. An anarchic state system is a crucial pre-requisite for the development of global capitalism for two main reasons: first, because the creation of an economic surplus is not absorbed by an over-large and unwieldy imperial state; and, second, because 'capitalism as an economic mode is based on the fact that the economic factors operate within an arena larger than that which any political entity can totally control. This gives capitalists a freedom of manoeuvre that is structurally based' (1974: 348). Thus because capitalists can move freely between different states, each state is compelled, through time, to respect the needs of capital because they are dependent on capitalist revenues to fund their military activities. Accordingly states do not stifle capitalist development but seek to enhance it by conforming to the needs of the bourgeoisie. Put differently, the balance of power between competing states in a multi-state system is the vital pre-requisite for the development of capitalism (Wallerstein 1974: chapter 3).

In making this claim, Wallerstein draws perilously close to the neorealist argument that Max Weber occasionally made: that the anarchic competitive system of sovereign states determined the rise of European capitalism (Weber 1978: 353–4). He also pre-empted Tilly's (1975b) neorealist argument that strong state formation occurred through the process of resolving fiscal–military crisis (Wallerstein 1974: chapter 3). But Wallerstein firmly closed this 'neorealist avenue' off by insisting that the inter-state system is determined by the CWE rather than the other way round. The inter-state system is merely the political organisation of the CWE. Or, as he consistently put it: 'The political superstructure of the capitalist world-economy is an inter-state system' (Wallerstein 1984: 14, 29, 38–9, 46). This indeed takes us back to a reductionist 'base–superstructure model', albeit one that exists on a world scale (Skocpol 1977; Dale 1984: 206). But this raises another more serious problem regarding the internal logic of Wallerstein's theory. For if the anarchic multi-state system acts as a crucial pre-requisite for the rise of capitalism but is sociologically reduced to, or explained by, the emergence of the world economy, then we end up with a circular or tautological mode of reasoning: that the world-economy is called into existence by the world-economy. It was left for subsequent writers to resolve this problem (e.g. Chase-Dunn 1989: chapter 7, see below). Nevertheless, given that the inter-state system functions to reproduce the CWE, the next task must be to consider how this happens. An important process here is that of the rise and decline of hegemonies, an area of analysis that has subsequently emerged within IPE.

Capitalist long cycles and international hegemony
Because much of WST's approach to hegemony mirrors the work of Robert Cox, with which I have already dealt, I shall confine my brief discussion to considering the key differences. For Cox, the hegemonic world order can be understood only through the prior concept of the relations between classes within the domestic 'historic bloc'. By contrast, Wallerstein focuses on the requirements and logic of the structure of the CWE to explain hegemony, and more specifically on a set of deterministic economic cycles that lie at its heart. The basic laws of motion of the CWE are based on fifty-year-long 'Kondratieff price cycles'. These involve an up-phase of rising prices and economic boom

(the first twenty-five years) and a subsequent twenty-five-year down-phase, in which prices decline and recession prevails. The rise of a hegemon is determined by two processes, both of which are determined by these long-wave cycles. First, the end of a long cycle leads to a world war or hegemonic war. This signals the end of a hegemonic order and enables a new hegemon to emerge. Secondly, in the subsequent up-phase the hegemon extends its rule over the world-economy. Thus the end of a long cycle led to the Thirty Years' war (1618–48), which was resolved by the rise of the United Provinces to hegemony, the decline of which was secured in the subsequent downphase after 1672. The almost-thirty-year Napoleonic Wars (1792–1815) brought Britain to hegemony which peaked in the up-phase (1846–73), and declined in the subsequent down-phase (1873–96). Between 1914 and 1945 another thirty-years' war (albeit in two phases) ended with the rise of US hegemony, which peaked in the subsequent up-phase (1945–67), and declined in the ensuing down-phase (Wallerstein 1984: chapters 3, 4, 6, 1996b: 98–106). But note that not all down-phases end with the rise of a new hegemon. Thus Wallerstein argues that the cycles of hegemony are longer than those of the CWE, even though the former are fundamentally embedded in the latter (Wallerstein 1984: 17 – and see Goldstein 1988 for a remarkably detailed analysis which refines and applies the long wave approach to understanding hegemony and war in the inter-state system). The key point is that hegemony functions to reproduce the CWE because it ensures the rapid development of the world-economy.

Cox fundamentally rejects Wallerstein's approach first, because it downgrades domestic class relations as underpinning hegemony and international relations; second, because it embodies an *ahistoricist* or determinist conception of historical development which is based on rigid economic cycles and, third, because in Cox's words it embodies a 'structural–functionalist' approach, where hegemony and the inter-state system become functional to the reproduction of the CWE, and are accordingly treated in reductionist terms as mere political superstructures (Cox 1987: 357–8). By contrast, Cox rejects this reductionist approach to the world order, and insists that it has its own 'relative autonomy' (Cox 1986: 217–30). But the fourth difference between Cox and Wallerstein lies in their radically different theories of the state. In producing a strong third-image theory of IR, Wallerstein ends up by denying the state any international agential power. The sovereign state is unequivocally determined by the CWE. As he put it:

The development of the CWE has involved the creation of all the major institutions of the modern world: classes . . . and the 'states'. All of these

structures postdate, not antedate capitalism; all are consequence, not cause . . .
The state is the most convenient institutional intermediary in the establishment
of market constraints . . . in favour of particular [dominant class] groups.
(Wallerstein 1984: 29–30)

Wallerstein oscillates between granting the state a low to moderate
degree of domestic agential power. But the key point is that states are
denied international agential power, and are unable to shape the
international system, since they must conform to the requirements and
dictates of the CWE. Thus while Wallerstein differentiates strong and
weak states, nevertheless the degree of strength is assigned by a state's
position within the CWE – strong states reside in the core, weak states in
the periphery: 'A state is stronger than another state to the extent that it
can maximize the conditions for profit-making by its enterprises . . .
within the world-economy' (Wallerstein 1984: 5). This stands in clear
contrast to Cox, who ascribes a moderate domestic agential power and
moderate international agential capacity to the state, such that it has
some agency to shape the international realm.

By way of addendum: 'neo-classical' WST
Because an adequate discussion of what I call 'neo-classical WST'
would deserve a whole chapter, in what remains of this chapter I shall
simply outline some of the new and exciting directions that WST has
taken in the last ten years. The fundamental aspect that differentiates
classical from neo-classical WST involves the shift from economism to a
more complex approach. One example of this genre is found in Chase-
Dunn's important book, *Global Formation* (1989). This is a highly
eclectic work, which seeks to synthesise 'orthodox' modes of production
analyses with that of classical WST, and to thereby bring class relations
back in (Chase-Dunn 1989: 13–69). Moreover, Chase-Dunn produces
a relatively complex theory of the state and refuses to treat it as a simple
product of economic relations, granting it a moderate degree of domestic agential power or institutional autonomy (Chase-Dunn 1989:
chapter 6). In similar vein, he also resists Wallerstein's economically
reductionist account of the inter-state system, and insists that the CWE
and inter-state system are inextricably entwined such that neither has
primacy over the other (Chase-Dunn 1989: chapter 7). This argument
has been developed furthest by Giovanni Arrighi in his important book,
The Long Twentieth Century (1994). In effectively dispensing with the
base–superstructure model, he argues that there are two analytically
separate logics that inform the development of state behaviour in the
international system. First is the 'logic of territorialism', in which rulers
expand their territory as the principal means to expand their power;

second is the 'logic of capitalism', in which rulers seek to directly acquire capital in order to enhance their power (Arrighi 1994: 33). Given that these fundamental logics interface in different ways to produce different international outcomes, Arrighi is able to produce a sophisticated historical sociology of IR.

Another version of WST is evident in the important and genuinely innovative work of Frank and Gills (1996) as well as Janet Abu-Lughod (1989). The basic claim is that the capitalist world system has existed not for 500 years but for 5,000 (though Abu-Lughod traces it back to 1250 AD). In radical contrast to Wallerstein, they argue that the rise of the West did not occur because of the rise of a modern world system/ economy after 1500; it was merely the latest phase or shift *within the pre-existent world system*. As Frank put it, 'the world system was not born in 1500; it did not arise in Europe; and it is not distinctively capitalist' (Frank 1996: 202). And here, class struggles are yet more marginalised than in classical WST, given that in the pre-1500 period inter-elite struggles (between private and state elites) were more important than class struggles (Gills 1996: 130–6). To avoid any possible confusion, I suggest that Frank has now made the move from classical- to neo-classical- WST. In their defence of classical WST, Wallerstein (1996a) as well as Samir Amin (1996) have reiterated the basic claim that the world before 1500 was not specifically capitalist (being based on a tributary mode of accumulation), nor was it sufficiently integrated to constitute a world system along the lines of the modern CWE. In this way they defend classical WST's most basic claim: that the CWE is unique to the post-1500 world.

In conclusion, neo-classical WST has added considerable sophistica-tion to Wallerstein's approach and agenda, and has begun to move away from its predecessor's economism. Nevertheless the crucial point as far as this book is concerned is that the state will continue to be denied international agential power so long as the CWE and/or the inter-state system are accorded primacy. Perhaps, to the extent that neo-classical world systems theorists have tried to bring the national level back in, their analyses will necessarily oscillate between according the state low to moderate (though never high) international agential power.

Discussion questions

• How is it possible to discern two theories of the state in Karl Marx's works?

- What is the 'base–superstructure' model and how does it give rise to Marx's 'class-adaptive' theory of the state?

- Why does Lenin dismiss the 'relative autonomy' approach to the Marxist theory of the state?

- Why, in contrast to J.A. Hobson, does Lenin accord the state only moderate rather than high international agential power?

- Why in general for neo-Marxists is the 'base–superstructure' model, in Wood's words, 'more trouble than it is worth'?

- In what way does the modern capitalist state have a 'relative autonomy' from class interests, and why (in contrast to neorealists and Weberians) do Marxists refuse to accord the state a full autonomy?

- What are the similarities and differences between the Gramscian and neorealist theories of the state, hegemony and international relations?

- What are the differences between the neo-Gramscian and WST accounts of the state and international hegemony? Why is WST differentiated from 'orthodox' Marxism?

- Why is it argued that the form (though not the content) of Wallerstein's theory is identical to that of Waltz?

- What are the key differences between 'classical' and 'neo-classical' WST? Why does the latter, in contrast to classical WST, succeed in attributing moderate international agential power to the state?

Suggestions for further reading

While *The Communist Manifesto* (1848/1977) remains the most succinct introduction to Marx's (and Engels') historical work as well as containing the classic definition of the state, it is well worth following up with his classic essay, *The Eighteenth Brumaire of Louis Bonaparte* (in Marx and Engels 1970) which succeeds in producing a more sophisticated historicist approach to the state that was purposefully omitted in the *Manifesto*. Engels' essay on 'The Role of Force in History' (Engels in Marx and Engels 1970: 377–428) is the most sustained piece on IR written by either author. Lenin's *Imperialism* (1916/1933) provides a succinct classical Marxist theory of IR (though it contrasts with the more 'social-democratic' or 'revisionist' theory of imperialism found in Hilferding (1981). Moreover, Lenin's *State and Revolution* (1917/1932) provides an excellent introduction to the classical theory of the state. David McLellan has produced a highly readable and succinct summary of Marx's thought and theory of the state (McLellan 1975, – see also the various essays in McLellan 1983). Secondary introductions to classical and neo-Marxism's theories of the state can be found in Dunleavy and O'Leary (1987: chapter 5) and Held (1987: 113–21), while Frank Parkin's neo-Weberian discussion of neo-Marxist state theory (1979) is, though critical, nevertheless succinct and especially useful. Once these have been absorbed, the reader can proceed on to Jessop (1990), which provides a sustained defence of Marxist state theory, as well as providing a comprehensive survey of neo-Marxist theories of the state (see also Perez-Diaz 1978). As noted in the text above, the famous 'Miliband–Poulantzas debate' generated more heat than light, given that both authors argued pretty much the same thing. This debate is reproduced in Blackburn (1973: 238–62). On the different neo-Marxist theories of the state see the following: Mooers (1991) and Wood (1995) on 'political Marxism'; Poulantzas (1973) and Benton (1984) on 'Althus-serian Marxism'; Cox (1986, 1987, 1996), Hall and Jacques (1984) and Gill (1993) on neo-Gramscian Marxism; while Fred Block (1987) and Ellen Trimberger (1978) are significant contributions which seek to extend the 'relative autonomy' of the state as far as possible within a Marxist discourse.

While Wallerstein's, *The Modern World System* (1974) contains the original statement of classical WST, it is long and quite hard to follow. A better place to start is Wallerstein (1979: chapters 1 and 9; 1984: chapter 1; 1996b). Good secondary introductions are Holton (1985: 74–9), and especially Hobden (1998: chapter 7). A good way in is through some of the major critiques, beginning with Skocpol (1977) and Dale (1984), and then proceeding on to Brenner (1977). Once the reader is familiar with 'classical' WST, it would be well worth pro-ceeding on to what I call 'neo-classical' WST – especially Arrighi (1994), Chase-Dunn (1989) and Frank and Gills (1996).

5 Constructivism

Introduction

The purpose of this chapter is not to provide an exhaustive account of the various theories of the state found throughout the already burgeoing constructivist literature. Given that new variants are only now emerging, my purpose must be more modest. Here I present three distinct theories of the state, which cover many, though not all, of the variants found in the extant constructivist literature. Unlike previous chapters, I shall begin with a general introduction to constructivism, before proceeding to examine three key variants and their approaches to the state.

Constructivism versus 'rationalism'

In the past, IR scholars have tended to divide IR theory into three competing schools: liberalism/pluralism, realism and Marxist structuralism (Banks 1985). But the rise of constructivism reconfigures the traditional 'trichotomy' into a dichotomy, comprising constructivism on the one hand and 'rationalism' or 'neo-utilitarianism' on the other. Now realism, liberalism and Marxism are all placed in the one category of 'rationalist' or 'neo-utilitarian' approaches. Constructivists critique 'rationalist' theory on many grounds.

Constructivists begin by arguing that rationalist theory (not to be confused with English school rationalism) has been excessively *materialist* and *agent-centric*. For rationalists, IR appears as the product of agents (usually states) which are imbued with 'instrumental rationality'. That is, states always rationally pursue their power or utility-maximising preferences or interests. For rationalists, state preferences are unproblematic – they are 'exogenously' formed and are based on a power-maximising rationality. By this, they mean that states begin with a portfolio of specific interests *prior* to social interaction. However, the claim that rationalist IR theory tends to be overly agent-centric is, I would argue, much too bold and sweeping, as I have argued throughout this book – though it should be noted that not *all* constructivists make this claim (see e.g. Ruggie 1986, 1998; Reus-Smit 1996). The point that many constructivists seek to establish is that states are far more constrained than materialist theory recognises (again, and for similar reasons, this is a questionable claim). For constructivists, states are constrained by *social normative* structures. One of the fundamental 'givens' in materialist theory is the claim that states, or power actors more generally, know exactly what their interests are, and that they know how to realise them. But for constructivists, states do not *a priori* know what their interests are. Most importantly, constructivists argue that the identities of states are constructed through norms, which in turn define a state's particular interests. As norms reconstruct identities, so interests subsequently change, leading on to changes in state policy. Thus interests and identities are informed by norms which guide actors (states) along certain socially prescribed channels of 'appropriate' behaviour. Constructivists emphasise 'norms' rather than 'ideology', in that the former specifically refers to behaviour that is deemed to be 'legitimate' or 'appropriate'. While some constructivists emphasise the importance of structure over agency (e.g. Finnemore 1996), others emphasise the need to synthesise agency and structure, and engage in 'structurationist' theory (e.g. Wendt 1987; Onuf 1989). On this point, therefore, there is considerable heterogeneity within the literature as a whole.

A further difference between rationalism and constructivism lies in the constructivist claim that state interests and identities are much more *malleable* than is allowed for in rationalist theory. If rationalism presupposes the fixity of state interests and fails to problematise 'identity', constructivists insist that such interests are constantly changing as identities change in line with normative structural changes. Norms constantly mould and re-mould states through subtle processes of socialisation. This argument is especially emphasised by radical constructivists. But perhaps the most important difference between constructivism and rationalism lies with the degree of autonomy that theories ascribe to norms.

As figure 5.1 shows, constructivism accords much higher levels of autonomy to norms and ideas than found in materialist theory (leading many scholars to describe constructivism as 'idealism' or 'ideationalism'). For rationalists, norms are either *epiphenomenal* (i.e. are completely determined by, or derived from, the interests of power actors), or are accorded a 'relative autonomy' from power actors. Carr's analysis in *The Twenty Years' Crisis* is an important example of the former 'reductionist' approach. For Carr (1939), the norms of liberal internationalism

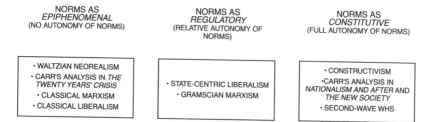

Figure 5.1 The different conceptions of norms found in rationalist (materialist) and constructivist theory

were functional to the maintenance of the dominance of the great powers in the international system. By contrast, Gramscian/Marxism and state-centric liberalism prescribe a relative autonomy to norms. Thus, for example, for neoliberals, although norms constrain states in the short run, nevertheless they are ultimately created by states and for states to maximise their long-run power interests (see Keohane 1984: 57–8; Axelrod 1986). At most, norms are conceived in rationalism as intervening variables that lie between the basic causal variables (i.e. power actors) and international outcomes. By contrast, constructivists insist that norms are wholly autonomous and can fundamentally shape the interests and identities of power actors. As figure 5.1 shows, such a position is also held by second-wave Weberian historical sociologists (e.g. Mann 1986) and, I would argue, classical realists (Morgenthau 1948/1978; Carr 1945, 1951).

Another way of differentiating the rationalist 'relative autonomy' approach from constructivism is to note the difference between *regulatory* and *constitutive* norms. Neoliberal institutionalism envisages norms as 'regulatory', whereby norms (embodied within international regimes) constrain or regulate states by changing the incentives that shape their behaviour. By contrast, for constructivists, constitutive norms 'do not simply regulate behaviour. They also help to constitute the very actors [e.g. states] whose conduct they seek to regulate' (Katzenstein 1996c: 22). That is, constitutive norms define the identity of a state. In sum, while the principal task for neorealists is to elaborate the methods through which states *defend* their national interests (e.g. Krasner 1978), by contrast, constructivists are concerned to reveal the normative processes which *define* the national interest. Moreover, constitutive norms channel state behaviour in ways that are often not consistent with any power-maximising interest on the part of states. Thus the 'logic of consequences' that rationalists implicitly focus upon is replaced by constructivists with a 'logic of appropriateness', in which norms prescribe the range of state behaviour that is deemed to be 'appropriate' (March and Olsen 1989). Accordingly, for what I call 'international society-centric' constructivists, the international realm is a *social* realm and is conceptualised not as a system but as an international *society*.

The notion of an international society found in international society-centric constructivism can be distinguished from the usage of the term within English school rationalism. For the English school, international society is a society of *autonomous states* in which non-state actors are unimportant, and where normative structures embody only regulatory norms – norms which are set up by states in order to promote orderly state behaviour (but see Dunne 1998 for a different reading). For constructivists, however, international society is primarily a normative structure comprising autonomous and constitutive norms which exist independently of states. Here, constructivists conceive the international realm as one of *obligation* rather than one of 'necessity' (neorealism) or 'possibility' (neoliberalism), or 'partial opportunity/partial constraint' (second-wave WHS). Thus, just as individuals and groups in domestic society are socialised by societal norms, so states are socialised by norms of obligation in international society. However, radical constructivists (postmodernists) take issue with this benign view of norms, arguing that norms are sites of exploitation and exclusion, as well as arenas of resistance and contestation.

As noted, there are many variants of constructivism, and it is already becoming apparent within the literature that there are different ways of categorising these – compare Adler (1997) and Ruggie (1998: 35–6) with the typology described here. My following three-fold typology is not meant to capture the full range of the variants found in the already proliferating constructivist literature, but is more modestly designed to convey some of the key ways in which constructivists analyse the state and IR. The three variants that I have chosen to single out are: *international society-centric constructivism, state-centric constructivism* and *radical constructivism* or *postmodernism*. I leave aside other writers who do not fit into the chosen categories, such as Ruggie (1998), Kratochwil (1989), Onuf (1989) and Reus-Smit (1999), and I choose not to focus on what has been termed 'holistic constructivism' which integrates the domestic and international realms (Price and Reus-Smit 1998). Finally, with respect to domestic agential state power (the ability to conduct policy free of domestic constraint) and international agential state power (the ability to conduct policy free of international constraint, and at the extreme to buck the logic of anarchy), constructivism produces at least three clear alternatives:

(1) The theory of the low domestic agential power of the state and high international agential state power, found in international society-centric constructivism

(2) The theory of the very low domestic agential power of the state but moderate international agential state power, found in radical constructivism.

(3) The theory of the low/moderate domestic agential power of the state and moderate/high international agential state power, found in state-centric constructivism.

International society-centric constructivism

The international normative socialisation of the state

This variant is perhaps the most common and one of the most coherent to have emerged in the last decade (e.g. Adler and Haas 1992; Sikkink 1993; Klotz 1996; Strang 1996; Finnemore 1996; Price and Tannenwald 1996). One of the clearest expressions of it is found in Martha Finnemore's book, *National Interests in International Society* (1996). Following many (though not all) constructivists, she suggests that traditional rationalist IR theory has been excessively agent-centric. Given her assumption that states do not always know what they want, the key question becomes: how are state interests *defined?* State identities and interests are defined by the normative structure of international society. This initially leads her to emphasise structure over agency.

The basic theoretical approach: the international structure

As figure 5.2 shows, Finnemore's key variable – international society – has, I suggest, two levels or tiers. The first tier is the normative structure which, I suggest, constitutes the 'deep structure' of international society. This embodies or contains many types of international norms which socialise states into following 'appropriate' behavioural patterns. In effect, Finnemore conceives of an international 'socialising principle', such that states are obliged to conform to benign international norms of 'civilised behaviour'. In her final chapter, Finnemore argues that although there are many norms that exist within the deep structure, she suggests that there are nevertheless three predominant ones: *bureaucracy* (i.e. bureaucracy is seen as the most appropriate way of exercising authority); *markets* (i.e. markets are seen as the most legitimate means of organising economic life); and *human equality* (entailing respect for human rights and broad notions of equality for all in political and

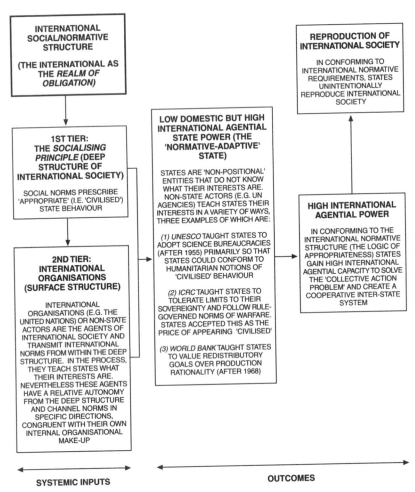

Figure 5.2 International society-centric constructivist theory of the state and IR (Finnemore)

economic life) (Finnemore 1996: 131–5; also Strang 1996: 45). In addition to the deep structure, Finnemore implicitly invokes a second tier – or what I call the 'surface structure' of international society – which comprises international non-state actors and international organisations. These actors are effectively the agents that transmit or diffuse the norms of the deep structure, principally by teaching states how to behave. In this way, international organisations are pro-active norm carriers. This conception echoes but does not perfectly replicate other conceptions, such as 'epistemic communities' (Haas 1992; Adler and Haas 1992), 'principled international issue-networks' (Sikkink 1993) or, 'norm entrepreneurs' (Florini 1996). Nevertheless, international organisations have a relative autonomy from the deep structure insofar as they channel norms in specific ways which are congruent with their own internal organisational structures. In sum, these two components of international society constitute the independent variable, while state behaviour constitutes the dependent variable.

One of Finnemore's primary aims is to demonstrate that state policies are *not* the outcome of national requirements (either on the part of the state or domestic power interests). The key point is to show that international forces can shape national policy (i.e. a 'second-image-reversed' approach), by teaching states what their interests should be. Of course, some rationalists have emphasised the importance of 'learning'. But Finnemore finds the rationalist concept of learning to be problematic because it is purposefully undertaken by states in order to overcome a problem or crisis and thereby enhance the power of a specific actor. By contrast, for Finnemore, international organisations have been 'active teachers' which guide states to initiate policies that are congruent with certain international norms of behaviour; and such behaviour might either fail to enhance the power of a particular actor, or it might even go against the actor's power-interests. Crucial to her international social-structural (systemic) approach is her claim that agent-centric approaches (which focus on the internal preferences of states and their constituencies) would expect policy-making to differ across states, given that states differ in their internal make-up. Reminiscent of Waltz, she shows that in the three chosen areas of policy, different states chose similar policies, suggesting that internalist/domestic variables are of little consequence. This implies the need to engage in international social-*systemic* analysis.

Three case studies in 'defining' national interests

Finnemore develops three case studies which focus on three different arenas of policy. Her method is to produce an 'ideal-type' constructivist argument which requires the initial discounting of any *instrumental rationality* on the part of states. Thus in each of her three case studies, she begins by demonstrating either that there are no power-maximising interests behind a certain state policy, or by showing that a certain policy might go against a pure power-maximising interest on the part of the state (as in the institutionalisation of norm-governed rules of war, as well as poverty alleviation).

The adoption of science policy bureaucracies by states, after 1955

Finnemore's first case study seeks to show that state structures are socialised by a norm-carrying international organisation, the United Nations Educational, Scientific and Cultural Organisation (UNESCO), which taught states how to develop science bureaucracies. She begins by asking: why did states develop science bureaucracies after 1955? She discounts what she calls 'demand-driven' variables (consistent with rationalist theory), such as the security needs of states, the developmental needs of modernising economies or the scientific preferences of domestic science communities. She then produces a 'supply-driven' explanation, in which she begins by showing that the development of science bureaucracies after 1955 correlated not with materialist power-maximising requirements, but with the pro-active push of international norms by the OECD and above all UNESCO.

Originally, UNESCO was set up to promote transnational scientific norms in order to advance global humanitarian norms, thereby making the world a safer place. States were to be denied a significant input into the development of such a scientific network, so that science would not be driven by the power-interests of states. However, Finnemore argues that owing to organisational changes within the structure of UNESCO, such a global norm was refracted and modified in a new direction. By the early 1950s with the onset of the Cold War and the emergence of the newly independent states, states came to demand greater representation within UNESCO. In 1954, UNESCO's internal structure changed, as states came to replace scientists as the organisation's core constituents. This led to a change in policy direction. Subsequently, UNESCO sought to pro-actively teach individual states to develop their own science policy bureaucracies. To this end, the organisation was highly successful: between 1955 and 1975 science policy bureaucracies had expanded from fourteen countries to some eighty-nine (Finnemore 1996: 39). Thus although the prime rationale for such 'educative' activity by UNESCO remained the same – to promote scientific thinking in order to advance humanitarian norms – the means by which this was achieved fundamentally changed as a result of organisational changes within UNESCO. And states came to accept UNESCO's teachings on the grounds that having a science policy bureaucracy was perceived as a necessary ingredient of what constitutes a 'modern civilised' state. Moreover, the 'authority' of UNESCO was crucial in persuading states to institutionalise such norms.

Tolerating direct limits to sovereignty: accepting rule-governed norms of warfare

Finnemore's second case study involves the process through which states came to accept rule-governed norms of warfare. Here she discusses the development of the Geneva Conventions which stipulate that states and their armies should protect the well-being of wounded soldiers in battle; should provide aid to prisoners of war; should provide humanitarian aid to non-state forces during civil conflicts; and should provide access and humanitarian treatment to political prisoners. In short, states should accept certain humanitarian rules of warfare which place limits on the exercise of sovereignty. Discounting demand-driven explanations is unnecessary because these norms of behaviour, by definition, would not aid the power-interests of states. How, then, did this all come about?

Again Finnemore focuses on the pro-active role of international organisations, in this case the International Committee of the Red Cross (ICRC). The ICRC, which was in turn promoted by the work of Henry Dunant, based itself on promoting humanitarian norms that prescribed wartime duties and responsibilities. In short, the ICRC prescribed what was appropriate behaviour for 'civilised' states engaged in war. States came to tolerate limits on their sovereignty as a 'price' worth paying in order to keep up the appearance of 'being civilised'. Thus, in contrast to neorealism, Finnemore argues that in this case states have taken on burdens which limit their most vital sovereign interests (i.e. the free exercise of state power during wartime) (Finnemore 1996: 72). Richard Price and Nina Tannenwald conclude similarly, in their study of nuclear and chemical weapons taboos, that 'the existence of prohibitory norms reveals that war is rarely absolute; instead it displays features of a social institution. Conforming to such norms occurs because states do not want to be classified as acting outside the bounds of "civilized" international society. "Society" not anarchy, is the source of constraining and permissive effects' (Price and Tannenwald 1996: 145; Finnemore 1996: 69, 87–8).

Tolerating limits to economic sovereignty: accepting redistribution over production values

Finnemore's final case study involves international political economy concerns. Here she focuses on why third world states came to accept the issue of poverty alleviation as an important norm of economic policy after 1968. Prior to 1968, there was little sign that such a norm was valued. The objectives of national economic policy had been to maximise national capital accumulation – that is, to prioritise production-over distributive-values. But by the 1970s economic developmental norms shifted from privileging production to ensuring welfare redistribution. How did this normative change come about?

Again there was no demand-driven logic identifiable, certainly not among states, since such a norm shift actually went against their immediate interests of maximising economic growth. Here, third world governments came to tolerate limits on their economic sovereignty, given that redistribution would necessarily impinge upon optimal-production criteria. The key international organisation here was the World Bank, which taught states to embrace this new norm. This was largely driven by the pioneering activities undertaken by the Bank's president – Robert McNamara. McNamara was driven by the normative belief that rich nation states had a duty or obligation to help alleviate poverty in third world countries. He set about increasing both aid and lending to the third world that was aimed at specifically targeted local areas. He also implemented a raft of policies connected to local infrastructural development programmes. As with UNESCO (though not the ICRC), the precise content of poverty alleviation policies that states came to employ was not simply a product of normative changes within the deep structure of international society, but also a product of the specific organisational structure of the World Bank within the surface structure.

The international society-centric constructivist theory of the state

For Finnemore, states are understood as normative-adaptive entities. States are socialised not by material structures but by the socialising principle of the international normative structure. In each case, states came to adapt their policies and domestic structures so as to conform to the international norms that prescribe 'civilised' state behaviour-norms that were transmitted to states through the 'teaching' activities of international organisations. It is implicit in her argument that states have only low domestic agential power. But the key issue concerns her approach to the international agential power of the state. Recall that Finnemore's principal objective is to accord greater weighting of 'structure' over agency. Has she succeeded? In terms of the definition of international agential power employed in this volume, the answer must be 'yes and no'. In the first instance, it is clear that states have no international agential power in that they are socialised by the structure of international society and have no power to affect this normative structure. Moreover, in the process, states often come to tolerate limits on their sovereignty. And in all three cases, states came to develop new policies not to maximise their power but rather to conform to what constitutes 'civilised' behaviour. Thus far, Finnemore has succeeded in emphasising international (social) structure while downgrading state-agency. But there is a clear paradox that emerges here. For in conforming to the international normative structure, states derive very considerable international agential power to overcome the collective action problem and thereby mitigate international anarchy. This suggests that benign global norms can re-educate states to cooperate and act in ways that enable them to 'buck the logic of anarchy'. Moreover, with respect to overcoming the collective action problem, Finnemore grants the state an even higher level of international agential power than that accorded by neoliberal institutionalism.

The two positions are compared in figure 5.3 (p. 156). For neoliberal institutionalists, states always have the choice to defect and follow short-term relative gains/self-help by ignoring state-created 'regulatory norms' embodied within international regimes. These norms do not inform the identity of states but act merely to enhance the long term power-interests of states. For Finnemore, states are deeply socialised by *constitutive* norms that actually create states' identity in the first instance. Crucially, these norms lead states to subconsciously choose to cooperate internationally even though they do not satisfy any power-maximising or utility-maximising interests: that is, cooperation is inscribed into the identity of the state. In this way, states can achieve more effective levels of cooperation than those envisaged by neoliberal institutionalism, precisely because the option of defection is greatly diminished.

Finally, it is important to note that while the analysis so far would clearly suggest a strong third-image approach, this is qualified in Finnemore's final chapter. A strong third-image constructivist approach would attribute a strong coherence and homogeneity to international norms. However she explicitly rejects a 'world-homogenisation process' on the grounds that global norms are not completely congruent – that is, different global norms are subject to contestation, often deep contestation (Finnemore 1996: 135–9). She therefore produces a 'weak' third-image approach.

Radical constructivism (postmodernism)

It is important to begin by noting that equating postmodernism and constructivism is controversial (but for a full justification of this, see Price and Reus-Smit 1998). Nevertheless, while I am treating post-modernism as one variant of constructivism it is important to note that it is a highly heterogeneous theory. And to satisfactorily convey the approach in its manifold variations would warrant at least one chapter,

NEOLIBERAL INSTITUTIONALISM

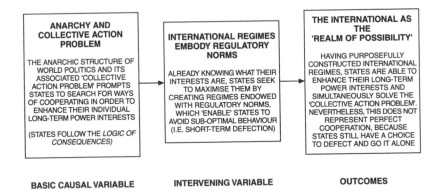

INTERNATIONAL SOCIETY-CENTRIC CONSTRUCTIVISM

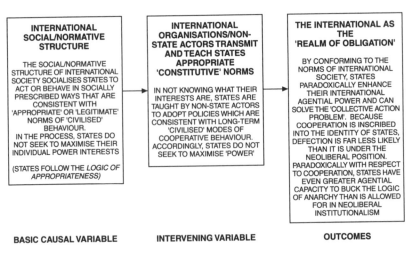

Figure 5.3 Differentiating international society-centric constructivism from neoliberal institutionalism

rather than only the present short section (but for two excellent introductions see Richard Devetak 1996 for a sympathetic treatment, and Darryl Jarvis 1998 for a more critical summary). Nevertheless, for the purposes of this book it *is* possible to extract or discern a basic approach to the state (without doing injustice to the many postmodern variants). And there can be little doubt that postmodernism produces new and important historically- and sociologically-sensitive insights into understanding the state and IR (see e.g. Ashley 1989; Der Derian and Shapiro 1989; Campbell 1990; Walker 1993; Bartelson 1995; C. Weber 1995; Doty 1995; Shapiro and Alker 1996). More recently, postmodern feminists have extended this agenda in new and exciting ways (e.g. Elshtain 1992; Peterson 1992b; Sylvester 1994) (for excellent introductions to feminism more generally, see Tickner 1992; True 1996 and Steans 1998). Moreover, I readily concede that my earlier dismissal of postmodernism as 'nihilistic' was unfair (Hobson 1997: 278).

It is testimony to the richness of constructivism as a heterogeneous body of sociological thought (of which I see postmodernism as a variant) that some of its variants produce quite distinct insights. Figure 5.4 juxtaposes radical constructivism with international society-centric constructivism (as well as with neorealism). We noted on p. 149 that for the international society-centric variant, global norms tend *on the whole* to be positive, benign and increasingly inclusionary. Accordingly the construction of state identities often tends to be positive. By contrast, radical constructivism always views the construction of state identity in negative terms. That is, the process of state identity formation necessarily leads to exclusion, repression, violence and the marginalisation of minorities. Moreover, the two variants can be radically differentiated in terms of the degree of international agential power accorded to states.

State identity formation and international relations

Radical constructivists begin by unpacking or deconstructing the state. In contrast to materialist IR theory – most especially neorealism – they insist that the state cannot be simply equated with sovereignty which confers upon it a fixed and stable presence or meaning. Sovereignty is not a material foundation but a social construct. More specifically, 'state sovereignty', 'state identity', 'state boundaries', 'state legitimacy' and the 'domestic political community' or 'nation' that the state allegedly represents, must be analytically differentiated from each other, rather than unproblematically fused into a 'finished' or 'complete' totality known as the 'sovereign state'. The appearance of a 'complete' or 'exclusive' state, differentiated from 'other' states in the international

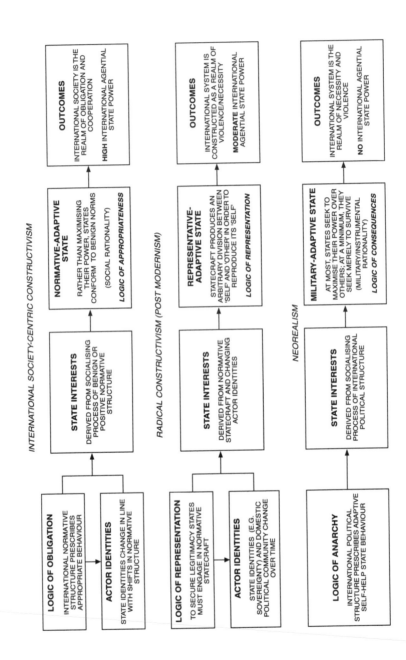

INTERNATIONAL SOCIETY-CENTRIC CONSTRUCTIVISM

LOGIC OF OBLIGATION

INTERNATIONAL NORMATIVE STRUCTURE PRESCRIBES APPROPRIATE BEHAVIOUR

ACTOR IDENTITIES

STATE IDENTITIES CHANGE IN LINE WITH SHIFTS IN NORMATIVE STRUCTURE

STATE INTERESTS

DERIVED FROM SOCIALISING PROCESS OF BENIGN OR POSITIVE NORMATIVE STRUCTURE

NORMATIVE-ADAPTIVE STATE

RATHER THAN MAXIMISING THEIR POWER, STATES CONFORM TO BENIGN NORMS

(SOCIAL RATIONALITY)

LOGIC OF APPROPRIATENESS

OUTCOMES

INTERNATIONAL SOCIETY IS THE REALM OF OBLIGATION AND COOPERATION

HIGH INTERNATIONAL AGENTIAL STATE POWER

RADICAL CONSTRUCTIVISM (POST MODERNISM)

LOGIC OF REPRESENTATION

TO SECURE LEGITIMACY STATES MUST ENGAGE IN NORMATIVE STATECRAFT

ACTOR IDENTITIES

STATE IDENTITIES (E.G. SOVEREIGNTY) AND DOMESTIC POLITICAL COMMUNITY CHANGE OVER TIME

STATE INTERESTS

DERIVED FROM NORMATIVE STATECRAFT AND CHANGING ACTOR IDENTITIES

REPRESENTATIVE-ADAPTIVE STATE

STATECRAFT PRODUCES AN ARBITRARY DIVISION BETWEEN 'SELF' AND 'OTHER' IN ORDER TO REPRODUCE ITS 'SELF'

LOGIC OF REPRESENTATION

OUTCOMES

INTERNATIONAL SYSTEM IS CONSTRUCTED AS A REALM OF VIOLENCE/NECESSITY

MODERATE INTERNATIONAL AGENTIAL STATE POWER

NEOREALISM

LOGIC OF ANARCHY

INTERNATIONAL POLITICAL STRUCTURE PRESCRIBES ADAPTIVE SELF-HELP STATE BEHAVIOUR

STATE INTERESTS

DERIVED FROM SOCIALISING PROCESS OF INTERNATIONAL POLITICAL STRUCTURE

MILITARY-ADAPTIVE STATE

AT MOST, STATES SEEK TO MAXIMISE THEIR POWER OVER OTHERS; AT A MINIMUM, THEY SEEK MERELY TO SURVIVE (MILITARY/INSTRUMENTAL RATIONALITY)

LOGIC OF CONSEQUENCES

OUTCOMES

INTERNATIONAL SYSTEM IS THE REALM OF NECESSITY AND VIOLENCE

NO INTERNATIONAL AGENTIAL STATE POWER

Figure 5.4 Differentiating constructivisms from neorealism

system is in fact an illusion: an illusion that is the product of successful 'statecraft', or what might be better labelled *normative statecraft*. Cynthia Weber (1995) also refers to this process as that of 'writing' the state. Nor is the state unproblematically representative of a domestic political community or the nation, as rationalists assume.

'Normative statecraft' refers to the process by which the state creates an *imaginary* domestic political community or nation that *appears* as unified and harmonious. The political community or nation is according to Benedict Anderson (1983) *imagined* because it does not exist as a complete or unified totality, given that it is incoherent and constantly fragmenting. And the nationalistic feeling of 'togetherness' is imagined because the members of a nation do not actually know most of the people that supposedly comprise it. Because the political community – or that which is to be signified by the signifier (i.e. the state) – does not properly exist given that its boundaries are constantly fracturing, the state must 'fix' or stabilise domestic society with a unitary appearance, without which there is no 'foundation' which the state can represent. How is this achieved?

In following what Cynthia Weber (1995) calls the 'logic of representa- tion', states must draw and make a whole series of arbitrary distinctions and divisions. Most fundamentally, this involves creating a highly arbitrary distinction, or drawing a boundary between 'inside' and 'outside'; in which the former *appears* as the realm of peace and order, and the latter the realm of necessity and violence (Ashley 1989: 300–13; Campbell 1990; Walker 1993: chapter 8; Bartelson 1995: 83–4; Weber 1995: chapter 1; Devetak 1996: 199–200). This involves creating a false distinction between 'self' and 'other'. That is, states tend to create the appearance of a *threatening* 'other', against which the 'self' is defined negatively. In constructing an 'other' that appears threatening, the state is able to confer the appearance of unity upon the 'self' – i.e. a domestic population. But the state must also draw boundaries within society in order to repress those groups that do not conform to the pure notion of the self. These 'deviant groups' become internal 'others' (to which I return shortly). In short, the self is defined negatively against the other(s) both inside and outside society, in order to create the appear- ance of unity. But how does this process of statecraft and the logic of representation relate to international relations?

Perhaps the key point here that opens radical constructivism up to IR is that in the process of constructing a fixed coherent national identity, states make or construct a world of 'others' which *appears* threatening, and consequently makes the state's task of military preparation appear as a natural imperative of foreign policy. Thus the appearance of the international realm as one of necessity and violence is the result not of an 'external' or objective logic of anarchy (as in neorealism), but rather the result of an internal process of state identity-construction as undertaken through normative statecraft. That is the 'hard' sovereign boundaries that 'divide' hostile states are really only imagined through statecraft. 'The constant articulation of danger through foreign policy is thus not a threat to a state's [military] existence [as in neorealism] . . . it is its condition of possibility [in the first place]' (David Campbell cited in Devetak 1996: 198). In this way, foreign policy is not only the result of normative statecraft, it is also a fundamental determinant of statecraft. Moreover, no sooner has unity and legitimacy been created and imagined, it once again fractures, requiring a renewed process of normative statecraft in order to create a new 'fixed' meaning to sovereignty, identity and the political community. Thus the task of 'completing' the state and domestic political community is not achieved once and for all (in contrast to traditional rationalist IR theory that presumes that such an unproblematic finished state appeared in 1648); it has to be constantly made and remade, imagined and re-imagined in order to produce the appearance of a state that is legitimate, natural and 'complete'. It is therefore, the successful process of 'writing' the state (i.e. normative statecraft) that produces the illusion of sovereignty as finished, or what Doty refers to as the *sovereignty effect* (Doty 1996: 121–4). At this point it is important to iron out one common area of confusion. Radical constructivists are often described as 'nihilistic' given their insistence that states, nations (and all social forms, for that matter), are 'not real'. But this criticism is incorrect. What they mean by this is simply that the state and all social forms do not exist as fully complete or finished entities whose legitimacy is unproblematic and fixed once and for all. Moreover, they are unequivocal that the consequences of normative statecraft – political repression, racism, genocide and war – are effects that are so appalling that it becomes imperative to do away with the state.

Writing the state and punishing states as 'others'

An important application of this approach to IR is found in Cynthia Weber's book, *Simulating Sovereignty* (Weber 1995). Weber's central task is to problematise sovereignty. If traditional IR theory assumes that the state/sovereignty couplet is natural and legitimate, and that sovereignty exists as an independent phenomenon that endows the state with a fixed meaning, she insists that the 'state' and 'sovereignty' should be analytically differentiated. Thus Weber opens up the 'black-box' of sovereignty, and reveals it as highly malleable and protean in nature. Sovereignty is not an objective category which acts as a referent for the state. Sovereignty itself must have a referent – that is, it must be grounded in a foundational 'truth', such as God or 'the people' that must be 'written' by the state through statecraft. And because such referents are themselves constructed, so sovereignty is ultimately a social construct (Biersteker and Weber 1996b).

Perhaps the key point for Weber is that a *crisis of representation* occurs when state *A* bases its mode of representation on a different foundation to that of state *B*. The crisis of representation occurs because new forms of political community within state *B* can pose an alternative to the mode of representation that exists within state *A*. In her three case studies, Weber shows how states are frequently 'threatened' by others, not in a military sense but because another state might found its 'self' upon an alternative mode of representation. Thus many of the states within the Concert of Europe in the early nineteenth century developed a mode of representation based on monarchical absolutism. But when *absolute* monarchy was challenged by the Spanish and Neapolitan revolutions in order to create a new mode of representation based on *constitutional* monarchy, the result was a 'representational crisis' in the remaining absolute monarchies. That is, the absolute monarchies felt threatened because the emergence of other more 'democratic' states posed an alternative form of governance. Accordingly, the absolute monarchies punished the 'deviant others' through military intervention. The same process occurred in the United States when the Bolshevik revolution occurred and a communist state posed a representational threat to US liberal capitalism. Thus in order to stabilise its rule at home, the United States sought to demonise and *punish* the USSR as the 'deviant other' in order to shore up its own mode of representation. It was this, argues David Campbell (1990), that led to the Cold War after 1947.

In this argument, Weber is able to undermine the traditional assumption that intervention and sovereignty are mutually exclusive. Weber shows that intervention actually constitutes the condition of sovereignty's existence. That is, to paraphrase Campbell, 'the constant articulation of foreign intervention is . . . not a threat to sovereignty but is its condition of possibility'. Intervention and sovereignty are necessarily entwined. This occurs because a state must take it upon itself to act as a 'disciplinary community' and punish those states that do not conform to the mode of sovereign representation found in the intervening state. It must do this if it is to continue to appear as representative of its own artificially created domestic political community.

Writing the gendered state and punishing women as domestic 'others'

As noted earlier, one of the fundamental aspects of creating an 'other' (in order to construct a 'self') is to punish those groups within society that do not conform to the pure notion of self. This leads states to create boundaries within domestic society to cordon off 'deviant others'. In particular, the state creates a self that is based on one racial group and one heterosexual masculine-gendered group. Thus deviant others – women, gays and 'domestic foreign aliens' – must be repressed in order to maintain the 'pure' self. It is important to note that the state is not a simple *instrument* of men's interests. The key point is that the practice of government is conducted *as if* heterosexual men's interests are the only ones that matter (Connell 1990). Moreover, men's interests are in any case socially constructed around a heterosexual masculine norm which embodies notions of paternal protection, aggression and militarism.

How, then, does the state construct women as a 'deviant other', and thereby keep them subordinate? Feminists of all persuasions argue that states construct an internal boundary line that separates the private sphere from the public. The public sphere is inherently masculine and represents the realm of work, production and government while, conversely, the private sphere is constructed as feminine and constitutes the realm of family and reproduction. The state must do this because the private world of women is equivalent to the world of states: both constitute 'others' which are constructed as threatening and must be repressed and controlled so that the state may create a homogeneous domestic political community and thereby provide a basis for its own legitimacy (True 1996: 231). The private sphere is repressed and separated from the public in numerous ways.

First, language is constructed *through* opposing or dialectical binary dichotomies (or what Peterson following Mies calls 'colonising dualisms') – mind/body, subject/object, reason/emotion, public/private, etc. (or what Derrida refers to as *logocentrism* – see Ashley 1989: 261–4). The former term represents dominant (or hegemonic masculine thinking) and the latter subordinate feminine thinking. The key point is that the masculine term is always privileged (or constitutes the 'colonising' term), while the feminine is constantly devalued or 'colonised' (Tickner 1988; Peterson 1992b: 12–13). Accordingly, this helps reproduce the divide between a masculine-based public sphere and a feminine-based private sphere. Secondly, the public sphere itself is monopolised by men, while women are relegated or confined to the private sphere. It is true that women can struggle for the right to enter into the public domain, 'but it is a space in which masculine values are valorized' (Steans 1998: 85). Moreover, feminists argue that conceptions of citizenship are based on masculinity (Pateman 1988). As Steans argues, citizenship has historically been based on notions of the 'warrior hero' and militarily defending the polity, practices that have been performed mainly by men (Steans 1998: chapter 4). Thirdly, because the private sphere is not valued by the state, it is separated out and repressed through both intervention and non-intervention (or malign neglect). States intervene and 'regulate' women through repressive laws concerning reproduction, marriage, divorce and property rights (Pateman 1988). But the state also represses women through its decision not-to-intervene in the private sphere (the policy of *malign neglect*). States uphold violence of men against women in manifold ways, not least by refusing to intervene within domestic disputes. Hence the state is indirectly complicit in gang rapes in the Western world, dowry deaths in India and clitoridectomies in Africa, all of which are simply allowed to go on. By not offering these women protection, the state represses the private sphere as the means by which it creates a homogeneous masculine self (Peterson 1992c: 46; Tickner 1992: 57–8). Thus for postmodern feminists, the process of normative statecraft involves the state conforming to a gendered logic. As Connell puts it, 'the state is constituted within gender relations as the central institutionalization of gendered power' (Connell 1990: 519; Peterson 1992c: 39, 45). But how does all this relate to IR?

As noted in the first half of this section, postmodernism argues that the international sphere is constructed by the state as the realm of violence and necessity as states set about creating a self. Thus an arbitrary inside/outside dichotomy is constructed (Walker 1993). In endorsing this argument, Peterson (1992b) talks about an implicit or imaginary 'sovereignty contract' drawn up between states, which stipulates that the use of international military force is a necessary evil not so much to protect the state from other states but to enable each state to consolidate and construct an imaginary unified domestic political community. But postmodern feminists have significantly supplemented this argument, by pointing out that the international sphere is constructed as violent in part because states have privileged constructed-masculine modes of thinking and behaviour. In privileging masculinised notions of aggression over accommodation and cooperation, warfare has been, and will continue to be, the natural preserve of states. Moreover, feminist theorists in general have provided a very strong critique of neorealist theory. In much the same way that Robert Cox (1986) has argued that neorealism is not in fact as scientific and value-free as it claims to be because it embodies a conservative set of political values, so feminists have persuasively argued that neorealism is not 'gender-neutral' as it implicitly claims to be, but is inherently value-laden insofar as it embodies and privileges conservative/masculine modes of thinking. Thus Ann Tickner and others have convincingly pointed to the various aspects of masculinist thinking – most notably the privileging of *reductionism*, *separationism* and *reification* – through which neorealist theory has been constructed. Thus neorealism embodies a *reductionist* theoretical approach which exaggerates and *reifies* the importance of anarchy, thereby downgrading the domestic and private spheres; *privileges* military force and power and downgrades empathy and cooperation; *separates* out the international and national spheres as two wholly discrete, *reified* realms and fails to recognise their mutual embeddedness; *reifies* the state's autonomy and in *separating* it out from the private sphere fails to recognise the gendered nature of states; and *reifies* 'objectivity' and 'military rationality', thereby downgrading the importance of morality (see especially Steans 1998: chapter 2; Tickner 1988, 1992: chapter 2).

Postmodernism and the theory of the state and IR

Finally, what of domestic and international agential state power? First, this variant grants the state the lowest level of domestic agential power found in any theory within the social sciences. Postmodernists deny that the state exists as a 'real' institutional or material form. All states are imagined. Moreover, radical constructivists argue that the 'sovereign state' is currently in crisis and its demise is daily becoming more apparent, as globalisation undermines the state both from within and without. Global processes are now impeding the ability of the state to reconstruct itself as a legitimate entity (see especially Camilleri and Falk 1991; Weber 1995; Shapiro and Alker 1996). However, the interesting point, with respect to the typology used in this book, is that this variant accords the state moderate international agential power. Why? Because IR and inter-state conflict is actually constructed by the state through normative statecraft. While international society-centric constructivism allows for a degree of high international agential power because it argues that states can come to cooperate and overcome the collective action problem, radical constructivism, by contrast, asserts that as long as states exist, warfare and violence will continue to constitute the 'normal' means by which IR is conducted. This is because states *must* create a 'threatening other' in order to construct an imaginary unified domestic political community (without which the state could not continue to exist). Or as the feminist Jean Bethke Elshtain puts it, 'Needing others to define ourselves, we will remain inside a state/nation-centred discourse of war and politics, for better and for worse, so long as states remain' (Elshtain 1992: 150). Thus the collective action problem itself is merely an artificial but inevitable construct that will remain so long as states continue to exist. In sum, states are caught up in cycles of international (and domestic) violence because of normative statecraft, which in turn leads to a masculinised state, which privileges repression and aggression against, rather than cooperation and empathy with, other states.

'State-centric' constructivism

A third variant of constructivism might be loosely labelled 'state-centric' (not to be confused with Wendtian statist-constructivism), which captures those theorists who focus on the importance of the national-domestic rather than the international sphere. Accordingly, they tend to focus on individual states or comparative analysis (e.g. Berger 1996; Herman 1996; Katzenstein 1996a; Kier 1996). Clearly the label does not equate with the neorealist notion of state-centricity. It is also important to note that within this broadly defined variant there exists a further set of variants or sub-sets. Differences exist not least between the emphasis placed on the importance of non-state actors, as well as the levels of domestic agential state power. In this section, I shall examine Peter Katzenstein's work as an example of this genre.

Constitutive norms and state structures in Japan: Katzenstein's Cultural Norms and National Security

In his important book *Cultural Norms and National Security* (1996a), Peter Katzenstein provides a micro-analysis, focusing mainly on Japan. He begins by rejecting *systemic* theorising of all kinds. And, in clear contrast to Finnemore's approach, he asserts that '[g]enerally speaking social norms in the international society of states are less dense and weaker than those in domestic society' (Katzenstein 1996a: 42, 20). Specifically, Katzenstein argues that systemic theory is inadequate not least because it 'black-boxes' the state, and fails to examine the complex relations within the state structure itself, as well as important state–society linkages and state–transnational linkages. Moreover, third-image theory tends to portray states as rational unitary actors, where state interests are assumed and are derived exogenously (i.e. prior to social interaction). But, Katzenstein argues, states differ internally in their make-up and, crucially, that this impacts upon their behaviour in the international system. And, in clear contrast to much of constructivist theory, Katzenstein examines the impact of a state's domestic agential power upon norms, as well as the impact of norms upon the state.

Japan provides a particularly useful case study as a means for developing both a critique of neorealism and establishing an alternative 'state-centric' constructivist approach. Japan is of special interest because, first, it has undergone a major paradigm shift in its external security posture – from having been militaristic before 1945 to being pacifist subsequently. Focusing on changing Japanese identity and social norms provides a more adequate explanation than does neorealism's emphasis on changes in the international distribution of power. Secondly, neorealism assumes that Japan should convert its economic power into military power and become a military great power or hegemon to complement its economic great power status. By contrast, Katzenstein shows why the nature of the domestic normative structure makes this an unlikely proposition. Thirdly, as Katzenstein shows, the story of Japan's foreign policy development presents a complex series of twists and turns which can be captured only by a complex second-image approach rather than a monolithic third-image analysis.

Katzenstein's basic theoretical framework

Katzenstein in effect conceives of a domestic normative structure which generates the Japanese state's identity at any point in time (figure 5.5). He focuses on three normative structures that inform state policy choices: economic security norms, external military security norms and internal security norms (though I shall focus only on the first two). In turn, each normative structure can take two main forms: norms can either be contested or uncontested. The basic formula is that where norms are uncontested, so state policy becomes flexible, and the state's domestic and international agential power is enhanced; conversely, where norms are contested, state policy becomes rigid, and agential power in the domestic and international arenas is diminished.

One of the most interesting aspects of Katzenstein's approach is to attribute to the state moderately high levels of domestic agential power or autonomy (see figure 5.6). In his model, normative structures and the state are fully embedded within each other. In clear contrast to Finnemore, the state is not purely derived from norms, but is both a product of and creator of normative structures. Moreover, unlike Finnemore, Katzenstein focuses on domestic state–society relations, as well as state–transnational relations that also shape state policy.

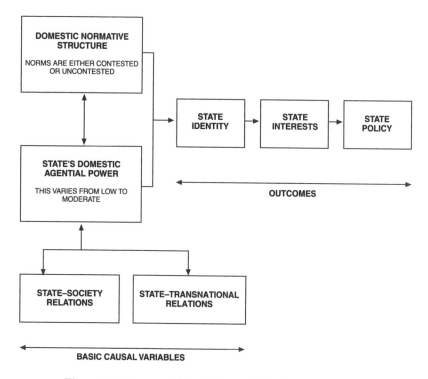

Figure 5.5 Katzenstein's basic theoretical schema

Policy choices: changes in external security posture

The most fundamental question that Katzenstein asks is: why has Japan shifted from a strong militaristic and imperialist foreign policy stance (prevalent before 1945) to a strong pacifist stance since 1945? To explain this, he shows how normative structures – in particular, those of economic as well as military security – have changed. Prior to 1945, economic security norms within Japanese society were *uncontested*. That is, there was a strong societal consensus for a strong pro-active state economic posture. This emerged especially after 1868. It emerged because of the widely held perception that Japan should seek to break its dependence on raw materials imports. Given the view that such a dependency made Japan vulnerable, it was widely accepted that a strong state was required that could propel Japan through the industrialisation process, so as to emerge as a strong economy that could be more self-sufficient, thereby being less vulnerable to foreign powers. Accordingly,

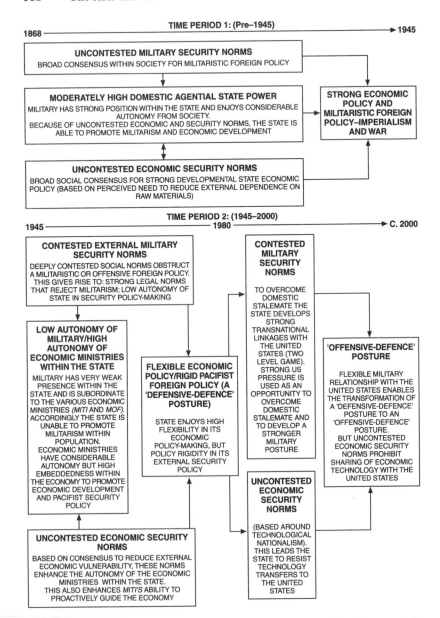

Figure 5.6 Katzenstein's 'state-centric' constructivist theory of the 'normative-adaptive' state

the state initiated a 'military-industrialisation' in order to 'catch up with the West'. But given that such uncontested economic security norms continue today, how does this explain why Japan was militaristic prior to 1945 and pacifist after that date?

The key point here is the changing nature of the military-security normative structure and its relationship to the state's domestic agential power. In the 1868–1945 period, military-security norms were uncontested – that is, there was a broad social consensus for a strong militaristic and imperialist foreign policy stance. Why? Here Katzenstein invokes the importance of the domestic agential power (i.e. autonomy) of the state. First, the state enjoyed a strong autonomy from society, such that the emperor's power and authority was supreme. In particular, within the state itself, the military acquired a high degree of autonomy, being insulated from both cabinet and parliament. Secondly, the military constantly interfaced with society and helped shape an uncontested militaristic normative structure. For example, the military imposed a system of conscription after 1873, and all manner of bodies promoted or inculcated a militaristic spirit into society (e.g. the Imperial Reserve Association and the Youth Association). In short, deliberate state policies were an important component in creating an uncontested security normative structure that promoted external militarism. Hence the state engaged in war and imperialism throughout the 1868–1945 period. But what led to the shift to pacifism after 1945?

As in the 1868–1945 period, economic-security norms have been uncontested (based on the continuing perception that the Japanese state should promote economic development in order to overcome external dependency on raw materials imports). This in turn has led to the predominance of the Ministry of International Trade and Industry (MITI) as well as the Ministry of Finance (MOF) within the state itself. Such uncontested norms have enabled the development of a strong, pro-active and highly flexible economic policy stance by the state. However, unlike in the 1868–1945 period, military-security norms have after 1945 been *deeply contested* mainly as a response to the horrors and shame of the Second World War. Accordingly the military's position within the state has been undermined and taken a back seat to MITI and MOF. Moreover, social and legal norms have prohibited a militaristic role in the international system. These include: *Article 9 of the Constitution* (the pacifist clause); the *three non-nuclear principles* (prohibiting any type of nuclear weapons policy); the *prohibition of arms exports* under certain circumstances; the commitment to a *military spending figure of only 1 per cent of national income*; and the creation of the *self-defence forces* in 1954, that can take no part in foreign 'adventures'. In short, the convergence of uncontested economic- and military-security norms prior to 1945 led to international militarism, while the convergence of uncontested economic-security norms and *contested* military-security norms after 1945 have led to a pacifist international stance (or what Katzenstein calls a 'defensive-defence posture').

Katzenstein reveals some important twists in the story, which cannot be captured by third-image analysis. First, he argues that although Japan has maintained its pacifist stance, nevertheless this does not imply an inert security posture. In particular, he points out that Japan's military power (measured in dollar spending) puts it within the top three in the world, and that Japan has shifted from a *defensive-defence* to an *offensive-defence* security posture. How has this occurred? Particularly since 1980, various prime ministers (especially Nakasone) have sought to strengthen the military power of Japan, albeit within the constraining parameters of social and legal normative structures. This has been made possible only because the state has in effect played a 'two-level game'. That is, the state has overcome strong domestic resistance to an offensive-defence posture by using external US pressure for a militarily stronger Japan as a 'resource' to achieve its objectives. This strategy is known in Japan as *gaiatsu*, whereby the Japanese government creates the appearance to its domestic community that it has no choice but to change military-security policy in order to conform to 'overwhelming' US pressure. This stands in contrast to the neorealist argument that Japan is remilitarising in the face of US demands for the end of 'free-riding'. Rather, Katzenstein argues, Japanese leaders have *chosen* to follow this path and have *used* US pressures as a resource to overcome domestic stalemate. Does this mean that Japan is now moving towards a possible *Pax Nipponica* (which could replace the declining *Pax Americana*), as neorealists often suggest?

Katzenstein denies this proposition by providing another fascinating twist in the story of Japan's post-1980 foreign policy stance. Thus while Japan has forged closer military ties with the United States, it has also been highly intransigent and inflexible in its economic relationship with it. US pressure has been equally strong, if not stronger, with respect to issuing demands for the Japanese to share their economic technology. But precisely because economic norms remain uncontested and stipulate a strong sense of 'technological nationalism' (as a continuing means to overcome external economic dependence on raw materials), so Japan has refused to share its economic technology. What this tells us is that Japan has only 'conformed' to US pressures in the military sphere because this suited it, enabling it to overcome domestic normative limits to a more assertive defence posture. Moreover, Japan is unlikely to have sufficient international agential power and assertiveness to play the role of hegemon. Ultimately, Japan is not prepared to consider hegemony because military-security norms remain deeply contested. The most that can be achieved on this front is the adoption of an 'offensive-defence' structure, as opposed to a purely offensive military stance (which is the leitmotif or fundamental pre-requisite for hegemony).

Katzenstein's state-centric constructivist theory of the state

One of the most interesting aspects of Katzenstein's approach is to pose a mutually embedded relationship between normative structures and the state's domestic agential power. In contrast to most constructivists, Katzenstein argues that the state can have different degrees of domestic agential power and that these impact upon norms, and vice versa. So, for example, in the 1868–1945 period, the state had a moderately high degree of domestic agential power and was able to develop a militaristic foreign policy. But this was reinforced by uncontested military- and economic-security norms. This, in turn, propelled a militaristic foreign policy. However, after 1945 contested military-security norms and uncontested economic-security norms undermined the autonomy of the military, and promoted the autonomy of the principal economic ministries within the state (MITI and MOF). This in turn led to a pacifist foreign policy stance (as well as a rapid rise to economic superpower status). In general, uncontested normative structures have led to policy flexibility (well exemplified by MITI's guidance of the economy since 1945); conversely, contested normative structures have led to policy rigidity. Even so, Japan has recently shifted to an 'offensive-defensive' posture, which has been achieved by the playing of two-level games by the state (which suggests that the state has a moderate degree of domestic agential capacity and is not merely a passive victim of domestic normative structure).

As regards international agential power, Katzenstein's position is complex, if somewhat unclear. Thus when military security norms were uncontested (and promoted a militaristic foreign policy), so the state eschewed international cooperation and implemented an aggressive and imperialistic foreign policy. This suggests only a moderate international agential power. Conversely, after 1945 the normative structure has led to a relatively passive foreign policy. In his comparison with Germany, Katzenstein argues that Japan has to an extent withdrawn from the international system, while Germany has sought to cooperate with other states in a 'Grotian community of states', which accords the German state a relatively high degree of international agential power. In short,

Katzenstein's argument well exemplifies Alexander Wendt's (1987) felicitous phrase: that 'anarchy is what states make of it', and that international agential power will vary across states. Either way, though, for Katzenstein, states are much freer of international structures than is the case in international systemic theory (as in Waltz or Finnemore).

Discussion questions

- What are the key differences between constructivist and 'rationalist' theories of the state and IR?

- How, if at all, does the constructivist definition of international society differ from that used by Hedley Bull and the English school?

- How does Finnemore end up by granting the state higher levels of international agential power than does Keohane?

- In terms of their theories of the state and IR, what are the key differences between international society-centric constructivism, radical constructivism and neorealism?

- Why is it that, for radical constructivists, war is ultimately not a threat but the condition of the state's reproduction?

- What do radical constructivists actually mean when they say that the state is not 'real'?

- What does postmodern feminist theory add to the radical constructivist theory of the state and IR?

- How does Katzenstein's 'state-centric constructivist' theory of the state and IR differ from that of Finnemore's international society-centric approach?

- Why has Japan according to Katzenstein shifted from a 'passive-defence' policy to an 'offensive-defence' policy since 1980, and yet is unlikely to shift to a hegemonic security policy?

Suggestions for further reading

One of the best ways into constructivism are the first and last chapters of Finnemore (1996). From there, the reader can follow up with summaries in Adler (1997); Ruggie (1998: 1–39); Price and Reus-Smit (1998); and the introduction to the Katzenstein edited volume (Katzenstein 1996c). Biersteker and Weber (1996a, 1996b) provide excellent introductions to constructivist approaches to state sovereignty; see also Wendt (1999). In addition to Finnemore (1996), other important examples of international society-centric theory are found in Adler and Haas (1992); Sikkink (1993); Klotz (1995); Strang (1996), Price and Tannenwald (1996). General summary statements on radical constructivism can be found in Devetak (1996) and, though from a more critical perspective, Jarvis (1998). The reader would do well to proceed on to Ashley (1989) and Weber (1995) for discussion of the state and IR, while Connell (1990) is useful for a more sociological discussion. Excellent introductions to postmodern as well as modernist feminist theories of the state and IR can be found in Peterson (1992a, 1992b); True (1996); Steans (1998) and especially Tickner (1992). And finally, for 'state-centric' constructivism, see Berger (1996); Katzenstein (1996a); Herman (1996); Kier (1996).

6   Weberian historical sociology

Introduction: the 'two waves' of neo-Weberian historical sociology

In the last decade, IR as a discipline has been undergoing a crisis as its master-paradigm, neorealism, is increasingly seen as limited, if not obsolete. Accordingly, IR is thought to have reached an impasse (Ferguson and Mansbach 1988; Halliday 1994). Why? It is perceived by critics that neorealism has many blind spots, four of which are: a lack of a theory of the state and an exaggeration of 'structure' to the detriment of 'agency'; an inability to theorise the integrated nature of global politics, given the assumption that there is a fundamental separation or dichotomy between the international and national realms; a lack of a theory of international change; and a static a-historical approach. One response to the crisis of neorealism made by some IR scholars has been to turn towards neo-Weberian historical sociology (WHS) to provide a way out of the impasse (e.g. Jarvis 1989; Halliday 1994; Hobson 1997, 1998a; Hall 1998; Hobden 1998; Seabrooke 2000). Thus WHS is thought to offer a theory of the state that is allegedly missing in neorealism, given that WHS problematises the state, and seeks to describe and explain its origins, powers and changing configurations over time. This also allegedly offers a means to go beyond neorealist structuralism by bringing 'agency' back in. Secondly, WHS advocates an intimate relationship between the internal and external realms, thereby offering a potentially rich 'integrationist' approach. While Waltz actually recognises that the international can shape the national, he nevertheless dismisses the possibility that the national can shape the international realm. Thirdly, WHS provides a theory of change, which allegedly helps counter neorealism's static approach. Accordingly, it claims to replace neorealism's 'continuity problematic' with an historicist approach.

But there is a double irony here in that, first neorealism *can* in fact shed *some* light in each one of these areas (see chapter 2 above) and, secondly, much of WHS, which is thought to provide a solution for some of neorealism's 'omissions', turns out to perfectly replicate neorealism. Indeed, while the 'promise' of WHS is to go beyond neorealism, many critics within IR have suggested that WHS has in fact failed to realise this ambition (e.g. Scholte 1993: 23, 96, 101–2, 112; Spruyt 1994; Halperin 1998). And despite its claim to be non-reductionist, various scholars have argued that the approach is in fact politically reductionist (e.g. Cammack 1989; Jessop 1990: 283–8; Fuat Keyman 1997: chapter 3). This chapter will argue that such criticisms are partly correct, but also partly incorrect. I argue that there have been 'two waves' of WHS. The 'first wave' (typified by Skocpol and Tilly) has in fact unwittingly applied neorealism to theorise state autonomy and explain socio-economic and political change, and thereby failed to live up to the 'promise' of WHS. However, I argue that a recent 'second wave' has sought to go beyond its first-wave predecessor (and hence beyond neorealism), and accordingly provides the most fruitful avenue for a non-realist and non-reductionist WHS approach to the state and IR. In sum, I argue that first-wave WHS effectively 'kicks the state back out', whereas second-wave WHS seeks to bring the state as an agent back in to the analysis of IR.

'First-wave' WHS: a neorealist international relations of domestic social and political change

Theda Skocpol's States and Social Revolutions: 'kicking the state back out'

One of the key first-wave WHS writers is Theda Skocpol, whose book *States and Social Revolutions* (1979) caused not only a stir in historical sociology, but subsequently provided a base for the integration of WHS into IR. Her explicit objective was to 'bring the state back in' as an agent into the analysis of social change (a phrase that she became famous for in her 1985 piece which went by the same name). Against liberalism and Marxism, Skocpol argued that social change (which she examines through the case study of social revolution) could not be understood in terms of domestic economic forces or national class struggles. Rather, social revolutions (and social change more generally) had to be understood through two key concepts: *state autonomy* and the military exigencies of the *international states system*. It was primarily this emphasis that opened up sociology to international relations, thereby enabling a dialogue between the two disciplines (Halliday 1994).

In contrast to Marxism, Skocpol argued that states could not be 'reduced to', but have a 'potential autonomy' from domestic class interests. States have interests which sometimes bring them into conflict with dominant classes, most especially in the sphere of taxation. In particular, when states go to war they need to increase taxation and/or push through economic reforms to enhance the state's military power base – reforms that often go against the interests of the dominant class. Moreover, in contrast to neo-Marxism's concept of the 'relative autonomy' of the state, Skocpol suggests that states do not always secure the long-term reproduction of the dominant class or the mode of production (MOP). Thus when states pursue their autonomous military interests, they sometimes suffer defeat in war, which in turn leads on to social revolution and the overthrow of the dominant class (Skocpol 1979: 24–33).

It might seem, therefore, that Skocpol has succeeded in 'bringing the state back in' as an independent autonomous power actor into the analysis of social change in that she grants the state 'potential' domestic agential power the ability to conduct policy free of domestic constraint). However, I shall argue that Skocpol reproduced the neorealist analysis of Waltz and especially Gilpin, such that I conclude that far from 'bringing the state back in', she has in fact, in typical neorealist fashion, succeeded only in throwing or 'kicking the state back out', thereby stripping the state of international agential power. As noted on pp. 7–8 above, international agential power refers to the ability of the state to conduct policy free of international constraint, and at the extreme to buck the logic of anarchy or the international structure. My claim is then based on the fact that, as with Waltz and Gilpin, Skocpol reduces the state to the international political system such that the state is discounted (albeit unwittingly) as an independent variable. At this point it is important to note that in order to fully understand the following discussion, it is vital to have first absorbed the discussion of neorealism in chapter 2 (see pp. 17–44).

Skocpol's neorealist theory of social revolutions

Figure 6.1 depicts the remarkable similarities between the analyses of Skocpol and Gilpin. Like Gilpin and Waltz, Skocpol subscribes to a 'passive-adaptive' theory of the state, in which the state's principal task is to adapt, or conform to the logic of the international political system and international military conflict between states. We noted in chapter 2 that Gilpin adopted Waltz's basic approach in that he privileges the logic of anarchy (and hence the adaptive state), but supplements this with a set of *intervening* variables which specify the actual processes through

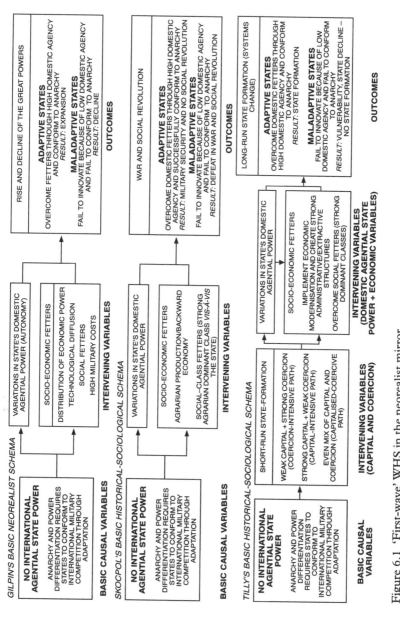

Figure 6.1 'First-wave' WHS in the neorealist mirror

GILPIN'S BASIC NEOREALIST SCHEMA

NO INTERNATIONAL AGENTIAL STATE POWER

ANARCHY AND POWER DIFFERENTIATION REQUIRES STATES TO CONFORM TO INTERNATIONAL MILITARY COMPETITION THROUGH ADAPTATION

BASIC CAUSAL VARIABLES

VARIATIONS IN STATE'S DOMESTIC AGENTIAL POWER (AUTONOMY)

SOCIO-ECONOMIC FETTERS

DISTRIBUTION OF ECONOMIC POWER

TECHNOLOGICAL DIFFUSION

SOCIAL FETTERS

HIGH MILITARY COSTS

INTERVENING VARIABLES

RISE AND DECLINE OF THE GREAT POWERS

ADAPTIVE STATES
OVERCOME FETTERS THROUGH HIGH DOMESTIC AGENCY AND CONFORM TO ANARCHY
RESULT: EXPANSION

MALADAPTIVE STATES
FAIL TO INNOVATE BECAUSE OF LOW DOMESTIC AGENCY AND FAIL TO CONFORM TO ANARCHY
RESULT: DECLINE

OUTCOMES

SKOCPOL'S BASIC HISTORICAL-SOCIOLOGICAL SCHEMA

NO INTERNATIONAL AGENTIAL STATE POWER

ANARCHY AND POWER DIFFERENTIATION REQUIRES STATES TO CONFORM TO INTERNATIONAL MILITARY COMPETITION THROUGH ADAPTATION

BASIC CAUSAL VARIABLES

VARIATIONS IN STATE'S DOMESTIC AGENTIAL POWER

SOCIO-ECONOMIC FETTERS

AGRARIAN PRODUCTION/BACKWARD ECONOMY

SOCIAL-CLASS FETTERS (STRONG AGRARIAN DOMINANT CLASS *VIS-À-VIS* THE STATE)

INTERVENING VARIABLES

WAR AND SOCIAL REVOLUTION

ADAPTIVE STATES
OVERCOME DOMESTIC FETTERS THROUGH HIGH DOMESTIC AGENCY AND SUCCESSFULLY CONFORM TO ANARCHY
RESULT: MILITARY SECURITY AND NO SOCIAL REVOLUTION

MALADAPTIVE STATES
FAIL TO INNOVATE BECAUSE OF LOW DOMESTIC AGENCY AND FAIL TO CONFORM TO ANARCHY
RESULT: DEFEAT IN WAR AND SOCIAL REVOLUTION

OUTCOMES

TILLY'S BASIC HISTORICAL-SOCIOLOGICAL SCHEMA

NO INTERNATIONAL AGENTIAL STATE POWER

ANARCHY AND POWER DIFFERENTIATION REQUIRES STATES TO CONFORM TO INTERNATIONAL MILITARY COMPETITION THROUGH ADAPTATION

BASIC CAUSAL VARIABLES

SHORT-RUN STATE-FORMATION

WEAK CAPITAL + STRONG COERCION (COERCION-INTENSIVE PATH)

STRONG CAPITAL + WEAK COERCION (CAPITAL-INTENSIVE PATH)

EVEN MIX OF CAPITAL AND COERCION (CAPITALISED-COERCIVE PATH)

INTERVENING VARIABLES (CAPITAL AND COERCION)

VARIATIONS IN STATE'S DOMESTIC AGENTIAL POWER

SOCIO-ECONOMIC FETTERS

IMPLEMENT ECONOMIC MODERNISATION AND CREATE STRONG ADMINISTRATIVE/EXTRACTIVE STRUCTURES

OVERCOME SOCIAL FETTERS (STRONG DOMINANT CLASSES)

INTERVENING VARIABLES (DOMESTIC AGENTIAL STATE POWER + ECONOMIC VARIABLES)

LONG-RUN STATE FORMATION (SYSTEMS CHANGE)

ADAPTIVE STATES
OVERCOME DOMESTIC FETTERS THROUGH HIGH DOMESTIC AGENCY AND CONFORM TO ANARCHY
RESULT: STATE FORMATION

MALADAPTIVE STATES
FAIL TO INNOVATE BECAUSE OF LOW DOMESTIC AGENCY AND FAIL TO CONFORM TO ANARCHY
RESULT: VULNERABILITY, STATE DECLINE – NO STATE FORMATION

OUTCOMES

which some states become adaptive or maladaptive. These comprise state autonomy (domestic agential state power) on the one hand and economic and social 'fetters' on the other. Gilpin argues that maladaptive states are unable to conform to anarchy because they have low domestic institutional autonomy and are consequently unable to overcome social fetters which block the development of state capacity. This results in great power decline and military vulnerability. Conversely, states are adaptive when they have high domestic agency or autonomy which enables them to overcome domestic fetters, thereby promoting survival and even the rise to great power. Domestic agential state power is an intervening variable because it is relevant only to the extent that it enables or hinders the state from conforming to the primary logic of anarchy; that is, it is ultimately reduced to the 'primitive' structure of the anarchic international system. In essence for Gilpin, as well as Waltz, states must be adaptive – that is, they must constantly upgrade and modernise their economies (i.e. emulate the successful practices of the leading states) so as to enhance their military power base; failure to emulate leads to military vulnerability. In addition, states must be able to maintain a sufficient rate of taxation in the face of domestic opposition. This is precisely the same schema that Skocpol employs, as figures 6.1 and 6.2 show. What Skocpol adds to Gilpin's analysis is the point that maladaptive states are punished not just through defeat in war but also social revolution.

Figure 6.2, which precisely mirrors Gilpin's theory of the rise and decline of the great powers (see figure 2.4, p. 34) depicts Skocpol's overall approach. In line with Gilpin, Skocpol adds a set of intervening variables which supplement the basic causal variable of anarchy. These comprise:

(1) varying domestic agential state power or varying institutional state autonomy
(2) internal social fetters (the power of dominant agrarian classes)
(3) the agrarian nature of the economy.

Skocpol's basic claim is that in order to conform to anarchy, states must enjoy high domestic institutional autonomy in order to push through economic and fiscal reforms against resistance put up by the various domestic fetters; failure to conform leads to defeat in war and social revolution. Thus in France and China, powerful noble dominant classes blocked the states' attempts at increasing taxation and modernising reforms, both of which were designed to enhance the states' military power base. These reforms were blocked because both states had insufficient domestic agential power or autonomy to overcome these powerful internal blockages or fetters. Because these 'proto-

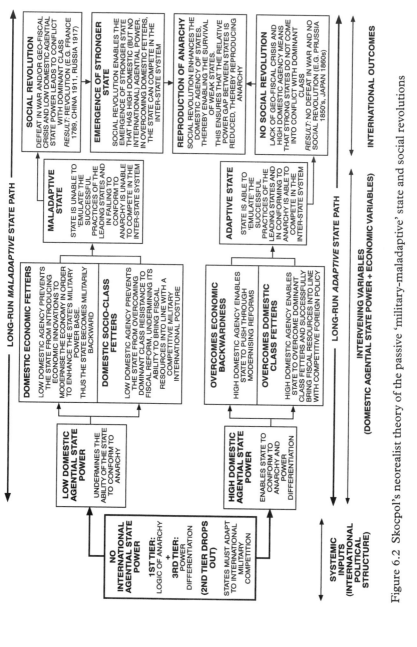

Figure 6.2 Skocpol's neorealist theory of the passive 'military-maladaptive' state and social revolutions

bureaucratic' states were inadequately centralised, they were unable to directly collect taxes from the provinces, and accordingly had no choice but to rely on the nobles to collect taxes, much of which were not passed on to the central state. Accordingly fiscal crisis set in, which undermined these states' ability to adequately compete internationally (since warfare required high amounts of taxation). In turn, military breakdown led to social revolution in France in 1789 and China in 1911. In Russia, the autocratic state did not face a strong dominant class (which had been weakened and made dependent upon the state for its income through state service). The main fetter in Russia was the backwardness of the agrarian economy which impeded the state's military capacity. Here the low domestic agential power (institutional autonomy) of the state prevented it from implementing sufficient modernising economic reforms so as to enhance its military power base (Skocpol 1979: 85–9). In contrast to Prussia and Japan, she argued in classic neorealist fashion that, 'the sluggishness of Russian agriculture after the [1861] emancipation fettered tsarist attempts to adapt imperial Russia to the exigencies of the modernising European states system' (Skocpol 1979: 109). Accordingly the maladaptive state was defeated in 1905 (against Japan). Moreover, military exhaustion during the First World War led on to social revolution in 1917.

By contrast, Skocpol points to the cases of Prussia and Japan, in which high domestic agential state power in the face of weak domestic fetters enabled them to adapt their societies in order to adequately compete in the inter-state system. Accordingly, neither state succumbed to defeat in war or social revolution. Thus as Skocpol put it, again in typical neorealist fashion, both Japan and Prussia 'adapted speedily and smoothly to international [military] exigencies through reforms instituted from above by autocratic political authorities' (Skocpol 1979: 110). Moreover she concludes that France, Russia and China

endured revolutionary political crises because agrarian structures impinged upon autocratic and proto-bureaucratic state organizations in ways that blocked or fettered monarchical initiatives in coping with escalating international military competition in a world undergoing uneven transformation by capitalism. (Skocpol 1979: 99, also 50, 110, 285–6).

Skocpol's neorealist theory of the state and the international system

Various IR scholars have suggested that Skocpol's theory of the state advances beyond neorealism, in large part because it focuses on developments within the 'second tier' (i.e. state–society relations), and that it specifies certain powers of the state (e.g. Halliday 1994). Steve Hobden's careful – and, indeed, highly sophisticated – interpretation argues that compared to neorealism, Skocpol develops a much richer theory of the state though a less systematic theory of the international system (Hobden 1998: 88–93, 178). But I argue here the inverse: that Skocpol precisely utilises Waltz's 'rich' definition of the international political structure, though she uses Gilpin's relatively crude and parsimonious neorealist theory of the state. Hobden's point, that for Skocpol 'there is no international system beyond war in her analysis' (i.e. that she reduces the system to war and that outside of war there is no system) poses an interesting challenge to my argument (Hobden 1998: 92). But my claim is that while Skocpol does indeed fail to explicitly develop a theory of the international system, nevertheless her approach and account of social revolutions proceeds *as if* she had done so. In short, a 'rich' neorealist theory of the international system is implicitly contained within her approach. How so?

First, with regard to the (European) international political structure, Skocpol states that it was one 'in which no one imperial state controlled the entire territory of Europe and her overseas conquests' (Skocpol 1979: 20–1). This is equivalent to Waltz's first tier – the ordering principle of anarchy. Skocpol's schema is equivalent because the anarchic system appears as a 'realm of (military) necessity' in which states must adapt through competition and emulation if they are to survive (as well as avoid social revolution). Moreover, when she discusses international relations she always equates it with an arena of conflicting and competing states (as Hobden argues). Secondly, power differentiation, or the uneven spread of military capacity among states (Waltz's third tier), is implicitly invoked as a central aspect of Skocpol's whole approach, because it was the fundamental military challenge that the stronger states posed that led on to defeat in war and social revolution in the weaker states. Thus relatively backward France faced the more advanced British and succumbed to military and political breakdown in 1789; backward China faced the more advanced states of the West and suffered similarly in 1911; and the under-developed Russian state was undermined by the more advanced German state during the First World War and accordingly suffered social revolution in 1917.

Skocpol might point to various arguments that she has made which seem to reject a neorealist definition of the international system. Thus in chapter 1 she specifies that the inter-state system is *interdependent* with the international economy and that neither are reducible to the other, which suggests a potentially non-realist approach. But this is little more than a red herring, because she argues throughout the book, as does Gilpin, that a state's position within the international economy is important only insofar as it enables or hinders that state from engaging in military competition. The international economic system does not acquire any causal autonomy in her approach, and remains outside of her theoretical framework (see also Hobden 1998: 88–90). In short, her implicit definition of the international system is precisely equivalent to that found in Waltz.

But the litmus test for this claim is whether the state as an agent in IR drops out as an independent variable. This can be rephrased: does Skocpol succeed in 'bringing the state back in', as she claims to have done (thereby implying a non-realist approach)? Surely it could be argued that her theory of the state is non-realist because, for her, the state responds to class pressures as well as international anarchy? Indeed, she conceptualises the state as 'Janus-faced' – as having a dual anchorage in domestic socio-economic relations on the one hand, and the inter-state system on the other (Skocpol 1979: 32). Thus when defining the state she quotes Otto Hintze, to the effect that two phenomena above all condition 'the real organization of the state. These are, first, the structure of social classes, and second, the external ordering of the states – their position relative to each other, and their over-all position in the world' (Hintze 1975: 183, cited in Skocpol 1979: 30–1, and 22, 29). Moreover, Skocpol would claim that she accords the state significant causal autonomy.

But I argue that while Skocpol opens up the 'black-box' of state and state–society relations, unlike Waltz, she does so in a way that is entirely congruent with Gilpin's 'modified neorealism'. As with Gilpin, a state's domestic agential power or autonomy, as well as state–society relations, are only *intervening variables*; that is, they are salient in her analysis only to the extent that they enable or prevent a state from conforming to anarchy and military competition. Thus high domestic agential power or institutional autonomy promotes adaptability, low domestic autonomy creates maladaptability. That is, states and states' domestic autonomy are reduced to the 'primitive' structure of anarchy. State autonomy and class forces therefore enable or constrain state adaptability, but they do not define state behaviour – that is left to the anarchic political system. For Skocpol, as for Waltz '[t]he game one has to win is defined by the [anarchic] structure that determines the kind of player who is likely to prosper' (Waltz 1979: 92, 128). Thus despite all the talk about state autonomy and state–society relations, reflected especially in the first part of Skocpol's definition of the state, it is ultimately all for nothing because the state is squarely reduced to the requirements of inter-national anarchy. As in Waltz, the state is but a mere passive victim of exogenous anarchy. Thus while Skocpol criticises Marxists for reducing the state to class interests, I suggest that she is also guilty of reductionism because she reduces the state to anarchy.

Surely, however, she succeeds in bringing 'class variables' into the analysis, because she argues that social revolutions occur only when peasant class forces mobilise against the state in response to adverse socio-economic circumstances. But the central argument of her chapters 4–6 is that the revolutions which began as class revolts against the noble dominant classes were hijacked by political elites which emerged during the revolutions. The key point is that these political elites did not fulfil or meet the requirements of revolutionary classes; rather, such classes were in effect used and mobilised by these political elites as they sought to centralise and enhance state capacity. Moreover, the revolution was ultimately crucial only because it undermined the social fetters that had made the state vulnerable to external attack in the first place. The final outcome of each revolution was a more centralised state which had sufficient domestic agential power or autonomy to push through reforms against weakened social groups in society, so as to make the state more competitive internationally (Skocpol 1979: 161–2). Revolutionary class movements turn out to be the unwitting agents of centralising political elites – they are functional to the enhancement of state capacity. This logically implies that class pressures have no determining influence on the state. Moreover, perhaps the central lesson of Skocpol's theory of social revolution is that states which conform to the social needs of strong domestic noble dominant classes will fail to conform to anarchy. Accordingly, they will be selected out by the anarchic system and punished through defeat in war and social revolution.

Skocpol's theory nicely complements Waltz's claim that adaptive state behaviour – emulation and balancing – serves to unintentionally reproduce the anarchic states system. This is because, for Waltz, these adaptive processes reduce the 'relative power gap' between states, thereby preventing any one state from transforming anarchy into imperial hierarchy. Social revolution turns out to unintentionally reproduce anarchy because it serves to strengthen the state's long-term military and political capacity, the better to conform to anarchy. Thus revolution unintentionally enables a reduction in the relative power gap between states because it allows even the weak states to maintain their existence in the long run, thereby reproducing the multi-state system.

In sum, it should be clear by now that while the state is granted varying degrees of domestic agential power or institutional autonomy, nevertheless the state has no international agential power either to determine the international political structure or mitigate its constraining logic. And given that domestic agential power or institutional autonomy is functional to a state's capacity to govern, and that a state's capacity to govern is determined by its ability to conform to anarchy, it seems fair to conclude that the state is ultimately reduced to anarchy. Thus the oft-made critique that Skocpol reifies the state and endows it with too much agency or voluntarism is incorrect. For the fact is that the state (i.e. the second tier of the international political structure) drops out as an explanatory variable and is stripped of international agential power. It was surely not for nothing that Skocpol (1979: 31) ironically, though correctly, described her theory of the state as '(neo)realist', even if she was unaware of the fatal ramifications this would have for her impassioned plea to 'bring the state back in'. Thus in the end, Skocpol unwittingly 'kicked the state back out'.

Charles Tilly's neorealist theory of states systems change (state formation)

Conventional understanding among IR scholars assumes that neorealism, especially in its Waltzian format, is unable to provide a theory of international change not least because of its emphasis on *static continuity* (Cox 1986: 243–5). Specifically, John Ruggie famously argued that by 'dropping' the second tier – the differentiation of the units (i.e. the state and state–society relations), Waltzian neorealism is unable to explain 'systems change', especially the transition from one form of states system to another (or what sociologists simply refer to as 'state formation'). This is because if the second tier drops out as an independent variable, and there is no change in the first variable (anarchy exists in both systems), this leaves only the third – the distribution of capabilities. And since no change is discernible there, Ruggie argues that Waltz is unable to explain the rise of the modern sovereign state system (Ruggie 1986: 141–52; Ruggie 1998: 132–3, chapters 5, 7). Accordingly, Ruggie concludes that neorealism 'contains only a reproductive logic, but no transformational logic' (Ruggie 1986: 152). But from our discussion so far, it should be clear that, *contra* Ruggie, neorealism *can* explain *historical systems change*. We noted in chapter 2 that Gilpin *is* able to explain historical systems change by invoking anarchy (the first tier) as the independent variable. For Gilpin, the anarchic system required states to adapt from feudal heteronomy to sovereignty in order to resolve fiscal crisis brought on by spiralling international military costs between 1550 and 1660. By implication, Waltz's emphasis on the logic of anarchy *is* also able to explain historical systems change; an ironic conclusion given that Waltz missed this point in his defence against Ruggie's critique (Waltz 1986: 323–30). Perhaps nowhere is the ability of neorealism to explain international systems change clearer than in the work of Charles Tilly.

Tilly charts two phases in the development of his thinking on state formation (Tilly 1990: 11–12). The early phase covered his pioneering edited volume *The Formation of National States in Western Europe* (Tilly 1975a, and 1975b, 1975c) as well as his famous piece 'War Making and State Making as Organized Crime', in *Bringing the State Back In* (Evans, Rueschemeyer and Skocpol 1985). The later phase allegedly opened with his book *Coercion, Capital and European States, AD 990–1990* (Tilly 1990). In fact, I shall argue that while the approach of his second phase succeeds in adding empirical sensitivity to his earlier work, it nevertheless remains confined within the same neorealist problematic of the early phase. And, overall, I conclude that Tilly, like Skocpol, Gilpin and Waltz, effectively 'kicks the state back out' by denying it any international agential power to shape the international political structure, let alone mitigate its constraining logic.

Two Tillys or one? A neorealist theory of systems change

In his 1990 book Tilly set out to overcome what he saw as the chief limitation of the argument made in his earlier work (found especially in his collaborative volume, 1975a). The principal limitation as he now saw it was that in his earlier work he had paradoxically formulated a *unilinear* path of state formation: 'paradoxically', because by specifying a single path that all states followed – one which ran from war to extraction and repression to state formation – Tilly and his colleagues had merely substituted a new unilinear story for the old traditional one (Tilly 1990: 11–12). The central rationale for his 1990 work was to describe and account for *variations* in state formation so as to overcome the problem of unilinearity. The objective here was to produce a *complex* or dual/non-reductionist theory of state formation in which two logics – capital and coercion – variously interact to produce different paths of state formation. Put in 'sociological' or 'IR speak', Tilly is implicitly trying to produce a complex approach that would go beyond the *parsimony* of neorealism (as well as Marxism, WST and liberalism) – although he never put it as such. But I argue that he failed to produce such a complex theory and in fact succeeded only in reproducing a reductionist neorealist logic, not least because his central question implied a neorealist answer (to which I return below).

Figure 6.1 (p. 177) depicts the remarkable similarities between the analyses of Skocpol, Gilpin and Tilly. Like Gilpin and Skocpol, Tilly subscribes to a 'military-adaptive' theory of the state, in which the

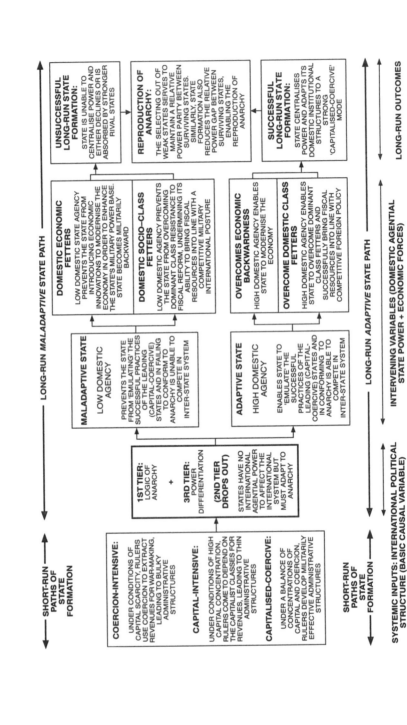

Figure 6.3 Tilly's neorealist theory of the passive 'military-adaptive/maladaptive' state in long-run state formation

state's principal task is to adapt, or conform to the logic of anarchy (i.e. international military competition between states).

Tilly's overall theory is summarised in figure 6.3 (which precisely mirrors Gilpin's theory of the rise and decline of the great powers and state formation, as shown in figure 2.4, see p. 34). In line with Gilpin and Skocpol, Tilly adds a set of intervening variables which supplement the basic causal variable of anarchy. These comprise: (1) varying domestic agential state power or institutional state autonomy; (2) internal social fetters (the power of dominant agrarian and capitalist classes); (3) the agrarian nature of the economy. For Tilly, the logic of anarchy is the basic variable. Thus states must upgrade their economies and administrations in order to increase taxation so as to conform to anarchy. In order to enhance taxation, states must centralise their power. To achieve this, states must enjoy high domestic agential power or autonomy in order to push through the required domestic reforms against the resistance put up by the various domestic fetters. Failure to conform leads to defeat in war and decline or even extinction.

Tilly's central question is in two parts, the first of which reads: 'what accounts for the great variation over time and space in the kinds of states that have prevailed in Europe since AD 990?' (Tilly 1990: 32, 54, 63, 190). This leads him to account for short-term variations in state formation trajectories. Tilly sets out to overcome the 'problem of unilinearity' by specifying three distinct paths or routes of state formation: the 'coercion-intensive', the 'capital-intensive' and the 'capitalised-coercive'. It is primarily at this point of his analysis that the varying configurations of capital and coercion become important. Thus one group of states employed a coercive-intensive path which included Russia, Hungary, Serbia, Sweden and Brandenburg. In these countries there was a distinct lack of either capital or commercialised production and trade. Here rulers sought to pacify the noble–aristocratic dominant class initially through violence (e.g. in Russia under Ivan III and Ivan IV, in the period 1462–1584), and later by making the nobility dependent on state service for their livelihood. A lack of concentrated capital forced rulers to use large doses of coercion against society in order to extract or, more accurately, squeeze, the required revenues for successful war-making. As a result, an absolutist despotic state emerged with a large bulky administrative structure (1990: 137–43).

The second route is characterised as 'capital-intensive', which in-cluded Venice, Genoa and the Dutch Republic (as well as various other urban confederations). The abundance of capital and merchants meant that rulers could easily extract taxation, such that the use of coercion was not necessary. Accordingly, no coercion under conditions of strong concentration of capital led to small or 'thin' state institutions. However, in the process rulers became dependent on capitalists, such that capital came to dominate the state (1990: 143–51). The third route – the 'capitalised-coercive' – was characterised by states that held a balance between capital and coercion, typified by Britain and France. It is the discussion of this path that is most crucial to Tilly's overall theory of state formation. The capitalised-coercive path proved to be the most effective in terms of meeting international competition, and hence adapting to anarchy.

Thus far it would seem that Tilly has gone beyond the 'unilinear' and reductionist approach of his earlier work, in that different concentrations of capital and coercion explain different short-term trajectories of state formation. But it is the second part of his central question that really gives the game away: that despite the short-run variations in state formation, nevertheless he asks, 'why did European states eventually converge on different variants of the national state?' (1990: 32, 54, 63, 190). It is particularly at this point that the teleology and reductionism of his neorealist approach becomes apparent. For he argues that capital-intensive structures held their own for centuries 'until the *sheer scale of war* with nationally recruited armies and navies overwhelmed their efficient but compact military power (1990: 151, emphasis mine). And because of the massive costs of war, by the eighteenth and nineteenth centuries, the *large scale* commercial and industrial states began to militarily prevail within the international states system (1990: 15, 28, 63–6, 83–4, 187–91). That is, capital-intensive states lasted until the scale of war costs outflanked them and rendered them maladaptive. Moreover, it was not simply the lack of scale that mattered. A major reason why Venice and other capital-intensive states failed to adapt and develop was because they had insufficient domestic agential power to centralise state power against the various domestic fetters (1990: 160). Coercion-intensive states also had insufficient domestic agential power or autonomy to move against the nobles. Strong nobles acted as fetters to state formation because they failed to pass on much of the tax revenues that they had collected from the peasantry, thus starving the central state of sufficient revenues to wage successful war. At the extreme Poland, with its low domestic agential power in the face of a strong noble class, was selected out by the system to be tragically absorbed by its Russian, Austrian and Prussian neighbours (Tilly 1990: 139; 1975b: 44). By contrast, the capitalised-coercive states were better able to adapt to the increasing costs of war because of their greater scale, as well as their higher domestic agential state power and high concentration of capital.

It should by now be apparent that Tilly has developed a reductionist neorealist explanation of state formation, in which the states that could adapt to anarchy and international military competition survived and developed (i.e. the capitalised-coercive states), while maladaptive states (i.e. capital-intensive and coercion-intensive forms) were unable to conform to anarchy and were accordingly rendered obsolete. Moreover, at this point Tilly, without realising it, contradicts a major aspect of his argument. He asserts throughout the book that state formation occurs as an *unintended* consequence of war-making; that state formation was never designed or engineered by rational states (also 1975c: 633–6). But it is apparent that intentional 'emulation' is, as in Waltz, a vital aspect of Tilly's actual model. Thus he argues that although individual states followed different *short-term* paths, in the long run all states that survived did so because they had *emulated* the successful practices of the leading (capitalised-coercive) states. As he put it '[d]riven by the pressures of international [military] competition . . . all three paths eventually converged on concentrations of capital and coercion . . . From the seventeenth century onward the capitalized-coercion form proved more effective in war, and therefore provided a *compelling model* for states that had originated in other combinations of coercion and capital' (1990: 31, emphasis mine). Moreover, elsewhere, he approvingly cites the neorealist George Modelski, to the effect that states must 'imitate' the successful practices of the leading great powers (1985: 185). Some 300 years of 'adaptive emulation' as the basis of state formation clearly implies a very high degree of 'engineering' and 'intentionality' on the part of rulers!

In sum, we can see that there is after all only one Tilly. Thus while he can indeed account for different state formation trajectories in the short run, nevertheless, in the long run it is the state's ability to adapt to a single logic – that of international military competition under anarchy – that accounts for the final outcome of state formation: the capitalised-coercive 'national state'. In the long run, then, as in neorealism, warfare dictated a system of 'like-units'.

Tilly's neorealist theory of the state and IR
As in his earlier work Tilly implicitly invokes Waltz's definition of the international political structure. Thus he differentiates China from Europe in that the former was an imperial state system with one centre, whereas '[i]n Europe, fragmentation into multiple competing states has prevailed over all of the last millennium' (1990: 128, 4, 23). And 'national states always appear in competition with each other . . . they belong to [an anarchic system] of states' (1990: 23). Moreover, Tilly

describes the system of states as one whose 'operation [or logic] constrains the actions of its members' (1990: 37). Thus anarchy and the competitive drive between states accounts for state formation in Europe. Conversely, the imperial (single) state system of China accounts for that state's failure to develop into a modern centralised form. It is clear that Tilly is implicitly invoking Waltz's 'first tier' (the ordering principle of anarchy). Moreover, the central recurring argument is that the dominant great powers 'set the terms of war, and their form of state became the predominant one in Europe', precisely because they held a superiority in war capability (1990: 15). Thus the more powerful states provide a compelling model for the others to emulate. Here Tilly is implicitly invoking Waltz's third tier (power differentiation). In short, Waltz's first and third tiers form the very foundation or sub-structure of his whole analysis. However, Steve Hobden might dispute this claim, because he correctly points out that at various moments Tilly defines the international system in non-realist, or quasi-constructivist ways (Hobden 1998: 106–16). But my point is that these moments are irrelevant precisely because they lie *outside* of his theory of state formation.

Moreover, Tilly further replicates Waltz's framework in another key respect. We noted in chapter 2 that Waltz argued that adaptive state behaviour served to unintentionally reproduce the anarchic multi-state system. Tilly unwittingly adds state formation to this list. Thus as states centralised their power by emulating the successful practices of the leading states in order to conform to anarchy, so they guaranteed their survival, thereby unintentionally securing the reproduction of the multi-state system. Moreover, the anarchic system naturally selects out the weaker species of states (e.g. Poland), thus serving to reduce the 'relative power gap' between the surviving states, thereby ensuring the continued reproduction of the anarchic states system.

But the central question is: does Tilly (like Skocpol, Waltz and Gilpin) drop the second tier (state–society relations) as an independent causal variable, and thereby 'kick the state back out'? While Tilly very clearly opens up the 'black-box' and produces a very detailed and careful examination of state–society relations, nevertheless state and society are brought in only as *intervening* variables. Essentially, differences in state–society relations – that is, differences in the mix between capital and coercion at the domestic level – can indeed explain why there are, in the *early stages* of state formation, at least three different paths or variants. But the crucial point is that *in the long run* it is the logic of the anarchic international system (the first and third tiers) that explains why all states eventually converge on the (capitalised-coercive) national state form. As with Skocpol, Tilly invokes a neorealist theory of the adaptive and maladaptive state to explain state formation and, like Gilpin, adds in a further set of intervening variables, of which a state's level of domestic agential power is the most important and class and economic fetters are secondary. That is, the higher the institutional autonomy or the domestic agential power of the state to overcome domestic fetters that resist state formation strategies employed by rulers, the greater its ability is to centralise state power and enhance tax-revenue accumulation (i.e. successful state formation). In turn, suc-cessful state formation enables the state to conform to international military competition (Tilly 1975b: 21–5, 40–4, 71–4). Conversely, maladaptive states, imbued with only low domestic agential power, were unable to overcome domestic blockages to the enhancement of central state power, and accordingly failed to undergo state formation. As Tilly puts it 'over the long run, far more than any other activities, war and preparation for war produced the major components of European states. States that lost wars commonly contracted, and often ceased to exist' (1990: 28).

It might be replied that surely Tilly places considerable emphasis on the logic of capital in addition to anarchy. But as with Skocpol and Gilpin, capital is theorised only to the extent that it enables states to adapt to anarchy. States are primarily adapting to the logic of inter-national competition under anarchy rather than the logic of capital. Thus, as with Waltz, Skocpol and Gilpin '[t]he game one has to win is defined by the [anarchic] structure that determines the kind of player who is likely to prosper' (Waltz 1979: 92, 128). Tilly really gives the game away when he candidly says of his model that 'in its rasher moments . . . [first] state structure appeared chiefly as a by-product of rulers' efforts to acquire the means of war; and second . . . that relations among states, especially through war and preparation for war, strongly affected the entire process of state formation' (1990: 14). He was, after all, made famous by his pithy neorealist dictum that 'war made the state and the state made war' (1975b: 42).

In sum, Tilly replicates Gilpin's neorealist conception of the state: that states have varying degrees of domestic agential power (high or low), but no international agential power to either shape the inter-national realm or mitigate anarchy. And, as with Skocpol, given that domestic agential state power or institutional autonomy is functional to a state's capacity to govern, and that a state's capacity to govern is determined by its ability to conform to anarchy, it seems fair to conclude that the state is ultimately reduced to anarchy. In short, as for Waltz and Skocpol, the state is 'kicked back out' and drops out as an explanatory variable.

'Second-wave' WHS: a non-realist sociology of international relations

Introduction: towards a 'complex' theory of the state

Conventional understanding within IR assumes that a theory which focuses upon long-run historical change and changing configurations of state–society relations would almost by definition be non-realist. But analysing state–society relations does not insulate Weberianism from the neorealist charge. One might set out to produce a non-realist theory of state formation and for argument's sake write a 600–page book, with the first 599 pages detailing specific and myriad changes at the state–societal (second-tier) level. But if on the last page, the author were to claim that these internal developments occurred as the state sought to adapt or conform to international military competition and warfare, the theory would be unequivocally neorealist. The real challenge for developing a non-realist theory is *not* simply to produce a theory that details domestic changes, but to explain such developments *through a number of causal variables that cannot be reduced to the international structure.* This task takes us into the realm of what might be called 'second-wave WHS'.

Before considering 'second-wave WHS', it is worthwhile explaining *why* neorealist logic has proved so seductive to Tilly and especially Skocpol, as well as more generally among many WHS scholars. Answering this is in fact surprisingly simple. In general, WHS scholars originated in the discipline of sociology where the dominant paradigms have been liberalism and Marxism. Both perspectives have been found wanting by Weberian scholars primarily because they view the Marxist and liberal theories of the state as reductionist. Given their perception that the state has been marginalised within sociology, and given their predisposition towards anti-reductionism, Weberian scholars have sought to correct the imbalance and 'bring the state (as well as geopolitics) back in' to the analysis and explanation of social change. Thus as we noted, Skocpol famously sought to attribute to the state a 'potential autonomy' over class forces.

But my principal critique of Skocpol and Tilly, and of first-wave WHS more generally, has been that in trying to correct the lop-sided economistic accounts of Marxism and liberalism, they have gone too far the other way and have (usually unwittingly) fallen back on a crude and reductionist neorealist logic (see also Little 1994: 9–10; Buzan 1996: 60). Thus, ironically, for all the talk of states and state autonomy, neo-Weberians have usually, albeit unwittingly, kicked the state back out because they *reduce the state to the requirements of the anarchic international system*. In essence, for neorealists and particularly for first-wave WHS scholars, the state turns out to be little more than a transmission belt through which geopolitics reshapes and reconfigures state structures and state–society relations. But given that neo-Weberians are committed to developing a non-reductionist theory of the state and of domestic change, it is clear that first-wave WHS has failed to live up to its promise. Thus we should issue a word of warning to those IR scholars who are looking to WHS as an avenue out of the neorealist impasse: 'first-wave WHS' turns out to be a pathway back into a neorealist cul-de-sac (cf. Scholte 1993: 23). It is the dissatisfaction with the reductionist neorealist logic of first-wave WHS that has led to the calling for a 'second wave' of WHS in which the state must be genuinely 'brought back in' as a power source that cannot be reduced to any singular exogenous logic (Hobson 1998a, 1998b). The two waves can be differentiated in two key respects. First, second-wave WHS seeks to explain not just domestic processes of social change (as in the first wave), but also international relations. Secondly, second-wave WHS seeks to go beyond the neorealist approach of the first wave and accordingly bring the state back in as an agent in the international realm. Thus the primary purpose of second-wave WHS is to realise the unfulfilled 'promise' of first-wave WHS: namely *to 'bring the state back in' as an agent, but at the same time to note that states are also constrained by structures.*

Before examining the second-wave approach found in the works of Michael Mann and John M. Hobson, it is worth noting that Mann (as well as Hobson and many other neo-Weberians) has at times strayed into theory and explanations that are based on neorealist logic. I think it fair to say that there are two Manns: an *early* 'quasi-realist Mann' and a *late* 'non-realist Mann'. Neorealist logic is clearly discernible in his *States, War and Capitalism* (Mann 1988), as well as in significant parts of his major work, *The Sources of Social Power*, vol. 1 (Mann 1986), most especially his accounts of state formation and great power decline, both of which mirror Gilpin's analysis. Nevertheless I choose here to focus on those aspects of their work that suggest a way forward to a non-reductionist or non-realist theory of the state and international relations.

A general neo-Weberian theoretical framework: the shift to 'complexity'

In order to understand the non-reductionist theories of the state found in Mann and Hobson, it is important to begin by adumbrating the basic tenets of Weberian historical-sociology. I have derived this from the extensive and various writings of a broad gamut of writers, but most especially Weber, Elias, Hintze, Mann, Collins, Runciman, Gellner and Giddens. The most general statement that can be made is that the approach is committed to theoretical 'complexity' as opposed to 'reductionism'. The tenets of such a complex approach are captured in what I have elsewhere called the 'six general principles' of WHS (Hobson 1998a: 286–96). Weberians argue that an adequate theory of the state, and of society and international relations, must embody the following aspects:

(1) a study of *history and change*
(2) *multi-causality* (not one but many interdependent power sources)
(3) *multi-spatiality* (not one but many interdependent spatial dimensions)
(4) *partial autonomy* of power sources and actors
(5) *complex* notions of history and change (historicism)
(6) (non-realist) theory of *state autonomy/power*.

Taking each principle in turn, we note first the preference for studying *historical domestic and international change*. Here, neo-Weberians seek to show that modern institutions – social, economic and political – are not natural and inevitable but unique and historically contingent (cf. Cox 1986; Linklater 1998). By focusing on long-run changes in institutional forms, WHS offers a way beyond what Robert Cox calls 'problem-solving' theory or what Hobson refers to as the 'chronocentrism and tempocentrism of IR theory' (in which IR scholars assume that present institutions and developments are 'natural', and can be adequately explained and understood by analysing only the contemporary period, Hobson 1997: 19).

Principle (2) emphasises '*multi-causality*' in which there is not one basic source of power (or one basic causal variable) but many. Gellner (1988) and Runciman (1989) argue for three, though Mann prefers four. Mann's pioneering IEMP model, which specifies four sources of power – ideological, economic, military and political – insists that each has its own partial autonomy and, though influencing and mutually structuring each other, cannot be sociologically reduced to (i.e. wholly explained by) one single factor (Mann 1986: chapter 1; cf. Gellner 1988: 19–23; Runciman 1989: 12–20). This assumes that there are no clear boundaries between the different power sources and actors. While often all four power sources might equally affect social development, it is possible that at specific moments one or two power sources might be singled out as primary (though such primacy will only last for a short period). So, for example, Mann singles out economic and military power as the most important in the eighteenth century, though economic and political power were more important in the nineteenth century (Mann 1993). The commitment to 'complexity' is reinforced by principle (3) which emphasises '*multi-spatiality*', in which the various spatial levels – the sub-national, national, international and global – all affect and structure each other, such that none are self-constituting but are embedded in each other. In other words, each spatial dimension cannot exist without the others, they all support each other. I refer to this as the 'dual reflexivity' of the external and internal realms (Hobson 1997: chapter 1, 7). Thus there is no such thing as a pure 'society' or 'state' or 'international society' or 'global society' since these realms are mutually embedded in one another. It is this that leads Mann to proclaim that societies (and states) 'are constituted of multiple overlapping and intersecting sociospatial networks of power' (Mann 1986: 1). Principle (4) emphasises the '*partial autonomy*' of all power sources and actors. Power actors such as states and classes are not singular or unitary, imbued with absolute autonomy and power. Each power actor is *promiscuous* (Mann 1986: 17–28), or *systactic* (Runciman 1989: 20–7), or *polymorphous* (Elias 1978: 92); each power source and actor has multiple identities given that each is structured to some extent by the others. In this way, neo-Weberians problematise social and political actors as complex phenomena with multiple essences.

Principles (2–4) lead neo-Weberians to differentiate their 'complex' model of power from what they see as *the* fundamental limitation of traditional theory: its utilisation of a reductionist or 'base–superstructure' model (see figure 6.4). While some Marxist and neorealist theorists have undoubtedly gone beyond pure parsimony, Weberians usually insist that they have utilised *modified parsimony* rather than *complexity* (see pp. 10–11 for definitions). The Weberian approach can be diagrammatically represented as a complex set of overlapping matrices of power (see figure 6.4). No one power source is self-constituting: all power sources and actors as well as the various spatial dimensions are not independent but are interdependent and require each other for their existence (cf. Strange 1988: 24–34). In this formulation, the nature and identities of all actors are no longer static or fixed and pre-ordained by a single structure; they are rather highly *malleable*, with multiple identities. Just as global space can be envisaged as a cobweb of complex and multiple interactions (Burton 1972: 16) so for WHS, power actors are not akin to billiard balls but entwine; and they do not clash in dramatic ways, but more mundanely 'interweave' within a complex cobweb (cf. Elias 1978: chapter 1, and 79–99, 154). Power sources and actors are reconfigured as 'impure'. As Mann puts it, actors can no longer be

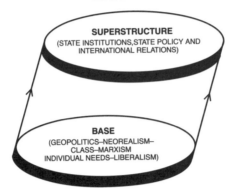

DEPENDENT VARIABLE

SUPERSTRUCTURE
(STATE INSTITUTIONS, STATE POLICY AND INTERNATIONAL RELATIONS)

BASE
(GEOPOLITICS–NEOREALISM–
CLASS–MARXISM
INDIVIDUAL NEEDS–LIBERALISM)

INDEPENDENT VARIABLE

Reductionist, parsimonious models of power and causality which according to neo-Weberians exist in Marxism, liberalism and neorealism (Base determines superstructure)

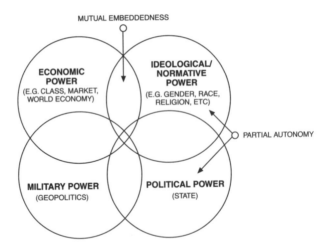

MUTUAL EMBEDDEDNESS

ECONOMIC POWER
(E.G. CLASS, MARKET, WORLD ECONOMY)

IDEOLOGICAL/ NORMATIVE POWER
(E.G. GENDER, RACE, RELIGION, ETC)

PARTIAL AUTONOMY

MILITARY POWER
(GEOPOLITICS)

POLITICAL POWER
(STATE)

ALL SOURCES ARE PARTIALLY AUTONOMOUS INTERDEPENDENT VARIABLES
Non-reductionist/complex model of power and causality–neo-Weberianism (Each power source shapes and is shaped by all others – hence the overlaps)

Figure 6.4 The neo-Weberian 'complex' model of power and causality compared with the Weberian depiction of traditional theory

likened to 'billiard balls, which follow their own trajectory, changing directions as they hit each other'. Rather '[t]hey entwine, that is their interactions change one another's inner shapes as well as their outward trajectories' (Mann 1993: 2). Thus a change in one power source necessarily stimulates changes in all of the others. Equally, the overlaps of the power sources can expand and contract. One example of this (found in the work of Mann and Hobson, see below) is their claim that the more political power (the state) overlaps or is embedded within economic and social power, the stronger the state and society become (e.g. early twentieth century Britain). Conversely, the more the overlap contracts between the two (i.e. the greater the isolation of the state from the economy and society), the weaker both state and society become (e.g. Tsarist Russia).

Principle (5) emphasises *complex notions of change*, such that history is not subject to continuity and repetition, but is subject to sudden and often random discontinuities, as the various sources of power interact to produce unintended consequences of action. Most importantly, social development is not pre-ordained and unilinear. Rather, 'the sources of social power are "tracklaying vehicles" – for the tracks do not exist before the direction is chosen – laying different gauges of track across the social and historical terrain' (Mann 1986: 28). In place of neorealism's 'continuity' problematic, WHS argues that both societies and international politics are best understood as 'immanent orders of change' (Elias 1978: 149).

This all culminates in principle (6) which emphasises a *non-realist theory of the state and state power*. Many scholars assume incorrectly that neorealism has no theory of the state, and that WHS is of interest because it can provide one. This is incorrect on both counts: not only does neorealism have a theory of the state, but it is one that is precisely equivalent to that of first-wave WHS. The real problem with neorealism is not that it fails to develop a theory of the state, but that such a theory *fails to attribute international agential capacity to the state*. By contrast, second-wave WHS *can* provide a synthesis of 'agency and structure', by demonstrating that structures constitute states and that states-as-agents also constitute structures. When listed on p. 194 above, 'non-realist' was bracketed. This is because most neo-Weberians do *not* explicitly seek to produce a non-realist theory of state power and autonomy. But I argue that failure to produce a non-realist theory of international agential state power undermines the whole neo-Weberian enterprise. Why? First, failure to do so effectively negates the important Weberian commitment to 'bring the state back in' *as an agent* (i.e. without reducing it to an exogenous power source), since in first-wave WHS the state is reduced to the structure of the international political system. And, secondly, failure to produce a non-realist theory of the state ultimately contradicts the fundamental Weberian commitment to *complexity*, as outlined in the six principles of WHS. This is because reducing the state to anarchy leads away from complexity back to the parsimonious 'base–superstructure' model. More generally it can quite legitimately be asked: if WHS cannot provide an alternative to neorealism, why should IR scholars turn away from the (neorealist) *status quo*? (Hobden 1998: 11). The next section outlines a 'second-wave' approach which not only produces a non-realist theory of agential state power, but also retains the full integrity of all six principles of the general Weberian approach.

Michael Mann's non-reductionist theory of state power: the 'polymorphous' state

I begin with a discussion of Mann's theory of the state found in his second volume of *The Sources of Social Power* (Mann 1993), and supplement it with the argument found in chapter 1 of *States, War and Capitalism* (Mann 1988). None of the theories of the state examined in this book thus far have sought to problematise the specific domestic powers of the state. This is Mann's first task.

In his 1988 work, he argued that standard statist theory envisages state autonomy (which is equivalent to the notion of high domestic agential state power or institutional state autonomy used throughout this volume), as a 'zero-sum contest' between state and society. This is captured in his notion of 'despotic power' which refers to 'the range of actions which the elite is empowered to undertake without routine, institutionalized negotiation with civil society groups' (Mann 1988: 5). But he argues that there is another form of state power that has been ignored by standard statism – what he calls 'infrastructural power'. This refers to 'the capacity of the state to actually penetrate civil society, and to implement logistically political decisions throughout the realm' (Mann 1988: 5, 1993: 55). For Mann, infrastructural capacity is 'power-neutral' in that it does *not* imply a contest between state and social actors in which one wins out at the other's expense. But one of Mann's major points is that a state has high governing capacity to the extent that it can realise its policies by being able to reach into society. Conventional theory assumes that traditional states were strong because they had relatively high despotic power. But Mann argues that such states were in fact feeble: monarchs could indeed roar 'off with his head', but if the person wasn't in range, there was little that the monarchs could do to enforce their arbitrary whims (Mann 1988: 5). In practice, traditional states were unable to rule directly, and had to rely on the nobles (i.e. *territorial federalism*, or what Anderson, 1974, calls *parcellised sovereignty*). By contrast, most modern states have insignificant despotic power but enjoy high infrastructural reach into society, enabling them to govern more directly and, therefore, far more effectively than their 'brash' predecessors.

In his 1993 volume, Mann develops this approach much further. He begins by differentiating two types of statism: 'true elitism' and 'institutional statism'. True elitism, characteristic of first-wave WHS and neorealism envisages, first, a unified and coherent state elite, which implements an unproblematic and singular conception of the national interest (i.e. military survival). Secondly, true elitism views the state as autonomous to the extent that it *confronts and conflicts* with social actors within civil society, which is generally equivalent to what Mann calls 'despotic power'. Against this neorealist/elitist theory of the state he offers an 'institutional statist' approach, the essence of which is, first, that 'the state' cannot be conceived of as a rational coherent entity that acts according to a single rationality (e.g. capitalist, or militarist, or democratic or patriarchal, etc.), but is a complex phenomenon that is fractionated with multiple identities (as captured in Mann's theory of the 'polymorphous' state, see below). And, secondly, domestic agential state power or autonomy is not something which is used *against* society (as is conventionally assumed), but implies cooperation with social actors. It is important to note, however, that Mann's notion is different from the common understanding of institutional statism. For example, it is generally thought that Skocpol is one of the chief proponents of institutional statism (e.g. Pierson 1996: 89–91). But in Mann's usage of the term, Skocpol's early (though not later) work would be located within 'true elitism', given her equation of state autonomy with despotic power.

A revised theory of domestic agential state power or autonomy
The notion of state power as embodied in collective/cooperative relations with society is captured in Mann's later definition of infrastructural power. In his 1988 book, 'infrastructural power' was understood merely as a technical or logistical capacity, or reach into civil society (Mann 1988: 5, 1986: 170, 477). But in his 1993 volume, it is redefined as power through or *with*, as opposed to power *against* or *over* society. Now '[i]nfrastructural power is a two-way street: [i]t also enables civil society parties [i.e. interest groups] to control the state, as Marxists and pluralists emphasize' (1993: 59). This contrasts with Giddens' notion of the 'surveillance' powers of the state, which implies a degree of despotic

power in which a strong state is able to manipulate society; a power that is present in democratic societies but is maximised under totalitarian regimes (Giddens 1985: chapter 11). For Mann, despotic and infra-structural power are mutually exclusive. The source of a state's domestic autonomy rests in the ability of the state to link *with*, rather than against, strong social power forces. Throughout the book, Britain and Prussia are viewed as the strongest states owing to their embeddedness within their respective dominant classes (Mann 1993: chapters 4, 6, 8, 13). This is a critical move in the shift to a non-reductionist theory of domestic agential state power or autonomy, because it links state power with society, such that the state cannot be reduced to the system of states, but also responds to and grounds itself in domestic socio–class relations.

This is reflected in Mann's latest definition of the modern state. In his earlier work he reproduced the classic Weberian definition of the modern state which constitutes: (1) a *differentiated* set of institutions and per-sonnel embodying (2) *centrality* in the sense that political relations radiate outwards from the centre to cover (3) a *territorially demarcated* area over which it exercises (4) a monopoly of *authoritative binding rule-making*, backed up by a monopoly of the means of physical violence (Mann 1988: 5; cf. Weber 1978: 54–6). However, in Mann's 1993 discussion, this definition has been subtly but dramatically reworked. Points (1) and (3) remain the same but points (2) and (4) now read: '(2) centrality in the sense that political relations *radiate to* and from a center'; and that the state holds '(4) *some degree* of authoritative, binding rule-making, backed up by *some* organized physical force' (Mann 1993: 55, emphases mine). Thus political relations also radiate *into the centre from civil society* (as well as outward from the state), and the state has been substantially down-graded, having only 'some degree', as opposed to a dual 'monopoly' of authoritative binding rule-making and violence. Mann does this because he believes that states cannot be reduced to military power, and also because he is seeking to bring the impact of social forces into the definition of the modern state (1993: chapters 3, 11–14).

All this does not imply, however, that the state can be wholly reduced to class or social interests. The key that unlocks this new theoretical universe is Mann's emphasis on *collective power* as opposed to distribu-tive/zero-sum power: that is, power is at its most effective when it is developed in a collective or cooperative setting. In this formulation, state power and social/class power advance together, collectively. Thus it is *not* a *non-sequitur* to argue that states are autonomous even when they cooperate with the dominant class. This notion of social embeddedness is examined further in chapter 13, where Mann produces an account of bureaucratisation that adds a twist to the conventional Weberian account. Following Weber, neo-Weberians have generally argued that the modern state is *institutionally differentiated* from society, such that the state follows a public or *formal/instrumental* rationality that is distinct from the *substantive* or *value* rationality found in the private sphere of civil society (Poggi 1978; Weber 1978: 978–90; Evans 1995). It is this institutional separation from society which is thought by most Weberians to be the source of autonomous state power. But Mann argues that as late as 1914 (and even today), state administrations were not wholly insulated, but had a strong element of social power. In 1914, noble class power and aristocratic values seeped into administrations, especially with respect to the making of foreign policy (Mann 1993: chapter 13, and 49–51, 69–75, 419–26, 749–57), thus opening up the way for a part-constructivist theory of the state, as Hobden also points out (Hobden 1998: 135–41). In contrast to conventional Weberian theory, Mann argues that the infusion of social power and values within the bureaucracy was a source of strength not weakness: '[w]hether states could act effectively and cohesively depended as much on officials being embedded in and expressing the national cohesion of dominant classes as on their own bureaucratic capacities' (1993: 474). This is all drawn together in Mann's theory of the 'polymorphous' state, which is a vital aspect of his non-reductionist theory of domestic agential state power or autonomy (1993: 75–88).

The state as 'polymorphous'
According to Mann, traditional theory argues that the state 'crystallises' in one specific form – as capitalist (Marxism), as democratic (pluralism), as militarist (neorealism), as patriarchal (feminism), or as normative (constructivism). But, for Mann, the state does not crystallise consistently as one but as many forms. This emerges from the assumption that the state is situated within a complex multi-power universe (which is derived from Weberian principles (2) and (3) mentioned above). The state crystallises at the centre of a *number* of these complex power networks. It 'crystallises' in a myriad of forms, the six most important (for the period down to 1914), or what Mann calls 'higher-level crystallisations' comprising: capitalist, militarist, representative, national, ideological–moral and patriarchal forms of power. In line with realists, Mann accepts that states responded to international military competition; in line with Marxists, that these states were also capitalist; in line with feminists, that these states were also patriarchal; and implicitly in line with constructivists, that social identities and norms also influence the state.

Some non-Weberian critics would then ask their standard (reductionist) question: which of these power forms is the most important (inherently assuming that one source of power must be more important than all others)? In short, they would want Mann to choose one as the most significant. The major point that Mann seeks to make is that the problem lies in the question. The answer is that none of these crystallisations can be singled out as primary: the search for primacy, like the quest for the holy grail, is futile. The rejection of an 'ultimate crystallisation' model of the state, or equally of domestic and international relations, derives from the second general principle (multi-causality), which posits that there is not one source of power that is ultimately determining, but four, none of which can be reduced to the others (see figure 6.4). Secondly, power actors and power sources rarely clash in 'head-on confrontation' mainly because they mutually structure each other. Accordingly, such 'promiscuity' implies that states will rarely have to make an ultimate choice between the different sources of power or power actors. In this way, partially autonomous states are constituted through a multiplicity of partially autonomous non-state power sources – economic, ideological/normative and military – just as partially autonomous non-state actors and structures are constituted through politics (the state), economics, geopolitics and ideology/norms.

In the process, state and social theory become radically transformed. No longer do we need to search for a single state identity, nor do we need to reduce all politics to a single or primary essence. We can now envisage multiple state identities. Thus '[t]oday, the American state might crystallize as conservative–patriarchal–Christian one week when restricting abortion rights, as capitalist the next when regulating the savings and loans banking scandal, as a superpower the next when sending troops abroad for other than national economic interests' (Mann 1993: 736). The problem now is to analyse how the state shapes the other power sources, as well as how they in turn shape the state. So, for example, by 1914 states employed their power to coordinate social and economic life, in the process territorialising or 'caging' social actors, thereby subtly transforming their interests and identities into national–territorial conceptions (1993: chapter 8). Here the influence of the state upon capitalism was not to undermine it in head-on conflict, but to subtly redefine notions of capitalist interest. Thus capitalism and 'capitalist interests' are not self-constituting and defined in pure terms by the MOP (as in Marxism). The developmental path of capitalism was subtly 'retracked' in new directions by the state and geopolitics. Moreover in chapters 17–19 Mann argues that the actions and behaviour of the working class and peasantry were also shaped in significant ways by the particular form of state – what he earlier called 'ruling class strategies' (1988: chapter 7). As he put it '[t]hese [class] interactions were not like billiard ball collisions . . . [C]lasses . . . entwined "non-dialectically" with authoritative political crystallizations, thus helping to shape one another. Actors' very identities and interests were changed behind their backs by the unintended consequences of [state] action' (Mann 1993: 725). Again, class interests could not simply be 'read off' from the mode of production, because they were subtly retracked by all manner of non-economic forces, especially the state.

But Mann does not fall back on a crude political reductionism, as some of his critics have charged (e.g. Scholte 1993: 23, 96, 101–2; Fuat Keyman 1997: 73). For the state cannot be conceptualised as a rational autonomous entity imbued with a single essence, because capitalism also retracked the development of the modern state. Moreover, aristocratic normative values held by bureaucrats, and especially statesmen and diplomats, helped channel and construct the state's foreign policy choices (Mann 1993: 49–51, chapters 8, 21). In addition, the development of the modern state was influenced after 1700 not just by war and capitalism but also by working-class movements and party democracy, to emerge by 1914 as a more complex 'diamorphous' entity': part military and part civilian (1993: chapters 13–14). In sum, Mann conceives of the state as having varying degrees of domestic agential state power. Moreover, states and their varying relations with society also autonomously impact upon and affect international relations (1993: chapter 21, 1996). It is this point that provides the starting point for Hobson's work.

John M. Hobson's 'non-realist theory of international agential state power': resolving the 'agent–structure dichotomy'

Although Mann does analyse IR, he is primarily interested in developing a non-reductionist theory of the state and applying this to understanding domestic social change. The central objective of my book, *The Wealth of States* (1997) is to specifically develop a 'non-realist theory of (international agential) state power' and apply this to international relations. Thus I set out to develop a neo-Weberian approach that, in contrast to first-wave WHS, could *not* be likened to a 'neorealist wolf dressed up in sociological sheep's clothing'. I argue that the *key* problem with neorealism is *not* that it fails to develop a theory of the state, but rather that its theory of the state is inadequate because it denies the state any agential power in the international system. This is because for Waltz (1979) the 'second tier' of the international political structure (i.e. the state and state–society relations) is purposefully omitted, or 'dropped' as an independent variable, thereby stripping the state of international agential power. Accordingly, neorealism reifies international structure at the expense of state-agency. A corollary of this is that neorealism also utilises what I see as the defunct 'base–superstructure' model of power and causality. What is needed is a *complex* approach that brings the state as an agent into international relations: an approach that reintegrates the partially autonomous state alongside partially autonomous non-state actors/structures within a complex social universe.

Neorealism in all its variants *separates* the state from society, such that the state acquires *absolute* levels of domestic agential power or autonomy from social actors. It is true that Gilpin and Krasner talk about varying state–society relations, unlike Waltz, but domestic class interests are understood only as fetters that impede the state from adequately conforming to anarchy. For them, a strong state must achieve autonomy over, or insulation from, social interests in order to conform to international anarchy. The game is still dictated by anarchy. In the process, neorealism operationalises a 'separationist' problematic that exaggerates the importance of boundaries. Not only are states strictly separated from each other as well as international non-state actors by non-permeable external sovereign edges, but there is also an invisible boundary between state and society. Perhaps the key to my approach is to depict states as variously embedded or integrated within domestic social relations as well as international relations, which in turn analytically presupposes a 'breaking down' of these artificial boundaries. Moreover, state strength – the capacity to govern effectively – can be achieved only through a deep embeddedness within society (also Weiss and Hobson 1995; Weiss 1998). In this formulation, strong social forces do not act merely as a constraint on domestic state agential power but also enable or enhance state governing capacity. The paradox of my argument is that 'to bring the state into IR' as an independent agent, it is essential to 'bring society (and international society) back in'. Thus in effect, *inter alia*, I trace the 'social sources of state power'. In contrast to the traditional conception of state autonomy, found in neorealism and first-wave WHS, strong social actors do not undermine state power, but can enhance it.

But it also helps to note that this approach is quite different from Marxism, liberalism and crude interdependence theory. As in neorealism, these approaches set up a problematic 'either/or' logic, in that they assume a trade-off between state power and social forces: if international social forces are strong, state capacity is assumed to be low or declining. I replace the binary approach of traditional theory with an inclusive 'both/and' logic, such that strong states and strong social forces go hand-in-hand. A non-reductionist theory of the state rejects asking the question, 'state *or* non-state forces', as in traditional reductionism and as in the first state debate, but calls for an analysis of 'state *and* non-state actors'. Thus in bringing non-state forces back in, I insist that 'the state should not be kicked back out' (Hobson 1997: chapter 7).

In producing a non-realist theory of international agential state power, I seek to operationalise all six principles of WHS and achieve genuine complexity. In my 1997 book I used a *fiscal–sociological* approach which emphasises multi-causal and multi-spatial variables: specifically, economic, military and political forms of power – class, geopolitics and state capacity – as well as developments occurring at the international, national and sub-national spatial dimensions. The case study of international trade regime change – specifically the transition from free trade to protectionism in the late nineteenth century – requires a *fiscal–sociological* approach, because I argue that states resorted to tariff protectionism mainly to enhance tax revenues. Such a link is made on the grounds that tariffs are a form of taxation – specifically 'indirect' taxation. This case study is useful insofar as it entails an 'integrative' approach, which produces what Jarvis calls a 'fit' between the multiple power and spatial variables (cf. Jarvis 1989: 291) – as depicted in figure 6.5.

State 'international agential' power and international trade regime change

In contrast to liberalism and Marxism, which argue that states raised tariffs after 1877 in order to promote the interests of various economic interest groups, I argue that states shifted to protectionism as they responded to governmental fiscal crisis. Fiscal crisis emerged through a variety of developments operating in all three spatial dimensions. Beginning on the top left-hand side of figure 6.5, developments in the international states system – the rising costs of war associated with the second military revolution – pushed states to increase expenditures. In addition, developments in the international economy – the Great Depression after 1873 – reduced government revenues, exacerbating fiscal crisis. Moreover, developments at sub-national levels variously impacted. In Germany, for example, the central Reich government had become extremely dependent upon revenues from the provincial state governments (the *Länder*), which served to reduce the autonomy of the executive in policy-making. Accordingly, Reich Chancellor Bismarck sought to find a new and independent source of revenue so as to reduce this political dependency – indirect taxes and tariffs fitted the bill.

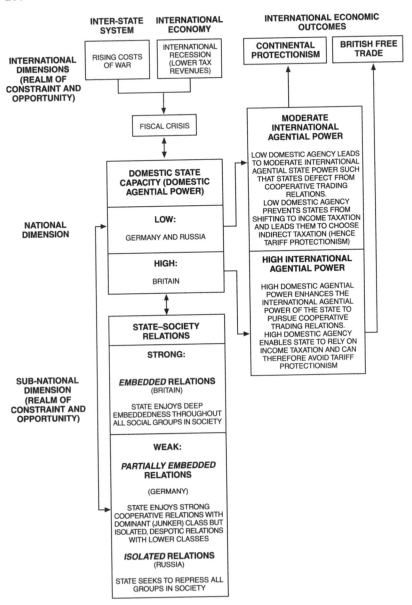

Figure 6.5 John M. Hobson's 'second-wave' Weberian theory of the state and international trade regime change

Most importantly, in contrast to neorealism, I argue that while international geo-fiscal pressures were an important determinant of fiscal crisis, nevertheless they provided only a part of the overall explanatory schema. In addition to the various 'cost-push' forces that prompted fiscal crisis, I also specify significant 'revenue-pull' objectives on the part of states. It is a vital part of the argument that 'incoming' cost-push pressures emanating from the international system were refracted in different policy directions by each state. This was due to the different degrees of domestic agential state capacity and varying configurations of state–society relations found in each country.

For clarification purposes, I analytically differentiate three categories of state power (even though they are all linked):

(1) *Governing capacity* or *domestic agential state power*: that is, the ability of a state to effectively govern, which is enhanced when the state is deeply embedded within a broad range of domestic social actors. While this shares some things in common with Peter Evans' (1995) concept of 'embedded autonomy', it also departs from it in at least two fundamental ways. First, I argue that states are most effective when they are embedded across a *broad* range of social actors rather than exclusively within the dominant class. And, second, *contra* Evans' *grave-digger* thesis, state autonomy is not undermined in the long run as social actors strengthen their power but is enhanced. In the long run, Evans presupposes a zero-sum game contest of power between social actors and the state – a position which I argue characterises only weak, despotic states rather than strong cooperative states (cf. Weiss 1998: 34–7).

(2) More specifically, governing capacity is derived from the configuration of a state's *domestic institutional power*, which comprises: *concentration, penetrative* (infrastructural) power, state *autonomy* (state–society relations) and *despotic* power.

(3) *The international agential power of the state*: states gain different degrees of international agential power depending on the degree of domestic agential power achieved. This is demonstrated in the (1997) case study on trade regime change.

A state's trading policy is shaped by its level of domestic governing capacity, which is in turn determined by the specific configuration of its various institutional powers. The first institutional aspect of power refers to a state's 'concentration', which refers to the extent to which a state is fiscally centralised. In federal systems the central government is only weakly fiscally centralised. In the nineteenth century, there was a strict fiscal division of labour between the central government and the provincial state governments, such that the latter held a virtual monopoly of direct taxation (mainly land taxes), while the former held a virtual monopoly of indirect taxes. Accordingly, in federal systems, central governments tended to rely on tariff protectionism for their revenues. This helps explain why Germany, Austria, Canada, Australia, Switzerland and the United States were protectionist. Conversely, the central states in unitary systems (e.g. Britain and Russia) had a choice between indirect and direct forms of revenue. Because Britain chose to increase income taxes to provide the required revenues, it was able to avoid indirect taxes and therefore maintain free trade. Nevertheless, the high concentration of the state is a necessary though not sufficient variable, not least because 'unitary' Russia (as well as Italy and France) relied on indirect taxes and tariffs for much of its revenues. To explain this, we need to examine the other forms of state institutional power.

Britain was able to shift to income taxation after 1842 because, first, it had high 'penetrative' power (the ability to reach into society in order to extract and collect taxation), which is a vital pre-requisite for an income tax. Tsarist Russia lacked such power, which blocked the introduction of an income tax. Secondly, the most important factor was a state's *autonomy*: that is, the degree to which the state was broadly embedded in society. Why was Britain able to maintain free trade from 1846 down to the First World War? This was possible, first, because fiscal crisis did not emerge until the turn of the twentieth century (unlike for much of continental Europe). But when the fiscal crunch finally arrived, the British state responded by increasing the income tax. This was possible only because the Liberal government, unlike the despotic Russian government, was *deeply embedded in both the dominant capitalist class and the working classes*. This enabled the state to play off the two classes in order to enhance its various interests in the domestic and international settings. By funding the new Dreadnought and old age pensions' expenditures through higher income taxes levied upon the richest groups in society, the government maintained working-class consent for its policies. The key point, though, is that the state had the dominant classes over a barrel because it could play off their contradictory 'polymorphous' interests. Because the dominant classes wanted free trade for their commercial ventures, but indirect taxation (i.e. tariffs) for personal tax reasons, they could not have it both ways: either they would have to accept higher income taxation if they wanted free trade (i.e. the 'fiscal price' of the Liberal government's policy package), or accept tariff protectionism if they wanted lower personal tax rates (i.e. the 'trading price' of the opposition Conservative party's policy package). In the end the Liberal government won out, and went against the long-run fiscal interests of the dominant classes, but retained their (grudging) consent by maintaining their trading interests through free trade. This contrasts with the Russian state. In seeking to maximise its despotic power, autocracy repressed both the dominant and subordinate classes through indirect taxes, and therefore resorted to protectionism.

Finally, moving to the bottom part of figure 6.5, I note the impact of societal forces in the making of taxation and trade policy. Class forces were an important factor in Britain's desire to maintain free trade, which was largely supported by both the dominant and subordinate classes. The German state, being embedded in the dominant Junker class, raised tariffs in 1885, 1887 and 1902–6 partly to meet the trading requirements of the Junkers – as Marxists and liberals argue. Nevertheless, it would be wrong to assume in the cases of Britain and Germany that the state acted *purely* in the interests of their various class-constituencies, as Marxists argue. Like the British dominant classes in 1909, the German Junker class was *cross-pressurised* in 1879, wanting free trade for commercial purposes but indirect taxes and tariffs for personal taxation reasons. The state was able to persuade the Junkers to accept tariff protection because of the non-commercial benefits that this entailed (i.e. lower personal taxation and the development of a more right-wing government coalition), even if this class did not favour tariffs for commercial purposes until 1885. The state went further in the 1890s, when it lowered grain tariffs at a time when the Junkers were clamouring for higher rates of protection. In short, embeddedness does not entail complete subordination of the state to the needs of classes. Thus the relationship between states and dominant classes in Britain and Germany was *competitive-cooperative* (as opposed to being purely cooperative). Moreover, Tsarist autocracy was isolated and used tariffs against all classes, such that the state's relations with the dominant and subordinate classes were purely *competitive*.

A clear paradox emerges at this point: the deeper a state's embeddedness is, the greater its governing capacity becomes. That is, the British state's deep embeddedness in social networks conferred upon it greater ability to push through its desired reforms to enhance its governing capacity. By contrast, the *partial embeddedness* of the German state and the *isolation* of the Russian state undermined their governing capacity. This was because Britain's high governing capacity enabled the income tax, which was far more fiscally productive than the indirect tax base that Russia and Germany relied upon. This became evident during the First World War when, in contrast to Britain, the German and Russian states were militarily undermined and subsequently overthrown through domestic revolution. But the central conclusion of this analysis is that the nature of the units were fundamental variables in shaping the international system. The deep embeddedness (and therefore high governing capacity) of the British state was the key to its free trade policy; by contrast, the various degrees of isolation (and therefore the low governing capacity) of the German and Russian states was crucial to their choice of tariff protectionism in the international political economy.

A 'non-realist theory of international agential state power' and international relations: towards resolving the 'agent–structure' dichotomy

The central objective of my analysis is to provide a solution to the 'agent–structure dichotomy'. International-systemic theory is capable of producing only a 'passive-adaptive' theory of the state which denies the state any agency to determine IR. But rather than correct the imbalance by exaggerating a state-as-agent problematic, I seek to provide a structurationist synthesis of agency and structure. This is achieved by bringing the partially autonomous state back in *alongside* the structures of the MOP, world economy and international state system, and emphasising both the *co-constitution* of state and society/international society. Thus the state resides within an international/national vortex, in which all three spatial realms are mutually embedded such that they shape and determine one another – thereby providing the 'fit' that Jarvis (1989) calls for. Is this manoeuvre equivalent to merely taking the various bits of each theory – class, international state system, capitalist world economy – and sticking them altogether in some sort of arbitrary grand synthesis? This is not the case because bringing in more variables requires a *major ontological reconfiguration* of the nature of the agents and power structures. Not only do the different power and spatial realms mutually entwine and become *partially autonomous* rather than absolutely autonomous, but 'structures' are no longer simply conceived as anthropomorphic and 'all-constraining' in nature. Structures become *double-edged*, such that they 'enable' as well as 'constrain' state capacity. International and national 'structures' are now (re)viewed as 'realms of opportunity' as well as 'realms of constraint'. In this way, domestic and international society become *partial resource pools* into which states-as-agents dip so as to enhance their power or interests in both realms. Above all, the state is a spatially *Janus-faced* entity, with one face looking to the international and global realms and the other facing the domestic arena. This enables the state to play off the different realms and power sources in order to enhance its multiple interests, which in turn leads to changes in the domestic and international 'spheres'.

In typical structurationist style, the argument operates in two phases. In the first phase I bracket the agential story and focus especially on the international realm as a 'realm of constraint'. Here I focus on increasing military costs at the international level entwined with international economic recession, which led on to fiscal crisis. This required states to adapt if they were to remain competitive. The strong state – Britain – was able to raise the income tax through social embeddedness and hence maintain free trade. Conversely, the weak states of Germany and Russia had isolated relations from society (especially the lower classes) and chose indirect taxes and tariffs. However, if we ended the story here, we would have developed only a modified neorealist argument. The next part of the story brackets structure and focuses on agency. The story here is that each state had its own particular domestic objectives, none of which had anything to do with international structural forces. Here, the international economy provided a resource pool into which states-as-agents dipped in order to push through particular domestic reforms. The federal 'partially embedded' German state taxed international trade to enhance its 'concentration' (i.e. its fiscal and political autonomy from the *Länder* after 1878), as well as to enhance its despotic power by repressing the lower classes and to promote the dominant class's fiscal and trading requirements through regressive tariffs. The unitary 'isolated' autocratic Russian state sought to enhance its despotic power domestically *vis-à-vis* the lower and dominant classes. By contrast, the unitary 'embedded' British state was primarily interested in enhancing its overall governing capacity. By refraining from taxing trade and maintaining free trade, the state – or the Liberal government – was able to push through the income tax against the long-term fiscal interests of the dominant classes, thereby enhancing its fiscal/governing capacity (given that the fiscal yield of the income tax was far superior to that of an indirect tax base). This enabled the government to attract the working-class vote and ensure the government's re-election in 1910. This was accepted because the dominant classes recognised that the price of their desired free trade was the income tax. Thus when we combine these two stories, we move to a structurationist theory of the state and IR, which goes beyond neorealist structuralism.

A major part of the argument is that domestic politics influenced international trade such that 'domestic embeddedness' (Britain) led to free trade, while 'partial embeddedness' (Germany) or 'isolation' (Russia) led to tariff protectionism. Accordingly, Waltz might counter this by suggesting that I have produced a 'theory of foreign policy' rather than a theory of the international system. But in reply I suggest that the reason why tariff protectionism emerged throughout the European continent after 1877 was because the *general threshold of state governing capacity across all states* was moderately low. Low state capacity led to a general reliance on indirect taxes, which in turn translated into a continental-wide shift in trade regimes from free trade to tariff protectionism. Here, I argue that it is the general level of state governing capacity that is crucial: when the general level is low, protectionism prevails (e.g. in late nineteenth-century Continental Europe and in the post-1945 third world); when the level is high, free trade prevails (e.g. in the post-1945 first world). Moreover, the distribution (and general threshold) of governing capacity is substantially related to the specific state–society relations within each of the units (see chapter 7 for a fuller discussion).

In sum, therefore, two concluding points are of note. First, I argue that Waltz's second tier must stay in. The internal properties of states as well as state–society relations constitute important variables for explaining IR. Indeed, a state's domestic relations impact upon its international agential power. Thus the British state enjoyed high international agential power in the early twentieth century precisely because it had high domestic agential capacity given that it was deeply embedded in a broad range of social forces domestically. This enabled it to shift to the income tax and thereby ignore increasing indirect taxes and tariffs. In turn, this led it to pursue the international cooperative policy of free trade. Conversely, the German and Russian states had only low governing capacity and were relatively isolated from domestic social forces. Accordingly they chose regressive indirect taxes and tariffs. In turn they had only moderate international agential power, and in choosing to defect from cooperative trade relations with other states followed a protectionist trading policy. The second concluding point is that states are not passive victims of exogenous structures (i.e. *Träger*), but are agents which not only constitute other power actors and domestic and international structures, but are simultaneously constituted by them (for a fuller discussion of this, see chapter 7, pp. 223–35). I therefore reject the state duality of 'international anarchy' and 'sovereignty' in favour of a 'dynamic duo' (Hobson 1997: 272–5). Paradoxically, therefore, the logic of this position is that if we downgrade the ontological importance of anarchy and state sovereignty we can reintegrate the international and national dimensions as mutually reflexive and thereby 'bring the state and state-society complex back in' as partially autonomous forces.

Finally, Fuat Keyman (1997: 84–5) argues that, in general, WHS is inadequate because it fails to adequately synthesise 'agency' and 'structure'. In particular, he claims that the state is *reified* as an all-powerful agent to the detriment of 'structure'. Thus, first, he claims that the state-as-agent is reified or accorded primacy over domestic structures (cf. Risse-Kappen 1995a: 18). But second-wave WHS is able to synthesise agency and structure. For Mann as well as myself, state power is embedded within social power: state–society relations are a crucial aspect of state agential power in the international system (also Weiss 1998). The second source of WHS' 'state reification', according to Fuat Keyman, exists in the alleged tendency to view international structures as purely 'enabling', with no notion that they can 'constrain' states. In point of fact, it is the other way round: first-wave WHS reifies structure (anarchy) at the expense of agency (states). But in second-wave WHS, international structures are *both* enabling *and* constraining. Thus states in the late nineteenth century were partially constrained by the inter-state system and accordingly sought new revenues in order to meet fiscal crisis – a crisis which was imposed upon states in part by the structural requirements of the international military system. But at the same time, states could use the international economy as a 'resource pool' in order not just to meet fiscal crisis but also to push through various domestic reforms, which satisfied both the state as well as some classes, though not others. In the process, the 'agential' state came to restructure the international economy. In sum, the state not only responds to structural 'requirements' at the international and domestic 'level', but also uses these realms as resource pools to reconfigure these structures. The state is not, therefore, reified as an agent at the expense of structures, but is conceived as embedded within such structures, which partially constitute and are partially constituted by the state. All this suggests what I call the theory of the 'constitutive state', which is contrasted with the neorealist theory of the 'passive-adaptive state' and the neoliberal institutionalist theory of the pure agential state (and is pursued further in chapter 7).

Discussion questions

• Why have some IR theorists recently turned towards WHS?
• How did Skocpol help promote an expansion of the boundary of HS to incorporate IR theory?
• On what basis is it claimed in this book that Skocpol and Tilly succeeded only in 'kicking the state back out'?
• Why is it argued that 'first-wave' WHS fails to realise the key theoretical ambitions (namely the 'six principles') of neo-Weberianism?

- What is the 'polymorphous' state, and does it enable Mann to successfully produce a non-realist and non-reductionist theory of the state in domestic politics?
- How, if at all, does Hobson's 'second-wave' theory of the *constitutive* state go beyond the reductionist neorealist theory of the 'adaptive state'?

Suggestions for further reading

The best place to start for a general introduction to WHS from an IR perspective is Hobden (1998). It is vital to note that sociologists are in danger of being outflanked by IR theorists 'within their own backyard'. IR theorists are able to show some of the problems that historical sociologists can run into when they invoke the international realm but do not sufficiently ground their concept of the international within IR theory. Hobden's book reveals these pitfalls (as indeed does this present chapter). Short summary statements of WHS from an IR perspective can be found in Jarvis (1989), Hobson (1998a), Griffiths (1999: 233–51) and, though from a critical perspective, Cammack (1989), Jessop (1990: 275–88) and Fuat Keyman (1997: chapter 3). Readers might also want to review the summary literature on the 'international–national connection' (see Almond 1989) and 'second image-reversed' theory (Gourevitch 1978). For detailed accounts of the application of WHS to IR, see Mann (1993: chapters 8, 21), Halliday (1994: chapters 4–6); Hobson (1997) and Seabrooke (2000). From the sociological side of the 'boundary', readers would do well to look at the general formulations of the Weberian and neo-Weberian approaches (which also contain much on the state), see Hintze (1975), Elias (1978, 1994), Mann (1986, 1988, 1993), Giddens (1984, 1985), Collins (1986) and Runciman (1989). The best and most succinct discussion of the rise of the modern state is still Poggi (1978). While Skocpol (1979) remains the classic text of 'first-wave' WHS within Sociology, for 'second-wave' state theory within Comparative Politics and Sociology, see Mann (1993), Evans (1995), Weiss and Hobson (1995) and Weiss (1998).

Part 3

Conclusion: proposing a 'structurationist' theory of the 'constitutive' state and global politics

Summarising the 'second state debate'

What have we learned in this book so far? I will first summarise the second state debate and extract five generic 'theories' of the state that can be discerned within IR theory. I argued in chapter 1 that IR has in fact had two 'state debates' running in parallel, even though the second state debate has remained obscured. The structure of the first state debate presents us with the orthodox view of IR theory: that neorealism is state-centric while liberalism, Marxism and constructivism are essentially 'society-centric'. But I suggested in chapter 1 that this received picture emerges because IR theorists have ignored what I have called the 'international agential power' of the state. The central message of this book is that the first state debate presents an inadequate framework for understanding IR theory and its various approaches to the state. The irony of the first state debate is that, arguably, it is not even about the state, given that both sides reify international structure over the state-as-agent (i.e. the economic structure for radical pluralists and the political structure for neorealists). Indeed, for neorealists the state is no less imprisoned within an international structure than it is for radical pluralists. In the end, then, both sides deny the possibility that states can shape the international realm, or even construct policy free of international structural constraints. The second state debate goes beyond the first debate, because it locates IR theory within the agent–structure problematic.

It has been the argument of this book that when we relocate theory within the agent–structure debate, and introduce the concept of the international agential powers of the state, we necessarily reconfigure the received picture of IR's approach to the state. In chapter 1 I defined the international agential power of the state as the *ability of the state to make foreign policy and shape the international realm free of international-structural requirements or the interests of international non-state actors*. And at the extreme, high international agential power refers to *the ability of the state*

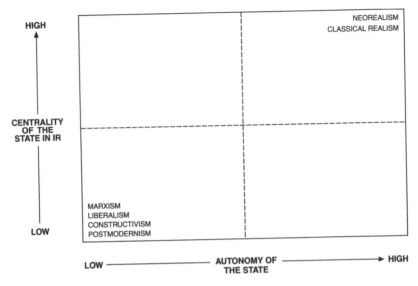

Figure 7.1 Configuring IR theory within the 'first state debate'

to mitigate the logic of inter-state competition and thereby create a cooperative or peaceful world. Applying this concept, we see that the received wisdom of how IR theory understands the state becomes precisely inverted. Figure 7.1 charts the conventional position of IR theory as it applies to the issue of the *centrality of the state* in IR and the *autonomy* of the state. This conventional position puts neorealism at the top so to speak, and Marxism, liberalism and constructivism at the bottom. But the second state debate inverts this picture and effectively 'turns IR theory upside down' (see figure 7.2). Now neorealism (as well as WST) is at the bottom, while some variants of constructivism and liberalism are at the top, and postmodernism (i.e. radical constructivism) and classical- and orthodox-Marxism are in the middle. That is, liberalism, constructivism, classical realism, orthodox Marxism and second-wave WHS all succeed in giving some international agential power to the state, while neorealism and first-wave WHS as well as world-systems theory all reify international structure and fundamentally deny the state any international agential power. This is the surprising or counter-intuitive conclusion of this book. But it is counter-intuitive only because IR theorists have confused a state's domestic agential power (or institutional autonomy) with a state's international agential power.

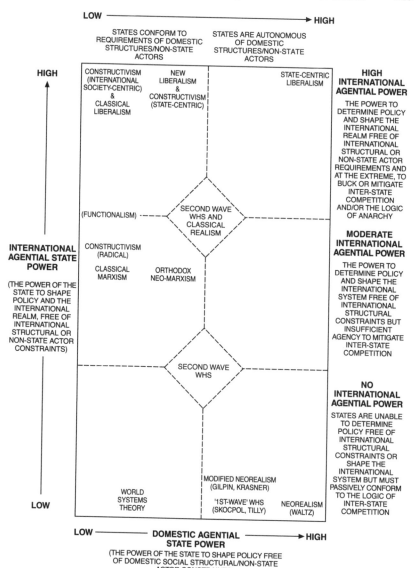

Figure 7.2 Reconfiguring IR theory within the 'second state debate'

Five generic forms of state theory in IR

I noted in chapter 1 how the first state debate became divided between two fundamentally opposing and intransigent opposites. One of the features of the second state debate, however, is that there are no longer two intransigent opposites that slug it out in a no-holds-barred contest. While we should be sensitive to the fact that each approach has many variants and sub-sets (as has been discussed in chapters 2–6), nevertheless it is possible to identify (through the lens of the second state debate), five clear generic forms of state theory within the IR discipline. I shall take each in turn before going on to consider one possible resolution to the second state debate (pp. 223–35). These approaches can be extracted from figure 7.2.

The passive-adaptive state with no international agency

Beginning at the bottom level of figure 7.2, we encounter international-systemic theory, which exaggerates the centrality of international structure and denies the state international agential power. These theories include Waltzian neorealism, modified neorealism (e.g. Gilpin Krasner), first-wave WHS and WST. While they all vary as to the degree of domestic agential power that they ascribe to the state, they all ultimately argue that states are in effect, *Träger* – that is, passive victims of international structure. The main difference between them lies in the particular structure that they privilege or single out. Neorealists and first-wave Weberians focus on the international anarchic political structure whereas world systems theorists privilege the capitalist world economy (CWE). The paradox here is that it is perfectly possible to accord the state high domestic agential power while simultaneously denying it any agential power in the international realm (as in neorealism).

The domestically-adaptive state with moderate international agential power

Moving up one level of figure 7.2, we come across the second type of theory. Here the state is granted moderate international agential powers but has only low or moderate domestic agential powers. Thus within the domestic realm, social structure takes precedence over the state-as-agent. The key formula here is as follows: that states must adapt or conform to the logic of domestic structures or non-state actors, but that in doing so, states gain a moderate degree of international agential power. Thus for Marxists, 'in the last instance' the state conforms to the domestic needs of the dominant economic class, but that in doing so, it gains moderate international agential power to create a conflictual inter-state system. Radical constructivists argue that states have barely any domestic agential power in that they must conform to the logic of representation: that states are imagined. But, again, as states engage in normative statecraft, so they come to separate themselves from other states. In the process, states create a violent world.

Finally, there is the marginal case of liberal functionalism which lies on the boundary of this and the third type of state theory. By and large liberal functionalists argue that modern 'comprehensive' states have only low domestic agency and must conform to the economic and social needs of individuals, but that they can create the foundations for the construction of a peaceful global order. Nevertheless functionalists fall short of granting the state high international agential power to create a fully peaceful international system, because ultimately the state acts as a fetter to global peace. Thus in the long run international functionalist agencies will outflank the sovereign state, rendering it increasingly obsolete until it eventually withers away.

The domestically-adaptive state with high international agential power

Moving to the top left-hand side of figure 7.2, we encounter the third generic type of state theory. This captures those approaches which argue that states have only low or moderate domestic agential power but have high international agential powers. Again, within the domestic realm, social structure takes precedence over the state, and the state is thereby denied high domestic agential power. Classical liberalism grants the state only very low domestic agency or institutional autonomy. That is, it must conform or adapt to the economic and social needs of individuals within society. However, in the process the state gains considerable international agential power such that it can shape or create a peaceful international system. Only when the state fails to conform to the domestic needs of individuals is a conflictual international system created. Although new liberalism grants the state moderate amounts of domestic agential power, nevertheless the state is still beholden to the economic requirements of individuals. But in conforming to the needs of individuals, states gain high amounts of international agential power to shape the inter-state system. Not least, states create international government which, in turn, enables the construction of a world of peaceful states.

The final example here is that of constructivism. International society-centric constructivism does not in fact pay much attention to the domestic agential power of the state, though it is clearly implicit that the state has only low amounts. But the key point is that it has an ambivalent position with regard to the degree of international agential power that it ascribes to the state. In the first instance, the state is granted only very low amounts given that the state must adapt or conform to the international social or normative structure. However, in conforming to the international normative structure, states gain very high degrees of international agential power because they can buck the logic of inter-state competition and solve the collective action problem. In the process, states can create a peaceful, cooperative and more equitable international social realm. Finally, state-centric constructivism (as in Katzenstein) grants the state a moderate degree of domestic agential power, although this is also grounded in domestic normative structures. Katzenstein's position is more ambiguous with respect to the international agential power of the state. States interpret the international system according to their own domestic normative structures. To borrow Wendt's (1987) phrase, 'anarchy is what states make of it'. In particular, the international realm does not constrain states, in turn implying a relatively high degree of international agential power.

The pro-active state with high domestic and high international agential powers

Finally, moving to the top right-hand side of figure 7.2, we encounter those theories which ascribe the state with both high domestic and high international agential power. In the process, state-agency is privileged and international structure is wholly downgraded. State-centric liberalism (neoliberal institutionalism and English school rationalism) is *the* outstanding example of this genre. We do, however, need to correct one misunderstanding (which was discussed in detail at the end of chapter 3). In the conventional literature it is generally assumed that both theories upgrade international institutions (regimes or norms) and downgrade the state. Thus it is generally thought that international regimes are ontologically central for neoliberal institutionalism, and that these regimes constrain state behaviour (pushing them to cooperate rather than conflict), in much the same way that international society is said to constrain states in English school rationalism. But I argue that, in both cases, it is the states themselves, imbued with high levels of international agential power, that set up international regimes or international societal norms, precisely so as to realise certain state objectives (namely 'order' for rationalists or the maximisation of long-term utility gains for neoliberals). In general, in this genre, states have their own interests which are not reducible to (i.e. explained by the needs of) domestic or international structures. Here, the state's international agential powers are reified at the expense of either domestic or international structures (and the international realm becomes a 'realm of possibility' rather than one of constraint or necessity).

The 'constitutive' state with varying domestic and international agential powers

The fifth generic brand of state theory can be found in both classical realism, but above all in what I have called 'second-wave' WHS. Classical realism can be situated only on the border of the second, third and fourth types because it argues that states have high domestic and high international agential power in the early periods (1648–c.1900) and then subsequently low domestic and moderate international agential power thereafter. But the most complex theory is that of second-wave WHS, which rests on the borders of *all* the other approaches. The next section is given over to developing this approach, not least as a means of reconciling the second state debate.

Proposing a sociological resolution to the 'second state debate'

It seems to me that there are basically three benefits in reconfiguring IR theory within the framework of the second state debate. First, it provides a more complete and nuanced picture of how the different theories of IR explain and theorise the state. Second, it produces a radically different picture of IR theory than that portrayed by the first state debate. In effect, it inverts the conventional picture, thereby standing IR theory on its head. Third, and perhaps most importantly, in strict contrast to its predecessor, the second state debate framework offers a way forward for the development of IR theory in general, and theories of the state in particular. I noted in chapter 1 that a principal limitation of the first state debate was that it led to two polar opposites such that it became impossible to effect a synthesis or resolution. This was essentially because the debate was founded on an exclusive or binary logic: either the autonomous state or not-the-state. The notion that both strong states and strong non-state actors could reside together within global or domestic space was not considered. The second state debate, by contrast, is interesting because it points to various possible resolutions. In particular, it suggests that resolution can be achieved by applying an inclusive or 'collective' both/and logic (as opposed to traditional binary logic). In what remains of this chapter I shall apply this inclusive approach in order to sketch out a possible sociological resolution to the second state debate. In applying a 'both/and' logic I suggest that we need to begin by rejecting pure agent-centric and pure structuralist theory and to effect a 'structurationist' synthesis. Here I draw upon and adapt the basic insights of a number of theorists most notably Anthony Giddens (1984); an analysis which is very much reinforced by Clark (1999) as well as Weiss (1999). Such an approach begins by noting two 'truisms' about social life: that

(1) human beings and their organizations [e.g. the state] are purposeful actors whose actions help reproduce or transform the society in which they live; and (2) society [international/domestic] is made up of social relationships, which structure the interactions between these purposeful actors. Taken together these truisms suggest that human agents and social structures are, in one way or another, theoretically interdependent or mutually implicating entities. (Wendt 1987: 337–8)

In this book I have effectively sought to problematise the state as a potential agent. Thus 'international life' embodies two 'truisms': that states are purposeful agents that shape and determine the international system within which they reside but that, conversely, the international system comprises all manner of relationships which shape and determine states. The structurationist resolution to the second state debate proposed here involves recognising these two fundamental aspects of international life. However, in attempting to synthesise agent-centric and structuralist theories we need to note that such a synthetic operation is an extremely delicate task; for as in human transplant operations, donor parts often do not take. The first task must therefore be to reconfigure the ontological nature of the agents (states) and structures so as to make them compatible, thereby preventing any potential rejection of the 'donor' by the 'host'.

Sketching a structurationist model of the 'constitutive' state and global politics

I begin by setting out a basic model that can be applied to theorising international and global relations. Here I take Waltz's theoretical model (see figure 2.2), but adapt and relocate it within a structurationist approach to the state and global politics. Applying the 'both/and' logic leads us to begin by noting that structures are 'double-edged' – that is, structures are both constraining and enabling. Global and international (and national) 'structures' are now viewed as both 'realms of opportunity' and 'realms of constraint'. International and transnational actors are similarly double-edged, enabling and constraining states. This is captured in the 'first tier' on the left-hand side of figure 7.3.

To an extent, states 'adapt' (i.e. conform) to these constraints, as

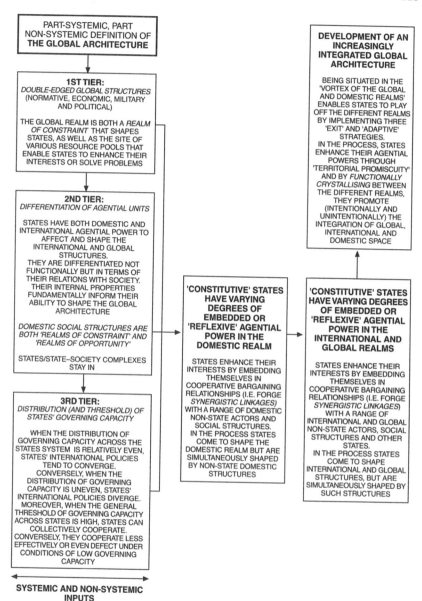

PART-SYSTEMIC, PART NON-SYSTEMIC DEFINITION OF **THE GLOBAL ARCHITECTURE**

1ST TIER:
DOUBLE-EDGED GLOBAL STRUCTURES (NORMATIVE, ECONOMIC, MILITARY AND POLITICAL)

THE GLOBAL REALM IS BOTH A *REALM OF CONSTRAINT* THAT SHAPES STATES, AS WELL AS THE SITE OF VARIOUS RESOURCE POOLS THAT ENABLE STATES TO ENHANCE THEIR INTERESTS OR SOLVE PROBLEMS

2ND TIER:
DIFFERENTIATION OF AGENTIAL UNITS

STATES HAVE BOTH DOMESTIC AND INTERNATIONAL AGENTIAL POWER TO AFFECT AND SHAPE THE INTERNATIONAL AND GLOBAL STRUCTURES. THEY ARE DIFFERENTIATED NOT FUNCTIONALLY BUT IN TERMS OF THEIR RELATIONS WITH SOCIETY. THEIR INTERNAL PROPERTIES FUNDAMENTALLY INFORM THEIR ABILITY TO SHAPE THE GLOBAL ARCHITECTURE

DOMESTIC SOCIAL STRUCTURES ARE BOTH 'REALMS OF CONSTRAINT' AND 'REALMS OF OPPORTUNITY'

STATES/STATE–SOCIETY COMPLEXES STAY IN

3RD TIER:
DISTRIBUTION (AND THRESHOLD) OF STATES' GOVERNING CAPACITY

WHEN THE DISTRIBUTION OF GOVERNING CAPACITY ACROSS THE STATES SYSTEM IS RELATIVELY EVEN, STATES' INTERNATIONAL POLICIES TEND TO CONVERGE. CONVERSELY, WHEN THE DISTRIBUTION OF GOVERNING CAPACITY IS UNEVEN, STATES' INTERNATIONAL POLICIES DIVERGE. MOREOVER, WHEN THE GENERAL THRESHOLD OF GOVERNING CAPACITY ACROSS STATES IS HIGH, STATES CAN COLLECTIVELY COOPERATE. CONVERSELY, THEY COOPERATE LESS EFFECTIVELY OR EVEN DEFECT UNDER CONDITIONS OF LOW GOVERNING CAPACITY

SYSTEMIC AND NON-SYSTEMIC INPUTS

DEVELOPMENT OF AN INCREASINGLY INTEGRATED GLOBAL ARCHITECTURE

BEING SITUATED IN THE 'VORTEX OF THE GLOBAL AND DOMESTIC REALMS' ENABLES STATES TO PLAY OFF THE DIFFERENT REALMS BY IMPLEMENTING THREE 'EXIT' AND 'ADAPTIVE' STRATEGIES. IN THE PROCESS, STATES ENHANCE THEIR AGENTIAL POWERS THROUGH 'TERRITORIAL PROMISCUITY' AND BY *FUNCTIONALLY CRYSTALLISING* BETWEEN THE DIFFERENT REALMS, THEY PROMOTE (INTENTIONALLY AND UNINTENTIONALLY) THE INTEGRATION OF GLOBAL, INTERNATIONAL AND DOMESTIC SPACE

'CONSTITUTIVE' STATES HAVE VARYING DEGREES OF EMBEDDED OR 'REFLEXIVE' AGENTIAL POWER IN THE DOMESTIC REALM

STATES ENHANCE THEIR INTERESTS BY EMBEDDING THEMSELVES IN COOPERATIVE BARGAINING RELATIONSHIPS (I.E. FORGE *SYNERGISTIC LINKAGES*) WITH A RANGE OF DOMESTIC NON-STATE ACTORS AND SOCIAL STRUCTURES. IN THE PROCESS STATES COME TO SHAPE THE DOMESTIC REALM BUT ARE SIMULTANEOUSLY SHAPED BY NON-STATE DOMESTIC STRUCTURES

'CONSTITUTIVE' STATES HAVE VARYING DEGREES OF EMBEDDED OR 'REFLEXIVE' AGENTIAL POWER IN THE INTERNATIONAL AND GLOBAL REALMS

STATES ENHANCE THEIR INTERESTS BY EMBEDDING THEMSELVES IN COOPERATIVE BARGAINING RELATIONSHIPS (I.E. FORGE *SYNERGISTIC LINKAGES*) WITH A RANGE OF INTERNATIONAL AND GLOBAL NON-STATE ACTORS, SOCIAL STRUCTURES AND OTHER STATES. IN THE PROCESS STATES COME TO SHAPE INTERNATIONAL AND GLOBAL STRUCTURES, BUT ARE SIMULTANEOUSLY SHAPED BY SUCH STRUCTURES

Figure 7.3 A structurationist theory of the state and global politics

structuralists argue (which is why I have located second-wave WHS on the border of the first and second generic types of state theory in figure 7.2). But at the same time, these structures and actors are not wholly 'self-constituting', but are partially shaped by states. Accordingly, states do not become 'passive victims' of structures and non-state actors. The international and global realms also become partial resource pools into which 'states-as-agents' dip so as to enhance their power or interests in both realms, or to solve problems that daily confront them (see pp. 203–13 above, where I discuss an example of this drawn from my own 1997 work).

Moving down to the 'second tier' (see figure 7.3), the principal difference between my approach and that of Waltz is that the 'units' – states and state–society complexes – do not drop out but stay in. As noted, international and global structures are not wholly separate from national level variables and are not self-constituting, but are partially shaped by the actions of states imbued with moderate–high levels of international agential power. Moreover, states vary in their capabilities and in their foreign policies depending on how well they are embedded within domestic and international society. Taking the case of trade policy in the 1879–1913 period, I argued that the strong domestic governing capacity of the British state (derived principally from its highly embedded relations with domestic social forces), enabled the state to extract income taxation and cooperate with both the working and dominant classes, which meant that it could avoid raising indirect taxes and tariffs. It thus gained high levels of international agential power and followed a cooperative free trade policy. Conversely, the low domestic governing capacity of the German and Russian states meant that they could not raise income taxation, but instead chose to repress various social actors in society through increasing regressive indirect taxes and tariffs (Hobson 1997, and pp. 203–13 in this volume). In the process they gained only moderate levels of international agential power and thereby defected from international cooperation, pursuing tariff protectionism rather than free trade.

At this point in the operation, however, we need to take extreme care. For one of the most problematic issues is how we theorise the state and its relations with social actors in domestic society. Unfortunately on this point, much (though not all) of IR theory remains silent, requiring us to turn to other disciplines, most notably Sociology, as well as Comparative Politics/Economics for insight. At the domestic level, there are a range of theories that emphasise the centrality of social structures, and accordingly tend to downgrade the domestic agential power of the state. Liberals and pluralists ultimately emphasise individuals or particular interest groups over the state. Marxists tend to emphasise the importance of class forces (though they do note that states have some autonomy in the short run), and postmodernists emphasise the importance of discourse and the 'logic of representation'. Conversely, at the other extreme are elitists, statists and first-wave Weberian sociologists, who tend to reify the state as an absolutely autonomous entity, such that the state is viewed as autonomous only when it can undermine the power of domestic classes (e.g. Krasner 1978; Skocpol 1979). Both extremes are problematic because they employ a binary logic or zero-sum conception of power: if states are strong, non-state actors must be weak; conversely, if non-state actors are strong, states must be weak. In short, for most theorists, there can only ever be a trade-off between state power and social power. The structurationist approach employed here employs an inclusive 'both/and' logic, such that strong states go hand-in-hand with strong societies. One way of conceptualising this is to recognise that states have 'embedded autonomy' (Evans 1995) or 'governed interdependence' (Weiss 1998), or what might be called in the context of this volume 'reflexive domestic agential power.' The difference between 'embedded autonomy' and 'reflexive domestic agential power' is that for Evans (1995), 'embedded autonomy' refers only to the ability of the state to embed itself in the capitalist class. But 'reflexive agential power' refers to the ability of the state to embed itself in a broad array of social forces, not just the capitalist class, as well as the ability of the state to embed itself within non-class structures (e.g. the normative structure of society). Earlier, I gave the example of how being embedded in both the working and dominant classes enabled the British Liberal government to play off the different classes and thereby push its preferred income tax policies through. Thus the more reflexive of society the state is, the greater its ability becomes to enhance its governing capacity; conversely the less reflexive or the more isolated the state is from society, the weaker its governing capacity becomes. In short, the state gains power when it collectively collaborates or makes 'synergistic linkages' with a broad array of social forces and non-state structures. It is therefore not a *non-sequitur* to argue that states can have autonomy or agency while at the same time being constrained by social forces (cf. Nordlinger 1981: 23–34). This is the 'paradox of state reflexivity' or the 'paradox of state strength' (see also Hobson 1997: 234–5, 238–9, 251–2; Weiss 1998, especially chapter 2; cf. Ikenberry 1986). A further difference between my approach and that of Evans is that I also emphasise the importance of the state's reflexive international agential power (see below).

In short, the state is rarely separated from society, but is more often than not variously embedded within, or 'reflexive' of, a broad array of social forces and structures. But while cooperating with social forces may enhance governing capacity, it also places limits upon or circumscribes parameters within which the state operates. For example, while absolutist states enhanced their power by cooperating with the capitalist class (which enhanced government revenues), nevertheless this required rulers to make all sorts of political concessions (bourgeois property rights, rule of law, etc.). I therefore define states as 'constitutive' in that they both constitute, and are constituted by, domestic social forces. This is why I have located the approach midway between those theories that accord the state only low or moderate amounts of domestic agential power and those that accord it absolute amounts (see figure 7.2).

Moving down to the 'third tier' (see figure 7.3), I replace Waltz's 'distribution of power' with the distribution (and threshold) of states' governing capacity. Governing capacity differs across states to greater or lesser degrees (and is derived from the degree to which the state is reflexive of society). Returning to my (1997) case study of trade policy, I argued that the uneven distribution of governing capacity led to varying trade policies in Europe: between 1879 and 1913 Britain followed free trade while much of continental Europe followed tariff protectionism. But also because the general threshold of governing capacity was low on the continent, states relied on indirect taxes and therefore chose tariff protectionism. However, after 1945, these differentials in governing capacity had broadly levelled out, and almost all first world states had attained high governing capacity, so their international agential power increased. Only then could states collectively sign up to a genuinely multilateral free trade regime. (Conversely, the low governing capacity of most third world states led them to defect and pursue tariff protectionism.) Of course neorealism emphasises the role of hegemony in the shift to free trade, and neoliberal institutionalists simply assume that free trade is a 'rational egoistic state strategy'. But my argument emphasises that states could move to free trade after 1945 only once their domestic levels of governing capacity had risen sufficiently to enable a shift to income taxation, thereby overcoming their dependence on indirect taxes and tariffs. And, moreover, the distribution of governing capacity had to be relatively even, because if some states had only moderate or low levels, they would have had to rely on indirect taxes and tariffs, and would therefore have defected from following collective free trade. This returns us to the point made above: that a state's degree of reflexivity within domestic society is fundamental to the degree of agential power that it gains in the international realm (requiring us to maintain the second tier as a vital aspect of our structurationist approach).

*Situating the 'constitutive' state within a 'neo-integrationist'
approach to global politics*

In the structurationist model of the state and global politics sketched out above, I began by bracketing the state's agential power and noted how the first tier (global and international structures) both enabled and constrained states. I then bracketed the effects of international and global structures and examined how the state can shape and affect the international and global structures (as well as how it shapes and is shaped by domestic structures). In this final section I combine these insights into one approach which I label 'neo-integrationist'. A neo-integrationist approach sets out to theorise the embedded relations or multiple linkages between the local/sub-national realm, the national (the state) and the international and global realms. It proceeds from two fundamental premises: (1) that the international/global realms both shape and are shaped by the national and sub-national realms and; (2) that the international, global and domestic realms are not discrete and self-constituting but are 'impure', such that they have only 'partial autonomy' given that they functionally entwine in complex ways (Hobson 1997: chapter 7, 1998a: 286–90). In short, my neo-integrationist theory entails an 'outside-in' and an 'inside-out' approach. Kenneth Waltz famously argued that '[s]omeone may one day fashion a unified theory of internal and external politics . . . [Nevertheless] students of international politics will do well to concentrate on separate theories of internal and external politics until someone figures out a way to unite them' (Waltz 1986: 340). This section argues that the time has now come to develop such a unified theory, and that we must do so if we are to produce a sructurationist theory of the state and IR (cf. Murphy and Tooze 1991). Moreover, in recent years others have sought to develop a 'neo-integrationist' theory of world politics (e.g. Evans, Jacobson and Putnam 1993; Risse-Kappen 1995; Keohane and Milner 1996), though it has been correctly noted that such theory is still only in embryonic form (Hasenclever et al 1997: 204). It should also be noted that neo-integrationist theory is not necessarily the same as globalisation theory, in that many theorists of globalisation actually reify the power of either global structures or the state and end up by effectively discounting the linkages between the state, the domestic, the international and global realms (Clark 1999; Hobson and Ramesh 1999; Weiss 1999).

Thus when we combine the two insights mentioned above ñ that states shape and are shaped by both the domestic and international/global realms ñ we can advance to a 'neo-integrationist' theory which can be applied not just to International Relations but also to Comparative Politics and CPE as well as Political Science, Sociology and Political Geography. Here I reject the claim that these realms are separate (as Waltz suggests), or that there is a one-way linkage between them (as, for example, in orthodox Marxism and classical WST), and suggest that there is a seamless web that envelops and binds each of these realms together. My structurationist solution to neo-integration theory begins by noting two points: first, that the internal and external realms are not self-constituting but are 'co-constitutive' such that we can discern a 'dual reflexivity' between them. Second, I note that the state resides within the 'vortex of the internal and external realms', which links up with the notion that the state is 'Janus-faced' (see also Ikenberry 1991: 161; Halliday 1994: 84–6; Hobson 1997: 246–69; Weiss 1998, 1999; Clark 1999). Combining these two insights suggests that the state is what I call 'territorially promiscuous' such that it can 'play off' both realms in order either to enhance its interests or to adapt or conform to the requirements of structures, which in the process leads to both realms becoming mutually embedded. This, in turn, presupposes recognising one further point: that states gain considerable agential power in both realms by virtue of their unique spatial location where, in contrast to non-state actors, the state resides within the 'vortex of the internal and external realms'. Put differently, the state derives considerable agential powers in the domestic and international/global realms through being 'territorially promiscuous'. In short, the state's unique territorial scope, which ranges across both the domestic and international/global realms, enables it to play the 'exit' strategy (though in practice, states employ three different types of exit strategy – see below). Thus when confronted with domestic problems (or challenges), the state can turn to the international realm to overcome or mitigate such problems, in much the same way that when it confronts international or global constraints (or challenges) the state can turn to the domestic realm. This indeed is the ultimate Bonapartist balancing act that states can achieve.

But if we focused only on the three 'exit strategies' that states pursue, we would produce a theory which exaggerated the agential power of the state and ignored the structural constraints that states face. In order to correct for such a potential imbalance and thereby retain an inclusive 'both/and' approach, we must also factor in the constraining influences that structures impart. This leads us to chart three 'adaptive strategies' that states employ so as to conform to the requirements of international/ global and domestic structures. By developing this argument we are able to develop both a structurationist theory of the state and global politics as well as to transcend what Ian Clark (1999) aptly refers to as the 'great divide' between the international and domestic realms, that has long dominated IR theory. Of what would such an approach comprise? The argument proceeds in three stages. First, I examine how the 'territorially promiscuous' state uses the international and global realms as 'resource pools', either to enhance its interests in the domestic realm or to buck the constraining logic of domestic structures (what I call the 'first exit strategy') or to adapt to the requirements of domestic structural imperatives (the 'first adaptive strategy'). Second, I examine how the 'territorially promiscuous' state uses the domestic realm as a resource pool either to enhance its interests in the international and global realms or to buck the constraining logic of international/global structures (what I call the 'second exit strategy') or to adapt to the requirements of such structures (the 'second adaptive strategy'). Finally, I briefly examine how the 'territorially promiscuous' state uses the international and global realms as 'resource pools' in order to buck or mitigate the logic of international or global structures (the 'third exit strategy') or to adapt or conform to the requirements of international or global structures (the 'third adaptive strategy').

States employ the 'first exit strategy' by dipping into the international or global 'resource pools' so as enhance their ability to push through domestic reforms and/or to buck domestic social structures. Thus, for example, to draw on the analysis made earlier, I noted how the Russian and German states dipped into the international economy and pursued tariff protectionism so as to push through their preferred domestic reforms (e.g. repressing the lower classes through regressive taxation/ tariffs). Conversely, the British state maintained free trade so that it could push through the income tax against the fiscal interests of the dominant economic classes (even if it maintained their 'trading interests' by retaining free trade). Similarly, states after 1945 came to cooperate with other states through the GATT free trade regime which enhanced their ability to resist the protectionist interest requirements of particular industrial domestic groups. Thus as states came to make 'synergistic linkages' with other states, so they could buck their domestic structures. Moreover, in the late twentieth century, many states have come to embed themselves in globalisation, such that by forging synergistic linkages with global capitalists, states have been able to enhance their interests at home. In the 1980s Singapore sought to attract global capital into the home economy, so that the state could lessen its dependence upon domestic capital (see Hobson and Ramesh 1999). More generally, states 'invoke' external crisis or external pressures (what the Japanese call *gaiatsu*) in order to shift the 'domestic terms of rule' in their favour, enabling them to push through reforms that otherwise might have been hard to promote (see also Putnam 1993; Katzenstein

1996a: chapter 6; Schoppa 1997). Such crises might be economic or military. Thus 'defeat in war' or meeting geopolitical requirements has often shifted the 'terms of rule' between the state and society towards the former. Tsarist Russia's defeat in the Crimean War in 1855, Prussia's defeat in 1807 and Japan's national humiliation at the hands of Commodore Perry (1853) enhanced these states' ability to push through various reforms in the ensuing period. In particular, in Japan and Russia, 'revolutions from above' were implemented in which the states went against the long-term interests of the dominant classes and transformed the domestic economy. Likewise, Japan, South Korea and Taiwan after 1945 were able to reform the economy in new ways in part because of the 'enabling' effects that the Second World War had created (Weiss and Hobson 1995). This suggests that the greater the 'reflexive international agential power' of the state (i.e. the more it is embedded within the dominant structures of international and global society), the greater its ability becomes to push through domestic reforms, as well as to maintain itself at the domestic level.

If we now bracket state agency, we can examine the 'first adaptive strategy' that states employ in which they dip into the international or global realms so as to adapt or conform to the needs or requirements of domestic structures or non-state actors. Thus the German state shifted back to tariff protectionism in the late 1870s in part to shore up the (fiscal) interests of the dominant (Junker) class, in much the same way that the British state maintained free trade from 1846 to 1913 in part to shore up the (trading) power of the dominant economic classes. Or, for example, after 1945, the US government has often changed the rules of international finance or international trade in part to shore up the interests of Wall Street or American industrialists. A further example concerns the relationship of states to international society. Those states that have embedded themselves in the dominant norms of international society (especially liberal democracy) have been better able to maintain themselves in the face of domestic political or revolutionary resistance; those that have bucked such norms have often been undermined through domestic revolution.

The 'second exit strategy' available to states involves them dipping into the domestic realm so as to enhance their interests in relation to, or buck the constraining logic of, international or global structures. As noted, once states had acquired highly reflexive domestic agential power so they gained highly reflexive amounts of international agential power and therefore came to mitigate or buck the logic of inter-state economic competition (associated with the structures of anarchy and global capital) by setting up a collective international free trade regime (GATT) after 1945. That is, the GATT itself could be created only once states' domestic agency had reached sufficiently high levels. Similarly, states have sometimes supported domestic capitalists in order to lessen their dependence upon global capital. This is precisely the strategy that Singapore followed after 1993 (Hobson and Ramesh 1999).

The 'second adaptive strategy' involves states dipping into the domestic realm so as to adapt or conform to the requirements of international or global structures. Thus for example, some (though not all) states in the late twentieth century have become 'internationalised' in that they have in part adopted neoliberal economic policies so as to conform to the imperatives of global capitalism – though the flip-side of this 'first-exit strategy' is that some states 'invoke' globalisation as an 'unavoidable imperative', thereby enabling them to push through neoliberal economic reforms against the interests of various social groups within society (see Ramesh 2000). Historically, absolutist states often cooperated with domestic capitalists so that they could enhance their government revenues, the better to conform to the structural imperatives of inter-state military competition. To a certain extent, Japan, South Korea and Taiwan after 1945 enhanced their domestic economies through pro-active state engagement and cooperation with the capitalist class (especially by integrating with the world economy through export-oriented industrialisation), not least to maintain their military power bases in the face of the logic of inter-state military competition (Weiss and Hobson 1995). And as Finnemore argues, in conforming to the dominant norms of international society, states have come to adopt science bureaucracies and have accepted that economic poverty should be alleviated by undertaking domestic reform (Finnemore 1996).

A 'third exit strategy' available to states involves the forging of synergistic linkages with other states and international non-state actors which enable states to either buck, or at least minimise, the constraining logic of international or global structures. The forging of international regimes or regional groupings such as the EU or the North American Free Trade Agreement (NAFTA) or the ASEAN Free Trade Area (AFTA) are typical 'collective strategies' that states employ so as to mitigate or lessen their dependence upon global structural constraints (Weiss 1998: 209–11; Hobson and Ramesh 1999). Moreover, after 1993 the Singaporean state encouraged domestic capital to 'go global' so as to buck or at least minimise the constraining effects of globalisation (Hobson and Ramesh 1999; cf. Weiss 1998: 204–11). Finally, the 'third adaptive strategy' involves forging synergistic linkages with other states, non-state actors or international organisations so as to conform to international or global structures. In the military arena, NATO and

ANZUS are good examples. And while the post-1945 free trade regimes (GATT and WTO) enable states to resist rent-seeking by their own industrial interest groups, these institutions also discipline states to commit to free trade and avoid the short-term option of defection and protectionism.

One of the most significant consequences of examining these three exit and adaptive strategies is to note how they enable the closer integration of the global architecture (see the middle and right-hand side of figure 7.3). Particularly important here is the notion that states 'functionally crystallise' – to adapt Mann's (1993) phrase – between global, international and domestic actors and structures, either to enhance their interests or to conform to the requirements of various structures. In the process, states have promoted (intentionally or unintentionally) through 'territorial promiscuity', the development of an increasingly integrated global spatial architecture. Ever since the seventeenth century states have sought to promote links between domestic and international capital, which has also significantly informed the development of global capitalism. Similarly, states have reformed their domestic realms so as to conform to inter-state military competition, thereby promoting a link between the international political structure and domestic society, just as most states have reformed their domestic societies so as to conform to the dominant norms of international society, thereby enhancing the linkages between the international normative structure and domestic society. In short, by playing the three 'exit' and 'adaptive' strategies, states have promoted (intentionally and unintentionally) the development of an increasingly integrated global spatial architecture.

Thus in developing a neo-integrationist approach, we need to advance to a position which gives relatively equal ontological weighting to international and global social, normative, economic and political structures on the one hand, but also the state and state–society relations on the other. As one theorist explains: 'one does not have to do away with the "state" to establish the influence of transnational relations in world politics' (Risse-Kappen 1995b: 15). Nor does one have to do away with global (or domestic) social structures to demonstrate the importance of the state. Thus the notion of the 'powerless state' is as much a 'myth' (Weiss 1998), as is the notion that states can make of structures whatever they choose. Globalisation makes of states what states make of it. Or put differently, global/international (and domestic) structures make of states what states make of them. Indeed the collective 'both/and' approach outlined here suggests that strong international agential state power goes hand-in-hand with both the strengthening and integration of states with the domestic, international and global structures. It is this that enables us to move beyond the traditional polarities between 'society-centrism' and 'international/global society-centrism' on the one hand and neoliberal 'agent-centrism' on the other. And in this way we can effect a synthesis between agent-centrism and structuralism, thereby enabling us to move beyond the sterility of the 'first state debate' and simultaneously to solve the 'second state debate'.

Discussion questions

• What, if any, are the limits of the 'first state debate' within IR, and what, if any, are the advantages of the 'second state debate'?

• What are the five generic theories of the state as revealed within IR's 'second state debate', and how does this debate turn IR theory upside down?

• How does the fifth generic form of state theory outlined in chapter 7 (pp. 223–35) resolve the second state debate? Does it succeed in this respect, and does it succeed in producing a viable alternative to the major theories of the state found in IR as well as Comparative Politics, CPE, Sociology and Political Science?

Suggestions for further reading

The main introductory readings on the 'agent–structure debate' are discussed at the end of chapter 1. Here, I shall point readers to works that are discussed in the second part of this chapter. On 'neo-integrationist' theory three different version can be found in: Evans *et al.* (1993), Keohane and Milner (1996) and Risse-Kappen (1995a). The introductions to each of these volumes are especially helpful. Excellent introductions to globalisation theory can be found in Barry Jones (1995) and Baylis and Smith (1997). The most comprehensive discussion of the various theories of the state and globalisation can be found in Clark (1999) – an analysis along with Weiss (1999) which reinforces the general argument outlined in this chapter. And see Halliday (1987, 1994: chapters 4, 6, 8, 9) which also echoes some of the arguments laid out here.

References

Abrams, Philip 1988. 'Notes on the Difficulty of Studying the State', *Journal of Historical Sociology* 1 (1): 58–89

Abu-Lughod, Janet 1989. *Before European Hegemony*, Oxford: Oxford University Press

Adler, Emanuel 1997. 'Seizing the Middle Ground: Constructivism in World Politics', *European Journal of International Relations* 3 (3): 319–63

Adler, Emanuel and Haas, Peter 1992. 'Conclusion: Epistemic Communities, World Order and the Creation of a Reflective Research Program', *International Organization* 46 (1): 367–90

Almond, Gabriel 1988. 'The Return to the State', *American Political Science Review* 82 (3): 853–74

1989. 'The International–National Connection', *British Journal of Political Science* 19(2): 237–59

Althusser, Louis 1969. *For Marx*, London: Allen Lane

Amin, Samir 1996. 'The Ancient World-Systems versus the Modern Capitalist World-System', in A.G. Frank and B.K. Gills (eds.): 247–77

Anderson, Benedict 1983. *Imagined Communities*, London: Verso

Anderson, Perry 1974. *Lineages of the Absolutist State*, London: Verso

Angell, Norman 1912. *The Great Illusion*, London: G.P. Putnam

Archer, Margaret S. 1995. *Realist Social Theory*, Cambridge: Cambridge University Press

Arrighi, Giovanni 1994. *The Long Twentieth Century*, London: Verso

Ashley, Richard K. 1981. 'Political Realism and Human Interests', *International Studies Quarterly* 25: 204–36

1986. 'The Poverty of Neorealism', in R.O. Keohane (ed.): 255–300

1989. 'Living on Borderlines: Man, Poststructuralism and War', in J. Der Derian and M.J. Shapiro (eds.): 259–321

Augelli, Enrico and Murphy, Craig N. 1993. 'Gramsci and International Relations: A General Perspective with Examples from Recent US Policy toward the Third World', in S. Gill (ed.): 127–47

Axelrod, Robert 1984. *The Evolution of Cooperation*, New York: Basic Books

1986. 'An Evolutionary Approach to Norms', *American Political Science Review* 80 (4): 1095–111

Axelrod, Robert and Keohane, Robert O. 1993. 'Achieving Cooperation under Anarchy: Strategies and Institutions', in D. Baldwin (ed.): 85–115

Baldwin, David (ed.) 1993. *Neorealism and Neoliberalism*, New York: Columbia University Press

Banks, Michael 1985. 'The Inter-Paradigm Debate', in M. Light and A.J.R. Groom (eds.), *International Relations*, London: Pinter

Barry Jones, R.J. 1995. *Globalisation and Interdependence in the International Political Economy*, London: Pinter

Bartelson, Jens 1995. *A Genealogy of Sovereignty*, Cambridge: Cambridge University Press

Baylis, John and Smith, Steve (eds.) 1997. *The Globalization of World Politics*, New York: Oxford University Press

Benton, Ted 1984. *The Rise and Fall of Structural Marxism*, New York: St Martin's Press

Berger, Thomas U. 1996. 'Norms, Identity, and National Security in Germany and Japan', in P.J. Katzenstein (ed.): 317–56

Biersteker, Thomas J. and Weber, Cynthia (eds.) 1996a. *State Sovereignty as Social Construct*, Cambridge: Cambridge University Press

1996b. 'The Social Construction of State Sovereignty', in T.J. Biersteker and C. Weber (eds.): 1–22

Blackburn, Robin 1973. *Ideology in Social Science*, New York: Vintage

Block, Fred 1987. *Revising State Theory*, Philadelphia: Temple University Press

Booth, Ken 1991. 'Security in Anarchy: Utopian Realism in Theory and Practice', *International Affairs* 67 (3): 527–45

Brenner, Robert 1977. 'The Origins of Capitalist Development: A Critique of Neo-Smithian Marxism', *New Left Review* 104: 25–92

Brown, Seyom 1995. *New Forces, Old Forces, and the Future of World Politics*, New York: HarperCollins

Bull, Hedley 1977. *The Anarchical Society*, London: Macmillan

Burchill, Scott 1996. 'Realism and Neorealism', in S. Burchill and A. Linklater (eds.): 67–92

Burchill, Scott and Linklater, Andrew (eds.) 1996. *Theories of International Relations*, London: Macmillan

Burton, John W. 1972. *World Society*, Cambridge: Cambridge University Press

Buzan, Barry 1996. 'The Timeless Wisdom of Realism?', in S. Smith, K. Booth and M. Zalewski (eds.): 47–65

Buzan, Barry, Jones, Charles A. and Little, Richard 1993. *The Logic of Anarchy*, New York: Columbia University Press

Camilleri, Joseph and Falk, Jim 1991. *The End of Sovereignty?*, Aldershot: Edward Elgar

Cammack, Paul 1989. 'Review Article: Bringing the State Back In?', *British Journal of Political Science* 19: 261–90

Campbell, David 1990. 'Global Inscription: How Foreign Policy Constitutes the United States', *Alternatives* 15: 263–86

Carr, Edward H. 1939. *The Twenty Years' Crisis 1919–1939*, London: Macmillan

1945. *Nationalism and After*, London: Macmillan

1951. *The New Society*, London: Macmillan

Chase-Dunn, Christopher 1989. *Global Formation*, Oxford: Basil Blackwell

238   References

Clark, Ian 1999. *Globalisation and International Relations Theory*, Oxford: Oxford University Press

Cohen, Gerry A. 1978. *Karl Marx's Theory of History*, Oxford: Clarendon Press

Collins, Randall 1986. *Weberian Sociological Theory*, Cambridge: Cambridge University Press

Connell, R.W. 1990. 'The State, Gender, and Sexual Politics', *Theory and Society* 19: 507–44

Cox, Robert W. 1986. 'Social Forces, States and World Orders: Beyond International Relations Theory', in R.O. Keohane (ed.): 204–54

1987. *Production, Power and World Order*, New York: Columbia University Press

1996. *Approaches to World Order*, Cambridge: Cambridge University Press

Dale, Roger 1984. 'Nation State and International System: The World-System Perspective', in G. McLennan, D. Held and S. Hall (eds.): 183–207

Der Derian, James and Shapiro, Michael J. (eds.) 1989. *International/Intertextual Relations*, Lexington: Lexington Books

Dessler, David 1989. 'What's at Stake in the Agent–Structure Debate?', *International Organization* 43 (3): 441–73

Devetak, Richard 1996. 'Postmodernism', in S. Burchill and A. Linklater (eds.): 179–209

Donnelly, Jack 2000. *Realism and International Relations*, Cambridge: Cambridge University Press

Doty, Roxanne Lynn 1996. 'Sovereignty and the Nation: Constructing the Boundaries of National Identity', in T.J. Biersteker and C. Weber (eds.): 121–47

Dunleavy, Patrick and O'Leary, Brendan 1987. *Theories of the State*, London: Macmillan

Dunne, Timothy J. 1997. 'Liberalism', in J. Baylis and S. Smith (eds.): 147–63

1998. *Inventing International Society*, London: Macmillan

Easton, David 1981. 'The Political System Besieged by the State', *Political Theory* 9 (3): 303–25

Ekelund, Robert B. and Tollison, Robert D. 1981. *Mercantilism as a Rent-seeking Society*, College Station, Texas: Texas A&M Press

Elias, Norbert 1978. *What is Sociology?*, London: Hutchinson

1994. *The Civilizing Process*, vol. 2, Oxford: Basil Blackwell

Elshtain, Jean B. 1992. 'Sovereignty, Identity, Sacrifice', in V. Spike Peterson (ed.): 141–54

Elster, Jon 1985. *Making Sense of Marx*, Cambridge: Cambridge University Press

Evans, Peter B. 1995. *Embedded Autonomy*, Princeton: Princeton University Press

Evans, Peter B., Rueschemeyer, Dietrich and Skocpol, Theda (eds.) 1985. *Bringing the State Back In*, Cambridge: Cambridge University Press

Evans, Peter B., Jacobson, Harold K. and Putnam, Robert D. (eds.) 1993. *Double-Edged Diplomacy*, London: University of California Press

Ferguson, Yale H. and Mansbach, Richard W. 1988. *The Elusive Quest*, Columbia, South Carolina: University of South Carolina Press

Finnemore, Martha 1996. *National Interests in International Society*, Ithaca: Cornell University Press

Florini, Ann 1996. 'The Evolution of International Norms', *International Studies Quarterly* 40: 363–89

Frank, André Gunder 1967. *Capitalism and Underdevelopment in Latin America*, London: Monthly Review Press

1996. 'Transitional Ideological Modes: Feudalism, Capitalism and Socialism', in A.G. Frank and B.K. Gills (eds.): 200–17

Frank, André Gunder and Gills, Barry K. 1996. *The World System – Five Hundred Years or Five Thousand?*, London: Routledge

Fuat Keyman, E. 1997. *Globalization, State, Identity/Difference*, Atlantic Highlands, NJ: Humanities Press

Gabriel, Jürg-Martin 1994. *Worldviews and Theories of International Relations*, London: Macmillan

Gellner, Ernest 1988. *Plough, Sword and Book*, London: Collins Harvill

Giddens, Anthony 1984. *The Constitution of Society*, Cambridge: Polity

1985. *The Nation State and Violence*, Cambridge: Polity

Gill, Stephen 1990. *American Hegemony and the Trilateral Commission*, Cambridge: Cambridge University Press

(ed.) 1993. *Gramsci, Historical Materialism and International Relations*, Cambridge: Cambridge University Press

Gill, Stephen and Law, David 1993. 'Global Hegemony and the Structural Power of Capital', in S. Gill (ed.): 93–124

Gills, Barry K. 1996. 'Hegemonic Transitions in the World System', in A.G. Frank and B.K. Gills (eds.): 115–40

Gilpin, Robert G. 1975. *U.S. Power and the Multinational Corporation*, New York: Basic Books

1981. *War and Change in World Politics*, New York: Cambridge University Press

1986. 'The Richness of the Tradition of Political Realism', in R.O. Keohane (ed.): 301–21

1987. *The Political Economy of International Relations*, Princeton: Princeton University Press

Goldstein, Joshua S. 1988. *Long Cycles*, London: Yale University Press

Gourevitch, Peter A. 1978. 'The Second Image Reversed: The International Sources of Domestic Politics', *International Organization* 32 (4): 281–313

Gramsci, Antonio 1971. *Selections from the Prison Notebooks of Antonio Gramsci*, London: Lawrence & Wishart

Grieco, Joseph 1993a. 'Anarchy and the Limits of Cooperation: A Realist Critique of the Newest Liberal Institutionalism', in D. Baldwin (ed.): 116–42

1993b. 'Understanding the Problem of International Cooperation: The Limits of Neoliberal Institutionalism and the Future of Realist Theory', in D. Baldwin (ed.): 301–38

Griffiths, Martin 1992. *Realism, Idealism and International Politics*, London: Routledge

1999. *Fifty Key Thinkers in International Relations*, London: Routledge

Groom, A.J.R. and Taylor, Paul (eds.) 1975. *Functionalism*, London: University of London Press

Guzzini, Stefano 1997. 'Robert Gilpin: the Realist Quest for the Dynamics of Power', in I.B. Neumann and O. Wæver (eds.), *The Future of International Relations*, London: Routledge: 121–44

1998. *Realism in International Relations and International Political Economy*, London: Routledge

Haas, Ernst 1964. *Beyond the Nation-State*, Stanford: Stanford University Press

Hall, Martin 1998. 'International Political Economy Meets Historical Sociology: Problems and Promises', *Cooperation and Conflict* 33 (3): 257–76

Hall, Stuart 1984. 'The State in Question', in G. McLennan, S. Hall and D. Held (eds.), *The Idea of the Modern State*, Milton Keynes: Open University Press: 1–28

Hall, Stuart and Jacques, Martin 1983. *The Politics of Thatcherism*, London: Lawrence & Wishart

Halliday, Fred 1987. 'State and Society in International Relations: A Second Agenda', *Millennium* 16 (2): 215–29

1994. *Rethinking International Relations*, London: Macmillan

Halperin, Sandra 1998. 'Shadowboxing: Weberian Historical Sociology vs State-centric International Relations Theory', *Review of International Political Economy* 5 (2): 327–39

Hasenclever, Andreas, Mayer, Peter and Rittberger, Volker 1997. *Theories of International Regimes*, Cambridge: Cambridge University Press

Held, David 1984. 'Central Perspectives on the Modern State', in G. McLennan, D. Held and S. Hall (eds.): 29–79

1987. *Models of Democracy*, Cambridge: Polity

Herman, Robert G. 1996. 'Identity, Norms and National Security: The Soviet Foreign Policy Revolution and the End of the Cold War', in P.J. Katzenstein (ed.): 271–316

Hilferding, Rudolf 1981. *Finance Capital*, London: Routledge

Hintze, Otto 1975. *The Historical Essays of Otto Hintze*, ed. Felix Gilbert, Oxford: Oxford University Press

Hirsch, Joachim 1978. 'The State Apparatus and Social Reproduction: Elements of a Theory of the Bourgeois State', in J. Holloway and S. Picciotto (eds.): 57–107

Hobden, Stephen 1998. *International Relations and Historical Sociology*, London: Routledge

Hobson, John A. 1896. *The Problem of the Unemployed*, London: Methuen

1900. *The Economics of Distribution*, London: Macmillan

1902/1968. *Imperialism: A Study*, London: George Allen & Unwin

1909. *The Crisis of Liberalism*, London: King & Son

1915. *Towards International Government*, London: George Allen & Unwin

1920. *The Morals of Economic Internationalism*, New York: Houghton

Hobson, John M. 1997. *The Wealth of States: A Comparative Sociology of International Economic and Political Change*, Cambridge: Cambridge University Press

1998a. The Historical Sociology of the State and the State of Historical Sociology in International Relations', *Review of International Political Economy* 5 (2): 284–320

1998b. 'For a "Second-wave" Weberian Historical Sociology', *Review of International Political Economy* 5 (2): 354–61

Hobson, John M. and Ramesh, M. 1999. 'Globalisation Makes of States What States Make of It', unpublished paper, University of Sydney, Department of Government

Hoffmann, Stanley 1981. 'Notes on the Limits of "Realism"', *Social Research* 48 (4): 653–9

Hollis, Martin and Smith, Steve 1991. 'Beware of Gurus: Structure and Action in International Relations', *Review of International Studies* 17 (4): 393–410

Holloway, John and Picciotto, Sol 1978a. 'Introduction: Towards a Materialist Theory of the State', in J. Holloway and S. Picciotto (eds.): 1–31

(eds.) 1978b. *State and Capital*, London: Edward Arnold

Holton, Robert J. 1985. *The Transition from Feudalism to Capitalism*, London: Macmillan

Howe, Paul 1994. 'The Utopian Realism of E.H. Carr', *Review of International Studies* 20: 277–97

Hurrell, Andrew 1990. 'Kant and the Kantian Paradigm in International Relations', *Review of International Studies* 16: 183–205

Ikenberry, G. John 1986. 'The Irony of State Strength: Comparative Responses to the Oil Shocks in the 1970s', *International Organization* 40 (1): 105–37

1991. 'The State and Strategies of International Adjustment', in R. Little and M. Smith (eds.), *Perspectives on World Politics*, London: Routledge: 157–68

Jarvis, Anthony P. 1989. 'Societies, States and Geopolitics: Challenges from Historical Sociology', *Review of International Studies* 15 (3): 281–93

Jarvis, Darryl S.L. 1998. 'Postmodernism: A Critical Typology', *Politics and Society* 26 (1): 95–142

Jessop, Bob 1984. *The Capitalist State*, Oxford: Basil Blackwell

1990. *State Theory*, Cambridge: Polity

Johnson, Chalmers 1982. *MITI and the Japanese Miracle*, Stanford: Stanford University Press

Johnson, Whittle 1967. 'E.H. Carr's Theory of International Relations', *The Journal of Politics* 29: 861–84

Jones, Charles A. 1998. *E. H. Carr and International Relations*, Cambridge: Cambridge University Press

Kant, Immanuel 1795/1914. *Eternal Peace and other International Essays*, Boston: The World Peace Foundation

Katzenstein, Peter J. 1996a. *Cultural Norms and National Security*, Ithaca: Cornell University Press

(ed.) 1996b. *The Culture of National Security*, New York: Columbia University Press

1996c. 'Introduction: Alternative Perspectives on National Security', in P.J. Katzenstein (ed.): 1–32

Keohane, Robert O. 1984. *After Hegemony*, Princeton: Princeton University Press

(ed.) 1986. *Neorealism and its Critics*, New York: Columbia University Press

1989. *International Institutions and State Power*, Boulder: Westview Press

1993. 'Institutionalist Theory and the Realist Challenge After the Cold War', in D. Baldwin (ed.): 269–300

Keohane, Robert O. and Milner, Helen V. (eds.) 1996. *Internationalization and Domestic Politics*, Cambridge: Cambridge University Press

Keohane, Robert O. and Nye, Joseph S. 1977. *Power and Interdependence*, Boston: Little, Brown & Co

Kier, Elizabeth 1996. 'Culture and French Military Doctrine Before World War II', in P.J. Katzenstein (ed.): 186–215

Kindleberger, Charles P. 1973. *The World in Depression, 1929–1939*, Berkeley: University of California Press

  1981. 'Dominance and Leadership in the International Economy: Exploitation, Public Goods, and Free Rides', *International Studies Quarterly* 25 (2): 242–54

Klotz, Audie 1995. *Norms in International Society*, Ithaca: Cornell University Press

Knopf, Jeffrey W. 1993. 'Beyond Two-level Games: Domestic–International Interaction in the Intermediate-range Nuclear Forces Negotiations', *International Organization* 47(4): 599–628

Krasner, Stephen D. 1976. 'State Power and the Structure of International Trade', *World Politics* 28 (3): 317–47

  1978. *Defending the National Interest*, Princeton: Princeton University Press

  1979. 'The Tokyo Round: Particularistic Interests and Prospects for Stability in the Global Trading System', *International Studies Quarterly* 23 (4): 491–531

  (ed.) 1983a. *International Regimes*, Ithaca: Cornell University Press

  1983b. 'Regimes and the Limits of Realism: Regimes as Autonomous Variables', in Stephen D. Krasner (ed.): 355–68

  1993. 'Global Communications and National Power: Life on the Pareto Frontier', in D. Baldwin (ed.): 234–49

  1995. 'Power Politics, Institutions, and Transnational Relations', in T. Risse-Kappen (ed.): 257–79

Kratochwil, Friedrich 1989. *Rules, Norms, and Decisions*, Cambridge: Cambridge University Press

Laclau, Ernesto 1971. 'Feudalism and Capitalism in Latin America', *New Left Review* 67: 19–38

Layder, Derek 1994. *Understanding Social Theory*, London: Sage

Lenin, Vladimir I. 1916/1933. *Imperialism*, London: Martin Lawrence

  1917/1932. *State and Revolution*, New York: International Publishers

Linklater, Andrew 1998. *The Transformation of Political Community*, Cambridge: Polity

List, Friedrich 1841/1885. *The National System of Political Economy*, London: Longmans, Green

Little, Richard 1994. 'International Relations and Large-scale Historical Change', in A.J.R. Groom and M. Light (eds.), *Contemporary International Relations*, London: Pinter: 9–26

Long, David 1996. *Towards a New Liberal Internationalism*, Cambridge: Cambridge University Press

Long, David and Wilson, Peter (eds.) 1995. *Thinkers of The Twenty Years' Crisis*, New York: Clarendon Press

Mann, Michael 1986. *The Sources of Social Power*, vol. 1, Cambridge: Cambridge University Press

1988. *States, War and Capitalism*, Oxford: Basil Blackwell
1993. *The Sources of Social Power*, vol. 2, Cambridge: Cambridge University Press
1996. 'Authoritarian and Liberal Militarism: A Contribution from Comparative and Historical Sociology', in S. Smith, K. Booth and M. Zalewski (eds.): 221–39
Mansbach, Richard W., Ferguson, Yale H. and Lampert, Donald E. 1976. *The Web of World Politics*, Englewood Cliffs, NJ: Prentice-Hall
March, James and Olsen, Johan 1989. *Rediscovering Institutions*, New York: Free Press
Marx, Karl 1867/1954. *Capital*, vol. 1, London: Lawrence & Wishart
1867/1959. *Capital*, vol. 3, London: Lawrence & Wishart
1967. *Writings of the Young Marx on Philosophy and Society*, ed. L.D. Easton and F.H. Guddat, Garden City, New York: Doubleday
Marx, Karl and Engels, Friedrich 1848/1977. *The Communist Manifesto*, Harmondsworth: Penguin
1969. *Selected Works*, vol. 1, Moscow: Progress Publishers
1970. *Selected Works*, vol. 3, Moscow: Progress Publishers
Mastanduno, Michael 1991. 'Do Relative Gains Matter? America's Response to Japanese Industrial Policy', *International Security* 16 (1): 73–113
McLellan, David 1975. *Marx*, London: Fontana
(eds.) 1983. *Marx: The First One Hundred Years*, London: Fontana
McLennan, Gregor, Held, David and Hall, Stuart (eds.) 1984. *The Idea of the Modern State*, Milton Keynes: Open University Press
Mearsheimer, John J. 1995. 'The False Promise of International Institutions', *International Security* 19 (3): 5–49
Miliband, Ralph 1973. *The State in Capitalist Society*, London: Quartet Books
Mitrany, David 1933. *The Progress of International Government*, London: George Allen & Unwin
1943/1966. *A Working Peace System*, Chicago: Quadrangle
1975. 'A Political Theory for the New Society', in A.J.R. Groom and P. Taylor (eds.): 25–38
Mooers, Colin 1991. *The Making of Bourgeois Europe*, London: Verso
Morgenthau, Hans J. 1948/1978. *Politics Among Nations*, New York: Alfred Knopf
Morse, Edward L. 1976. *Modernization and the Transformation of International Relations*, New York: Free Press
Mouzelis, Nicos P. 1986. *Politics in the Semi-periphery*, London, Macmillan
Murphy, Craig N. 1994. *International Organization and Industrial Change*, Cambridge: Polity
Murphy, Craig N. and Tooze, Roger 1991. 'Getting Beyond the "Common Sense" of the IPE Orthodoxy', in C.N. Murphy and R. Tooze (eds.), *The New International Political Economy*, Boulder: Lynne Rienner
Nordlinger, Eric A. 1981. *On the Autonomy of the Democratic State*, Cambridge, MA: Harvard University Press
North, Douglass C. 1981. *Structure and Change in Economic History*, London: Norton
Offe, Claus 1974. 'Structural Problems of the Capitalist State', in K. von Beyme (ed.), *German Political Studies*, vol. 1, London: Sage: 31–57

Olson, Mancur and Zeckhauser, Richard J. 1966. 'An Economic Theory of Alliances', *Review of Economics and Statistics* 48 (3): 266–79

Onuf, Nicholas G. 1989. *World of Our Making*, Columbia: University of South Carolina Press

Parkin, Frank 1979. *Marxism and Class Theory*, London: Tavistock

Pateman, Carole 1988. *The Sexual Contract*, Cambridge: Polity

Perez-Diaz, Victor M. 1978. *State, Bureaucracy and Civil Society*, London: Macmillan

Peterson, V. Spike (ed.) 1992a. *Gendered States*, Boulder: Lynne Rienner

1992b. 'Introduction', in Peterson (ed.): 1–29

1992c. 'Security and Sovereign States: What is at Stake in Taking Feminism Seriously?', in V. Spike Peterson (ed.): 31–64

Pierson, Christopher 1996. *The Modern State*, London: Routledge

Poggi, Gianfranco 1978. *The Development of the Modern State*, London: Hutchinson

Poulantzas, Nicos 1973. *Political Power and Social Classes*, London: New Left Books

Powell, Robert 1993. 'Absolute and Relative Gains in International Relations Theory', in D. Baldwin (ed.): 209–33

Price, Richard and Reus-Smit, Christian 1998. 'Dangerous Liaisons? Critical International Theory and Constructivism', *European Journal of International Relations* 4 (3): 259–94

Putnam, Robert D. 1993. 'Diplomacy and Domestic Politics: The Logic of Two-level Games', in P.B. Evans, H. Jacobson and R. Putnam (eds.): 431–68

Ramesh, M. 2000. *Welfare Capitalism in South East Asia*, London: Macmillan

Reus-Smit, Christian 1996. 'Beyond Foreign Policy: State Theory and the Changing World Order', in P. James (ed.), *The State in Question*, Sydney: Allen & Unwin: 161–95

1999. *The Moral Purpose of the State*, Princeton: Princeton University Press

Ricardo, David 1817/1969. *The Principles of Political Economy and Taxation*, London: Dent

Risse-Kappen, Thomas (ed.) 1995a. *Bringing Transnational Relations Back In*, Cambridge: Cambridge University Press

1995b. 'Bringing Transnational Relations Back In: Introduction', in T. Risse-Kappen (ed.): 3–33

Rose, Gideon 1998. 'Review Article: Neoclassical Realism and Theories of Foreign Policy', *World Politics* 51 (1): 144–72

Rosecrance, Richard 1981. 'The One World of Hans Morgenthau', *Social Research* 48 (4): 749–65

Rosenau, James N. 1980. *The Study of Global Interdependence*, London: Frances Pinter

Rosenberg, Justin 1994. *The Empire of Civil Society*, London: Verso

Roxborough, Ian 1979. *Theories of Underdevelopment*, London: Macmillan

Ruggie, John G. 1986. 'Continuity and Transformation in the World Polity: Toward a Neorealist Synthesis', in R.O. Keohane (ed.): 131–57

1998. *Constructing the World Polity*, London: Routledge

Runciman, W. Gary 1989. *A Treatise on Social Theory*, vol. II, Cambridge: Cambridge University Press

Rupert, Mark 1995. *Producing Hegemony*, Cambridge: Cambridge University Press

Scholte Jan Aaart, 1993. *International Relations of Social Change*, Milton Keynes: Open University Press

Schoppa, Leonard J. 1997. *Bargaining with Japan*, New York: Columbia University Press

Schwarzmantel, John 1994. *The State in Contemporary Society*, Hemel Hempstead: Harvester Wheatsheaf

Schweller, Randall L. and David Priess 1997. 'A Tale of Two Realisms: Expanding the Institutions Debate', *Mershon International Studies Review* 41: 1–32

Seabrooke, Leonard 2000. *The Victory of Dividends – Direct Financing and US Structural Power in the IPE*, London: Macmillan

Shapiro, Michael and Alker, Hayward R. (eds.) 1996. *Challenging Boundaries*, Minneapolis: University of Minnesota Press

Sikkink, Katharyn 1993. 'Human Rights, Principled-issue Networks and Sovereignty in Latin America', *International Organization* 47 (3): 411–41

Singer, J. David 1961. 'The Levels-of-Analysis Problem in International Relations', *World Politics* 14 (1): 77–92

Skocpol, Theda 1977. 'Wallerstein's World Capitalist System: A Theoretical and Historical Critique', *American Journal of Sociology* 82 (5): 1075–90

1979. *States and Social Revolutions*, Cambridge: Cambridge University Press

1985. 'Bringing the State Back In: Strategies of Analysis in Current Research', in P.B. Evans, D. Rueschemeyer and T. Skocpol (eds.): 3–42

Smith, Adam 1776/1937. *An Inquiry into the Nature and Causes of The Wealth of Nations*, 2 vols., ed. Edwin Cannan, New York: The Modern Library

Smith, Michael J. 1986. *Realist Thought from Weber to Kissinger*, London: Louisiana State University Press

Smith, Steve, Booth, Ken and Zalewski, Marysia (eds.) 1996. *International Theory*, Cambridge: Cambridge University Press

Spruyt, Hendrik 1994. *The Sovereign State and its Competitors*, Princeton: Princeton University Press

Steans, Jill 1998. *Gender and International Relations*, Cambridge: Polity

Strang, David 1996. 'Contested Sovereignty: The Social Construction of Colonial Imperialism', in T.J. Biersteker and C. Weber (eds.) (1996a): 22–49

Strange, Susan 1988. *States and Markets*, London: Pinter

Suganami, Hidemi 1986. 'Reflections on the Domestic Analogy: The Case of Bull, Beitz and Linklater', *Review of International Studies* 12: 145–58

Sylvester, Christine 1994. *Feminist Theory and International Relations in a Postmodern Era*, Cambridge: Cambridge University Press

Taylor, Paul and Groom, A.J.R. 1975. 'Introduction: Functionalism and International Relations', in A.J.R. Groom and P. Taylor (eds.): 1–7

Thompson, Edward P. 1978. 'The Poverty of Theory: Or an Orrery of Errors', in E.P. Thompson, *The Poverty of Theory and Other Essays*, London: Merlin Press: 193–397

Thrift, Nigel 1983. 'On the Determination of Social Action in Space and Time', *Society and Space* 1: 23–57

Tickner, J. Ann 1988. 'Hans Morgenthau's Principles of Political Realism: A Feminist Reformulation', *Millennium* 17 (3): 429–40
1992. *Gender in International Relations*, New York: Columbia University Press
Tilly, Charles (ed.) 1975a. *The Formation of National States in Western Europe*, Princeton: Princeton University Press
1975b. 'Reflections on the History of European State-making', in C. Tilly (ed.): 3–83
1975c. 'Western State-making and Theories of Political Transformation', in C. Tilly (ed.): 601–39
1990. *Coercion, Capital and European States, AD 990–1990*, Oxford: Basil Blackwell
Tooze, Roger 1977. 'The Progress of International Functionalism', *British Journal of International Studies* 3: 210–27
Trimberger, Ellen K. 1978. *Revolution From Above*, New Brunswick: Transaction Books
True, Jacqui 1996. 'Feminism', in S. Burchill and A. Linklater (eds.): 210–51
Van der Pijl, Kees 1984. *The Making of an Atlantic Ruling Class*, London: Verso
Vincent, R. John 1986. *Human Rights and International Relations*, Cambridge: Cambridge University Press
Wade, Robert 1990. *Governing the Market*, Princeton: Princeton University Press
Wæver, Ole 1996. 'The Rise and Fall of the Inter-paradigm Debate', in S. Smith, K. Booth and M. Zalewski (eds.): 149–85
Walker, R.B.J., 1987. 'Realism, Change and International Political Theory', *International Studies Quarterly* 31: 65–84
1993. *Inside/Outside*, Cambridge: Cambridge University Press
Wallerstein, Immanuel 1974. *The Modern World System*, vol. 1, London: Academic Press
1979. *The Capitalist World-Economy*, Cambridge: Cambridge University Press
1984. *The Politics of the World Economy*, Cambridge: Cambridge University Press
1996a. 'World System versus World-Systems: A Critique', in A.G. Frank and B.K. Gills (eds.): 292–6
1996b. 'The Inter-State Structure of the Modern World-System', in S. Smith, K. Booth and M. Zalewski (eds.): 87–107
Waltz, Kenneth N. 1959. *Man, The State and War*, New York: Columbia University Press
1967. *Foreign Policy and Democratic Politics*, Boston: Little, Brown
1979. *Theory of International Politics*, New York: McGraw-Hill
1986. 'Reflections on *Theory of International Politics*: A Response to my Critics', in R.O. Keohane (ed.): 322–45
Weber, Cynthia 1995. *Simulating Sovereignty*, Cambridge: Cambridge University Press
Weber, Max 1978. *Economy and Society*, 2 vols., Berkeley: University of California Press
Weiss, Linda 1998. *The Myth of the Powerless State*, Cambridge: Polity
1999. 'Globalization and National Governance: Antinomy or Interdependence?', *Review of International Studies* 25(5): 1–30

Weiss, Linda and Hobson, John M. 1995. *States and Economic Development: A Comparative Historical Analysis*, Cambridge: Polity

Wendt, Alexander 1987. 'The Agent–Structure Problem in International Relations Theory', *International Organization* 41 (3): 335–70

1991. 'Bridging the Theory/meta-theory Gap in International Relations', *Review of International Studies* 17 (4): 382–92

1999. *Social Theory of International Politics*, Cambridge: Cambridge University Press

Wheeler, Nicholas J. 2000. *Saving Strangers*, Oxford: Oxford University Press

Wight, Colin, 1999. 'They Shoot Dead Horses Don't They? Locating Agency in the Agent–Structure Problematique', *European Journal of International Relations* 5 (1): 109–42

Wight, Martin 1977. *Systems of States*, Leicester: Leicester University Press

Wood, Ellen M. 1995. *Democracy Against Capitalism*, Cambridge: Cambridge University Press

Young, Oran 1983. 'Regime Dynamics: The Rise and Fall of International Regimes', in S.D. Krasner (ed.): 93–113

Zacher, Mark and Matthew, Richard A. 1995. 'Liberal International Theory: Common Threads, Divergent Strands', in C.W. Kegley (ed.), *Controversies in International Relations Theory*, New York: St Martin's Press: 107–50

Index

units, 37; ordering principle (anarchy), 31; shift from heteronomy to sovereignty, 36, 184–91
modified parsimony, 10, 30
theory of hegemony, 38–44: altruistic (benign) hegemony, 40, 41; coercive (predatory) hegemony, 40; defined, 39–40; free-rider problem, 33, 41, 43; hegemonic regimes, 38–40, 94–5; hegemonic war, 35, 36; hegemony as self-liquidating, 41; interdependence, 38; limits of, 94–5; regimes, 38–9, 40, 41–3, 94–5; relative autonomy of regimes, 95; rise and decline of great powers, 31, 32–6; rise and decline of hegemonic regimes, 41–3; rise and decline of hegemony (cycle), 33–6, 38, 41–3
theory of the state (maladaptive), 31–6, 41–3: failure to emulate, 31, 32–5, 36; free-riding, 33; high military costs, 33; low domestic agential state power, 31–4, 42, 43, 44; strong domestic fetters, 32–5, 37, 42, 44
theory of the state (military-adaptive), 31–5, 36, 44; adaptation through emulation, 31–3, 35, 36, 42; high domestic agential state power, 32–4, 42; weak domestic fetters, 33, 34
weak third-image theory, 11, 30, 43–4
see also neorealism
Morgenthau, Hans J., 17, 45–55, 147
Murphy, Craig N., 128, 130, 132

Neoclassical realism, 44
neoliberal institutionalism
as a 'practical' mode of discourse, 102
as a non-systemic approach, 100–4
compared with neorealism, 38–9, 94–6, 96–104
conception of anarchy as malleable, 99, 101, 102
differentiated from constructivism, 147, 155, 156
in the first state debate, 102, 219, 222
in the second state debate, 6, 102–4
incommensurability with neorealism, 104
the debate with neorealism, 99–104
the international as the realm of possibility, 101, 102
theory of regimes: as relatively autonomous from states, 96–8, 102–3; as absolutely autonomous from anarchy, 96–8, 103; compliance mechanisms, 98–9, 101; cooperation

between states, 97–101; defection from cooperation, 98, 99; enhancement of domestic agential state power, 99, 101, 102–3; mitigating anarchy, 97, 101, 103, 104; norms as *regulatory*, 147; overcoming the collective action problem, 96–8, 101; prisoner's dilemma, 98–9; robustness (resilience) of, 97, 98
theory of the state (agential): defined, 104; high domestic agential state power, 6, 97, 101, 102, 222; high international agential state power, 7, 9, 38–9, 64, 65, 97, 101, 102, 103–4, 219, 222; maximisation of long-run (absolute) gains, 97, 98, 99, 100, 101, 102–4; states' insensitivity to unequal gains, 100; the rational egoistic assumption, 95, 97, 98, 101
neorealism
compared with classical realism, 17–19, 27, 45
compared with constructivism, 146–7, 148–9, 153, 158, 160, 163–4, 165–6, 170–2
compared with English School rationalism, 27, 89–90, 91, 93–4
compared with liberalism, 64, 65
compared with Marxism, 117, 119–21, 134–7
compared with modified neorealism, 30–2, 36, 37, 39, 43, 44
compared with neoliberal institutionalism, 38–9, 94–6, 96–104
compared with postmodernism, 149, 153, 160
compared with Weberian historical sociology, 30, 174, 175, 175–91, 192–3, 197–8, 199, 203–4
in the first state debate, 2–3, 217, 218
in the second state debate, 1, 5, 217, 218, 219, 220
incommensurability with neoliberal institutionalism, 104
general theory of the state: as sociologically reductionist, 23; billiard-ball analogy, 2–3, 18, 23; defined, 30, 104; high domestic agential state power, 5, 17, 18, 24–5, 28, 219, 220; low international agential state power, 7, 9, 17, 18, 19, 26, 28, 217, 219, 220; positional assumption, 18, 24, 41, 100, 104; relative gains, 18, 38, 97, 100; sensitivity to unequal gains, 100
international political structure, 19,

postmodernism
approach to the state: collective action problem as imagined, 165; construction of public/private distinction, 162–3; low domestic agential state power, 5–6, 164, 219, 221; moderate international agential state power, 8, 9, 158, 164, 218, 219, 221; normative statecraft, 157, 158, 159–60, 164; repression and punishment of 'other' states, 160–1, 164–5; repression and punishment of domestic 'others', 162–3; the state as imagined, 160
differentiated from international society-centric constructivism, 157, 158, 164
differentiated from neorealism, 158, 160, 163–4
in the first state debate, 5, 218, 219, 221
in the second state debate, 218, 219, 221
logocentrism, 162
the international realm as imagined, 159, 160, 164–5
the international as the realm of violence, 158, 159, 160, 164–5
see also postmodern feminism, radical constructivism
postmodern feminism
approach to international relations: critique of neorealism, 163–4; differentiated from international society-centric constructivism, 157, 158, 164; the international as the realm of violence, 163; the international realm as constructed and imagined, 163; the rejection of empathy and cooperation, 165
approach to the state: citizenship as constructed through masculine norms, 163; construction of language through 'colonising dualisms' (logocentrism), 162; construction of state identity as imagined, 162; construction of the public/private distinction, 162–3; decline of the sovereign state under globalisation, 164; heterosexual 'self', 162, 165; low domestic agential state power, 164; moderate international agential state power, 164; nation or domestic political community as imagined, 162–3; normative statecraft, 163; policy of malign neglect, 163; public realm as valorised in masculine norms, 162–3; repression/punishment of gays and

women as 'others', 162–3; writing the state, 163
see also postmodernism, radical constructivism
Poulantzas, Nicos, 125, 126, 127, 144
Price, Richard, 148, 149, 153, 172
public goods, 41

Radical constructivism
approach to international relations: crisis of representation, 161; critique of neorealism, 160; differentiated from international society-centric constructivism, 157, 158, 164; norms as exclusionary, 157; sovereignty/intervention as mutually inclusive, 161; the international as the realm of violence, 158, 159, 160, 164–5; the international realm as constructed and imagined, 159, 160, 164–5; the repression/punishment of 'deviant' states, 160–1, 164–5; the social construction of the collective action problem, 165
approach to the state: as a disciplinary community, 161; differentiated from international society-centric constructivism, 158; differentiated from neorealism, 158, 163–4; low domestic agential state power, 164, 219, 221; moderate international agential state power, 158, 164, 218, 219, 221; normative statecraft, 157, 158, 159–60, 164; sovereignty as a social construct, 157–8; sovereignty as highly malleable, 160–1; the construction of state identity as imagined, 160; the logic of representation, 158, 159; the nation or domestic political community as imagined, 159, 161, 164; the notion that the state as unfinished (incomplete), 157–8, 160; the repression/punishment of domestic 'deviant' others, 159, 162–3; writing the state, 159, 160, 161
in the second state debate, 218, 219, 221
see also constructivism, postmodernism, postmodern feminism

realism
differentiated from constructivism, 146–7, 148, 149, 153, 158, 160, 163–4, 165, 166, 170–2
differentiated from English School rationalism, 27, 89–90, 91, 93–4

256   Index

differentiated from Marxism, 117,
119–21, 134–7
differentiated from neoliberal
institutionalism, 38–9, 94–6, 96–9,
99–104
differentiated from postmodernism
(radical constructivism), 149, 153,
160
differentiated from second-wave
Weberian historical sociology, 30,
174–5, 192–3, 197–8, 199, 203–4
in the first state debate, 2–4, 31, 38,
217, 218
in the second state debate, 5, 217–20,
223
linkages with first-wave Weberian
historical sociology, 175–91
links with critical/constructivist theory,
17, 18, 19, 45, 50–2, 55–6, 59–61
theory of international relations: balance
of power, 49, 50; compensatory
diplomacy, 53–4; hegemonic regimes,
38–9, 41–3; international hegemony,
38–44; international political
structure, 19, 20–4, 27–30; rise and
decline of the great powers, 31, 32–6
theory of the state (adaptive): emulation,
26–7, 31–5, 36, 42, 44, 48–52;
balancing, 27–8; theory of the state
(agential), 46, 49, 50–5, 55–61
see also classical realism, modified
neorealism and neorealism
Reus-Smit, Christian, 146, 148, 172
Ricardo, David, 68, 69, 70, 105
Ruggie, John G., 28, 30, 36, 63, 146, 148,
172, 184

Schumpeter, Joseph, 69
second-wave Weberian historical sociology
(WHS)
bringing state and society back in, 204,
205
constructivist insight, 197, 201, 203
critique of (reductionist) base-
superstructure model, 195, 196, 198,
202, 204
critique of elitism, 198, 199, 227
critique of first-wave WHS, 197–8, 199,
227
critique of neorealism, 30, 192–3,
197–8, 199, 203–4
differentiated from Marxism, 192, 196,
202, 203, 205
differentiated from neoliberal
institutionalism, 228

fourth-image theory, 12
in the second state debate, 3, 5, 223–35
institutional statism, 199
non-realist theory of state power, 203–13
non-realist theory of the state, 197–8:
competitive-cooperative state-society
relations, 209; definition, 200;
diamorphous state, 203; domestic
agential state power, 5, 199, 206, 207,
212, 226, 228; *infrastructural*
(penetrative) state power, 198–9, 200,
207, 208; international agential state
power, 7–8, 9, 206, 207, 212, 226,
228, 232; linkage between domestic
and international agential state power,
207, 212, 213, 228, 232; *polymorphous*
state, 199, 201–3
six principles of (complexity), 193–8:
class power as *polymorphous*, 208, 209;
compared with critical theory, 194;
dual reflexivity, 195, 230; historicism,
194, 197; malleability of identities,
195, 202–3; multi-causality, 194–5,
201, 202, 205–7; multi-spatiality, 194,
195, 205–7, 229–35; *promiscuity* of
power and power actors, 195, 199,
202; rejection of an ultimate
crystallisation model, 202
states as *constitutive*, 224, 225, 226, 228:
ability to constitute structures, 213;
ability to play off different domestic
classes, 208–9, 227; ability to play off
the different realms (*territorial
promiscuity*), 210, 225, 230–5;
adaptation to structures, 211, 224,
225, 226, 230, 231, 232, 233–4;
creation of synergistic linkages with
non-state actors, 225, 227, 231, 233;
integration of the domestic and global
realms, 225, 234; three 'adaptive'
strategies, 225, 230, 231, 232, 233–4;
three 'exit' strategies, 225, 230, 231,
232, 233
state governing capacity, 198, 207
state governing capacity (high); caging of
social forces, 202; embeddedness/
reflexivity of the state (creation of
synergistic linkages with non-state
actors), 199, 200, 204, 206, 207, 208,
209, 213, 225, 227, 231, 233; high
infrastructural power, 198–200, 207,
208; state capacity through domestic
values/norms, 201, 203
state governing capacity (low): isolation
from social forces, 198, 199, 200, 206,
207, 209